NICOLE LEGERRA

The Big Light

Finding Grace in the Grit

Dedication
For everyone who destroyed me into the person I am today.
You left me in the dark, so I learned to carry my own light.
To the one searching for a way out:
let this book be your North Star.

Content and Trigger Warning

This book contains sensitive and potentially distressing material, including themes of child abuse, attempted suicide, domestic violence, trauma, grief, and depictions of severe mental health struggles including PTSD and depression. Reader discretion is advised.

As much as I want you to read and enjoy my book, your mental health matters more to me. Please proceed with caution and prioritize your well-being. If you or someone you know is affected by any of these topics, please seek support from a trusted individual or professional.

And if you or someone you know needs immediate mental health resources and support, please call, text, or chat with the 988 Suicide & Crisis Lifeline or visit www.lifeline.org for 24/7 access to free and confidential services.

It is my hope you find your own healing by reading this book, knowing you're not alone and I can help you find your light again.

Introduction

I had no intention of writing a book. But you see, this is an assignment I could not contend with. This is the kind of assignment I tried to bargain my way out of, but the Holy Spirit kept circling back, persistent as a debt collector, leaving me torn between the comfort of silence and this crushing obligation to speak. It means that there is something I am supposed to do through this book that I must sacrifice to help others, because that's what Jesus did—though some nights I lie awake wondering if this pain is truly necessary, and if excavating these memories serves any purpose beyond reopening old wounds. But then morning comes, and I remind myself: no matter what scars He forces me to trace with my fingertips, He will help me through each one. At least, that's the promise I cling to. The outcome is His job; my job is to be obedient, even when every instinct screams at me to run. You don't need to be Christian or even spiritual to read this; my hope is it helps your soul knowing you're not alone. For as many books as I have read, you would think it would be easy to sit and write one of my own. But my fingers hover over the keyboard, trembling between the urge to type and the instinct to run. One moment I'm convinced this story needs telling; the next I'm sick with dread at exposing wounds I've spent decades bandaging. Some nights I delete everything I've written. Some mornings I wake with sentences already formed. I had this overwhelming feeling for a long time—both a command and a warning—that I needed to do this. No matter how hard I tried to avoid it, I couldn't. I told myself I was too busy. I didn't know how to write a book. And, my favorite, who wants to hear what I have to say anyway? Those were not excuses; that was fear—or so I tell myself. Some nights I'm certain it's cowardice: fear of failure, or fear of being vulnerable. Other nights I wonder if it's actually wisdom keeping me from disturbing what should remain buried. My fingers trace the outline of that metaphorical headstone, and part of me longs to dig, to unearth what lies beneath, while another part whispers that some graves exist for a reason. Maybe I'm protecting myself. Maybe I'm hiding. Maybe I'm both. Fear lives in my body like an unwelcome tenant. At night, it wraps cold fingers around my throat while I try to sleep. During the day, it sits heavy in my stomach as I type these words, delete them, type again. President Roosevelt famously said we have nothing to fear but fear itself, but he never knew the kind of fear that leaves permanent fingerprints on your soul. Some fears are warning signals, like the smoke detector of the soul. Others are phantoms we conjure ourselves, whispering "what if" until our hearts race and our palms sweat, until we're fighting for breath against dangers that exist only in our imagination. This is not a book about overcoming fear. But I know how debilitating it can be. My own mind created a fear that grew. I've had such crippling panic and anxiety attacks that I've been held hostage by my own nervous system, trapped in moments where my body betrays me, convinced I'm dying while my mind races toward catastrophe. I've experienced moments when my chest constricts, my pulse thunders in my ears, and the world narrows to a pinpoint. The first time it happened, I was certain my heart was giving out. Even now, these episodes ambush me when my thoughts spiral into an endless parade of worst-case scenarios. My brain is wired to anticipate, to create flowcharts of possibility, to map every potential outcome. When something threatens to disrupt that careful order, terror blooms. This book represented exactly that kind of threat, hence my elaborate dance of avoidance. But the Spirit is persistent. I've learned there's something called "dissociative amnesia," where your mind becomes your protector by sealing away what it cannot bear to witness. Unlike simply forgetting where you placed your keys, this amnesia carves canyons through your timeline, entire seasons of your life vanish. It's not that you're avoiding difficult conversations; it's that your brain has built walls around memories too painful to hold. Those memories still exist somewhere inside you, like photographs buried in a box you've lost the key to-influencing you in ways you cannot name, from places you cannot reach. These buried memories exist beyond our reach, yet they pull invisible strings, making us dance to rhythms we don't understand years after the original wound. Therapists offer maps to these hidden territories, but no magic eraser to remove what happened. Whether in treatment or not, the mind makes this choice without consulting us—sealing away what it cannot bear to witness. Behind my own consciousness, I've constructed a vault of steel and silence. But now I find myself picking at the lock, searching for answers not just for my sake, but for yours too. Perhaps in my story, you'll recognize fragments of your own. Please stay with me while I pry open the rusted locks of memories I've sealed away. I'm about to share secrets I've guarded so closely that speaking about them feels like learning a foreign language. I survived all of it-beautiful moments that saved me and horrors that nearly didn't. That survival isn't just mine to keep; it might be the flashlight someone needs while fumbling in their own darkness. The journey to this moment has been long and winding. Even now, I'm unfinished, still being shaped by each new day. But I promise you-yes, YOU, the one reading these words right now, perhaps alone in a quiet room, or on a crowded train, or with your shoulders hunched against the weight of memories—you matter. You are worth more than all the stars scattered across the night sky, more than every grain of sand on every shore, more than you can possibly imagine in your darkest moments when the world feels impossibly heavy. You are worth more than you can possibly imagine. Let me be clear: writing these words terrifies me. Each sentence peels away another layer of the armor I've spent decades polishing the facade of someone who has it all together. What you'll find underneath isn't pretty. There are jagged edges where I've been broken, scars that never quite healed straight. But between those fractures, you'll also find hard-earned wisdom that no classroom could have taught me. I believe our greatest power lies in standing beside others when their knees are buckling. So I'm laying bare the ugliest corners of my life, the moments that nearly destroyed me, and the small miracles that didn't. Perhaps in seeing how I survived, you'll recognize your own strength waiting to be discovered. Because I see you. I am you. You see, everyone, and I mean everyone, has a story. And no matter how much you want to forget any part of it, or the whole thing entirely, I promise, one day your story will be someone else's survival kit. And I hope today I can be yours.

Chapter One

Websters defines light as something that makes vision possible. They also define darkness as the partial or total absence of light. If this is true, then light counteracts darkness enabling visibility. But it's our perception on which one of those we see.

As I lie upright on an emergency room gurney with my left arm extended on a table with a bright blue surgical draping covering me from my hand to my elbow, with the opening at my wrist. A doctor was pouring bottles of saline on the inside of my arm, and it felt warm with a slight sting. A nurse stood to the right of me asking me questions I don't recall except for one. "Did you do this to yourself?" I said "No, I did not. I was opening an old window, and the pane broke and cut me." I don't think she believed a word of what I was saying but even though I was barely conscious I knew if I told her yes I did do this, I was surely in the psych ward on at least a 72-hour hold or more. I didn't want to endure that, but I also didn't want to endure being alive either.

Being the oldest meant I was the designated caretaker and responsible for my younger sister and brother. A job thrust upon me before I could tie my own shoes or tell time on a clock with hands. My childhood prison was a narrow row home wedged between identical brick houses in South Philly, where the 1980s seemed to stretch on forever. South Philly exists in its own universe, a tiny corner of Pennsylvania that might as well be another country entirely. It is predominantly swarmed with Italian heritage, and names that either start or end with a vowel. You might have heard of the small movie franchise called, Rocky. I still consider it the greatest film ever made—the kind that pumps you full of so much hope and determination that by the end credits, you're shadow-boxing in your living room, convinced you could conquer the world with nothing but raw grit and a pair of worn-out sneakers. Well, that was all filmed in South Philly; even the run through the Italian market towards the classic Art Museum steps scene, which, trust me, is miles longer than the movie makes it seem, (and in converse for that matter). That's South Philly in a nutshell. The people, the culture, the cramped streets where everyone knows your business but nobody knows your secrets. Unfortunately, my life was neither a blockbuster film, or some epic tale of a comeback kid who works hard, gets a break and goes on to stardom. The way my life was playing out was more like a horror movie, and I just wanted to be anywhere, but there. As a kid in South Philly, you don't have yards, or a front lawn to play on, or even air conditioning; well except maybe a window unit or two if you're lucky. You don't even have a park or playground to go to that isn't scattered with trash or some beer cans left from teenagers trying to find some escape from this place. What you have is a "stoop" to sit on. All that means is your 3 or 4 front steps leading to your front door is where you had to just sit and be outside. Of course, kids ran the streets and caused trouble, and once we even had a brick thrown through our basement window. I'm pretty sure my dad pissed someone off. My sister and brother and I used to play school in that very basement with some old easel and chalk just to hide away from whatever yelling was happening either in, or outside our house, plus it was cooler down there. What I had wasn't a childhood, it was an apprenticeship in survival. While other kids played and got to have fun, the most pain they felt was skinning their knees on playground, but I studied the sound of my father's footsteps on the stairs, learning to distinguish drunk-angry from drunk-violent. My mother, with her collection of hidden bruises, taught me without meaning to that love sometimes meant staying when you should run. By six, I was already the designated grown-up for my four-year-old sister and three-year-old brother. I became an expert at reading a room, at anticipating the moment my father's beer-soaked rage would need a new target. I learned to place my small body between his fists and my siblings.

I went to a catholic elementary school, and if I am being honest, I don't even know if there were any public schools there. All I knew was nuns I was supposed to call "Sister", priests I was supposed to call "Father", and wore an ugly blue polyester uniform with a white Peter Pan collar and some beat up saddle shoes. I walked each day to and from school, and I had a few friends that lived in the better, more "wealthy" part of the neighborhood. The kind with air conditioning throughout the whole house. I just waved as I'd continue my dreaded walk home in fear, usually to find my dad sitting inside home from work, watching baseball...and as always, with a beer in hand. My dad, Bill, drank Schmidt's beer...by the case full. Back then, Schmidt's came in squat cardboard boxes with a tear-away panel on the side. When you pulled that cardboard tab, the cans would tumble out one by one, like bullets from a chamber. Each empty can meant another moment of dread as I waited for him to crush it and bark his next command. If I was anywhere near him in the moment that he "needed another" beer, he'd crush the can and hand it to me and tell me to "get me another one." No "please" or no, "honey can you please do daddy a favor"? No, just commands to get him alcohol… because he was an abusive drunk and I was terrified of him.

We had a neighbor that lived on the corner, about 3 or 4 row homes down, and her name was Annie. She was a sweet small white haired elderly woman who I believe was a tailor or seamstress of some sort. I remember going to her house many times for whatever reason served that day to distract us, probably to escape whatever terror my dad was causing in the moment of one of his drunken rages. She was always welcoming, and her house felt quiet and safe. I was too young to understand then, but looking back, Annie must have heard the shouting through those paper-thin row home walls. She never asked questions when we showed up at her door, just ushered us inside with warm hands and distractions ready—fabric scraps to play with, sometimes cookies that tasted like butter and safety. Her clock would tick steadily while somewhere down the street, time in our house had stopped completely due to my dad's drunken rages. But, Annie's wasn't the only safe place we went. My mom Louise would round us up and head to my aunt Franny's, and we'd show up on her doorstep whenever dad's shouting turned into something worse. Being with her older sister made mom's shoulders drop an inch, like she could finally exhale.

The journey to Aunt Franny's house remains a blank spot in my memory—whether we trudged those blocks on foot or if my mother somehow managed to drive us there through her tears. Those details disappeared into the fog that forms when your body stays perpetually tensed, waiting for the next explosion. But in that house, I had three boy cousins, who were rough but had a relatively normal life with a mom and dad that were in fact loud, (but so is every Italian you meet, or at least that I knew of) but relatively "normal." I just admired that type of existence since it was far from anything I knew. I'm sure at whatever moment my mom decided it was time to leave from the terror my dad was causing, she didn't have time to pack clothes for us, or maybe she just forgot pajamas. Because I wore my fair share of airplane and truck pajamas graciously lent to me by one of the boys. The row homes of South Philly were carbon copies of each other, a tradition dating back to William Penn's time. Builders saved money by constructing them in identical batches—same plumbing, same gas lines, same layout. Walk through any front door in my neighborhood and you'd find yourself in a narrow foyer with stairs directly ahead, living room to the left, and kitchen tucked away in the back like an afterthought. The staircase in my aunt's house was covered in crimson carpet so bright it hurt my eyes, with a banister painted hospital white. I spent hours perched on those steps, my small hands tracing the swirls in the carpet fibers, listening to the muffled voices of adults deciding our fate. Each time, I'd try to listen and wonder if we'd be going back home or somewhere else entirely. I'd run my small fingers over the exposed brick in her kitchen, tracing the letters of their last name that had been etched or painted there years before. To my small child self, this seemed like magic; their name would stay hidden inside those walls even if someone covered them up someday. It was the closest thing to forever I'd ever seen. Forever was a word that belonged to other people, like a toy I'd seen in a store window but never got to hold. I never remember sleeping there, nor anything fun we did while there, just that my dad wasn't welcome there, so we were safe, whatever that meant. It must not have meant much, or maybe my dad was an apologetic drunk, because eventually we'd go back home, every single time. It was more of a beat, leave, come home, repeat cycle my mom seemed to be stuck in. And by virtue of her being stuck, made me have no choice but to deal with the collateral damage of her choices, or lack thereof. I eventually became the target he decided to use for the duration of my life, and his.

My forever safe place was a home I could not only feel protected, but I knew without a doubt I'd be fed, loved, and not made to feel like a burden that I felt so too often. My Grandmom's house was that place for me. It never mattered when, what time of day or night, she was there. She was a petite woman, 4'11, maybe smaller, but to me she was larger than life. I know she was part of an army God had on this earth to make sure little kids like me felt His presence and love in any way possible. To me she was a living, breathing, walking angel. The visits to her house became so frequent that my memories of her peaceful home outshine the darkness that followed my father wherever he was. She despised him, and she tolerated nothing...so he'd never had the audacity to show up there; I was surely safe, and I felt that to my core. She always pleaded with my mom to stay and not go back, but old habits die hard I suppose. As if something was magically changing overnight, or maybe she was just scared for what he'd do if she didn't return. Fear of what he'd to my mom, or to us kids. And she was right.

When I was about 8 years old, I wound up with liver toxicity and had a week-long stay in the hospital. I was quarantined and closed in a separate room because no one knew what was causing this. Apparently, I was sick with a virus the week prior and whoever spoke to my mom finally figured out she that had basically overdosed me on children's Tylenol, which was causing my liver to fail. My mom didn't tell me I could have *died* until I was an adult, and if I'm honest, I'm not even slightly surprised. When it was determined I was not carrying some virus that could cause an outbreak, no longer a danger to the floor, hospital staff, or tri-state area, I was allowed to go to the play area they had. It had board games, and crafts, things to keep a kids mind off why they were there to begin with. To give them some normalcy during their either short stay or the now hospital they called home. I went to that very play area and found the game called "Guess Who." This is where you play your opponent and you try to guess the people by their facial features, and if you guessed right you got to put that person face down. You win when all the faces are down on your side. I didn't win, nor play with anyone, just flipped the people up and down as I sat there in a hospital play area, by myself. Maybe being isolated in a room alone was better, because at least there someone would have to take care of me. Being alone in an area meant for kids while you recover from a virus, while seeing other sick kids who might never leave that place left any fun to be desired. I assumed the teacher in my class was wondering where I was or maybe my mom told the school she almost killed me. Either way I was given a manilla envelope with a stack of handmade cards from my classmates that were made on various shades of construction paper. Some opened the right way, some backwards, and most just read "get well soon" with a picture of some strange stick figure drawing, signed your friend, (insert name here). I'm sure that was a project for the day, and they couldn't care less who I was or why I was sick. I don't remember the things you'd think I would. Like the doctors, nurses, leaving the hospital, and I don't even remember how sick I really was. What I do remember is going directly to my Gram's house when I was discharged. I don't know why we went there, and not directly home, or why I wasn't put into bed to rest, considering I was just released from a hospital and was on deaths door a week prior.

All I know is it was dark outside and walking into her house was the safest place I'd felt all week. She rarely put the big light on in the kitchen, she mostly used the dim light above the sink, but on this night the big light was on and it illuminated the entire room, and her face lit up with a smile that reached her eyes the moment she saw me standing there. Probably mostly due to being alive, but nevertheless, the big light was on as if to welcome me home. I walked into the kitchen and there was a pot of Kraft mac & cheese on the stove, just made staring at me in all its creamy orange perfection. I grabbed the biggest spoon I could find and ate it right from the pot. She never let me eat right out of the pot, but she knew they hadn't let me eat all week in that place, and I was starved!She stood next to me, her soft laugh warming the kitchen as she watched me devour the man and cheese. "I figured they weren't feeding you right in that place," she said, nodding knowingly. That night was the best mac and cheese

I'd ever eaten, and not because I was just hungry. It wasn't because she stayed next to me until my belly was full....it was because she turned the big light on, for me.

Chapter Two

Memory is fallible.

But science tells us that's because of the key role emotions play in making and storing memories. The reason for this is there's a region of the brain called the hippocampus, which plays an important role in this process of creating memories, either good or bad ones, but especially traumatic ones. This space in our brains has the job of taking things from short-term memory and then transferring them into long-term memories. So, when something elicits an intense negative emotion, like a trauma, it's even more likely to be hard-coded in the brain, like anchor memories. When the brain experiences a moment like this, the stress hormones, cortisol and norepinephrine, that are released during that terrifying trauma will render an experience vivid and memorable, especially the central aspect of this part of the brain; meaning only the most meaningful aspects of the experience are filed into your brain's memory filing cabinet. It also means that the most essential and frightening elements of the event will be stored in vivid detail and will be remembered for the duration of one's life. But this doesn't mean that these memories include every detail of the event. The brain holds on to the most important stuff at the expense of the peripheral details.

I say all that scientific stuff to say this. For me to tell you my story, I needed things that have happened to me to make sense of why I could only remember certain things and not others. I remember all the upset, the trauma, and the scary moments even from an early age because I was always in a state of high stress, so all that trauma is encoded in my brain's subconscious forever. A constant state of fight or flight. But it at least makes sense as to why I can only recall a few good memories and those places and people you will meet along this journey with me. But most of my early memory is slated in the space of trauma and the people that caused that far more often than those who didn't. I have no recollection of time or space, or anything good that ever came out of our 10th Street Philly rowhome. I know we were poor, dirt poor. Food stamps and welfare kind of poor. The kind of poor that you can only go back and see photos of the conditions you lived in and ask yourself as an adult, how was that okay? I fell down the outside steps when I was three years old and bit straight through my tongue, and I know for sure I did not go to the hospital because I have the scar to prove it.

I imagine it is exactly like the puncture that someone would voluntarily pay for nowadays, except their tongue has a metal bar in it. I'm sure by the looks of the house and the fact we had nothing, there was no way they could afford an ER bill. So, I sat with my tongue on ice and called my aunt, who told me funny stories to get me to laugh until I stopped crying. My mom told me that when I was an infant, my dad found $20 outside on the ground, but instead of formula for me or diapers, he went and bought a case of beer. This wasn't the first time either. Guess she wasn't very good at seeing the neon sign blinking that stared directly back at her.

I don't remember birthday parties, or really anything celebratory, except for one party at McDonald's. This is when they allowed you to hold birthday gatherings in their restaurants with a bunch of questionable children and whatever theme they decided to decorate their establishment in. No decorations at this gathering, but this one was one where you could bring your Cabbage Patch doll to the party. You know the dolls that all smelled like a baby and had yarn for hair and soft cloth-stitched-together bodies? They all came with an outfit and even "adoption papers" with their name on them that made it official that said children are now parents! Who decided on this idea? Also, who determined that the same kids who didn't know me from Adam and who wrote me get-well cards the year prior were going to gather at the local South Philly McDonald's for Happy Meals and to show off their dolls? And believe me, there were plenty of boys at the party too, not just girls. This was a craze like no other. If you were a kid growing up in the 80s, or a parent of a kid who grew up then, I'm sure you remember the intensity of the CBK craze. Everyone was elated to show off their newly purchased (that their parents stood in lines for hours to get) Cabbage Patch kids; not truly excited to be at my birthday party. Either you invite the whole class, or you don't invite anyone, isn't that the rule? I had no idea who these kids were, and if I did it was very short-lived. I'm pretty sure my Aunt Gio, my mom's oldest sister, put this endeavor all together. She was over the top and made sure I was always paid attention to because she knew the hell, we lived in. But you will get to know all about her a bit later. All I know was photos were taken of me at said party, with said dolls, with said classmates, and that's about all I know of it. I don't remember gifts, or even eating for that matter. Isn't it funny how your brain will remember the minor happiness among a giant mess? It's like when you go through a box of "memories" you kept that's shoved deep in the back of your closet somewhere and you haven't seen it in years, but somehow amid the mess that *is* your closet, you bumped right into it trying to find the other shoe you were looking for. You immediately forget the shoe you searched tirelessly for and excitedly open the box thinking you will be transported back in time somehow. But only to find things like an old mixed tape that you can't play because who owns a tape player these days…or the one napkin from that restaurant you went to on the date that you swore he was "the one"—he wasn't; or the pink envelope that enclosed the birth certificate of your very own Cabbage Patch doll. Mine was named Bonnie Bunny. She had blonde ponytails of yellow yarn and wore a maroon corduroy jumper with a striped shirt. I held on to her for dear life. She couldn't leave, couldn't be taken away, (nothing Aunt Gio did for me was ever questioned) and by the sheer fact that these dolls were a hot commodity in 1983 and I had one, made me feel relatively normal in comparison to the life I was experiencing at the time. I took her everywhere. I even took her to my Grams when my dad violently backhanded my mom across the face in front of us kids and then proceeded to break the glass coffee table while he was yet again in another one of his drunken rages. While my mom yelled, for what felt like the hundredth time, "that's it we're leaving!" Here we go again. All I could do was hold on to my little sister's hand while holding my baby brother. Being all but a child myself, I followed my mom out the door. This time the stay was longer. This time I had taken up residence in my uncle's old bedroom. Things must have been bad, or maybe, Gram refused to help my mom should she return.

My Grandfather Nicholas, God rest his soul, I never had the pleasure of meeting. He died five days before I was born. Had the funeral and bam, I decided that's the best time to come into the world. I've been told I was the miracle of joy everyone needed. Based on how my life has played out, I was a short-lived miracle for those who apparently needed one. My Pop was as Italian as they come; lineage is straight from Italy "off the boat" as they say. Even the photos I've seen of him, he looks like he's straight from every stereotypical Italian mobster movie ever known. He died young, in his 50s from many heart attacks, so my Gram was alone to deal with the mess my mom kept bringing home. My Pop would not have tolerated it; he loved my mom but despised my dad. The kind of despise where he'd grabbed her by both shoulders and begged her not to marry.

"that worthless drunk". I was the first granddaughter, so I'm sure that status would have come with some form of protection. But unfortunately, I didn't meet him, have his protection, nor did I know what it was like to be loved by a man who wasn't taking his wrath out on the first person he saw daily. I didn't have any protection from this life I was forced into, but at least being at my Grams offered me some shelter and safety from the outside world as I knew it. She still looked at me like I was the miracle she needed when she lost the most important person in her life, even when no one else did.

My uncle's old bedroom was exactly the way he left it, brown. Who loves brown? The walls were covered in brown paneling, floor to ceiling. The rug was brown, the dresser and headboard a dark brown, the bedding a brown pattern of some sort, and even the closet door, brown! Everything that was in that room was what we'd call today "vintage"; but nothing was vintage to me. It was just an old back of the house upstairs bedroom with zero air conditioning. There was a small black and white television on the dresser, you know the ones with the antenna you had to adjust at just the right angle to even get a picture. I guess parents who leave everything in their kids' rooms the same as when they physically left home give them some sort of moment in time that they want to remember. It's not as though my uncle was returning to reclaim his teenage bedroom or take the old musty stale *vintage* furniture anyhow. So, the brown room was mine for the duration. I don't know how long we were there this time, but it must have been long enough that I was allowed to put posters on the walls. Well, on the *brown paneling*. I had a giant poster of Michael Jackson from Human Nature right smack above where the TV was. He was in a white and yellow suit, and he was the most amazing, most popular music artist at that time; they called him the King of pop. My mom would have never gotten that for me; I'm sure that too was an Aunt Gio purchase. After finally settling into the stuffy brown room, with my Michael poster, Bonnie Bunny, and feeling a sense of comfort and protection, it eventually came to an end. My Michael poster didn't accompany me because I was certain I'd be back at some point soon. But we weren't. Instead, we were headed to New Jersey. What was in New Jersey? I don't recall why we moved there, maybe a job, maybe to get out of the terrible neighborhood, or maybe my parents thought this was some fix-it-all for the complete disaster that was our life. Nothing good ever came out of our small South Philly rowhouse anyhow. We were poor or at least I thought we were poor, but somehow, we had money to move? Dad's paychecks always disappeared into beer cans and broken furniture, but now suddenly there was enough for to move. It didn't make sense, but I was afraid to ask. I didn't have a say in the matter, or even the right to ask questions being only a kid, I had to roll with the punches, and I mean that both literally and figuratively. If you think of what I should have thought, it was "this means a new school, new friends, and a new start for our family!" But that was hardly the case. This meant taking my siblings and me so far away that we could not escape the temper of a man who had just finished a 12-pack of beer and was looking for a fight. This meant putting me in the direct line of fire for when he attacked my mom, and I was the only one there to defend her. This meant having to now protect my sister and brother from what they were too young to understand. This meant taking me away from the only people who had ever protected me and cared about what happened to me. This meant I was entirely alone to endure a war that was only just beginning. I don't remember anyone looking at a house, the process of buying said house, and I sure don't recall driving up to a home where it felt like something magical was about to happen to my childhood. What I do know is now we lived in a yellow house that had a kitchen with a breakfast "nook." It wasn't much of a nook as it was just a table with benches off the side of the kitchen. My sister Samantha and I shared a room; this was no shocker, we always have. I've never had my own room, ever. My brother Luke got his own room, and there was a powder room upstairs, and that was it. Seemed ok except through our closet door was a little door to an attic. The attic door loomed in our closet like a gateway to some nightmare, and my sister and I silently agreed never to touch it, not even on the bravest of days. My sister Sam used to put things in bags, specifically brown grocery bags. Random stuff, but random stuff people needed. Like a set of car/house keys kind of stuff. Any time anything went missing, we'd check her bag(s) first before calling it lost. Most of the time everything you were looking for was there, plus many items you say, "hey I was looking for this!". It was surely a phase; perhaps moving into a new environment, she took familiar things to comfort her. One night it was so bad, and I was terrified of what my dad might do to me because of the violent, intoxicated state he was in, that I asked her to hide and sleep in the closet with me. She took her brown bag, and we slept in the closet together. Despite our fears about what lurked behind that attic door, the closet felt like a fortress that night—the one place where not even my father's rage could reach us as we huddled together in the dark. In retrospect, it was probably the worst thing I could have done in the event anyone came looking for me or my sister. After all, my dad was a real-life scary living monster, the worst of them all. I lived in a constant state of fear and had to protect myself at any cost, and I'm only now in the third grade to give you some perspective on time. The mind is a complex organ that we can't even make sense of sometimes until after the fact. Surely my now 9-year-old old brain could not understand the agony I was essentially living in. My brother Luke was quiet. Always has been. He's much younger than me, 6 years to be exact; so, I didn't connect with him very well at all. Maybe it was because he was taking direct lessons from the man who was supposed to be his hero, but rather taking lessons from an abusive alcoholic father with a backhand that would lead anyone to the floor, or into a wall. It's no wonder my brother was always timid and shy. He witnessed so much he was afraid to speak for fear he'd be next. He never was. It was always me...very much always me. My parents' room was downstairs. And that meant my dad would have to chase me up the stairs when his temper flared up and he wanted to use me to "make an example" to my siblings. I was glad my room was on the second floor; that meant I was faster and I could hope to lock myself in my room before he got there. He never gave up, even though I was able to lock the door in time while even throwing a metal trash can at my head on the way up in hopes to stop me. No one picked up for me, no one talked him off whatever ledge he was on, and no one helped me when I was being attacked in yet another one of his drunken furies, at least not that I remember. He'd take off his belt and bind it together in a loop and crack it as if it were a whip, while banging on the door until I opened it; or else he'd bust the door in. By that time, he had nearly lost his mind, and my face was usually his retaliation for his upset at his hand and my body for his belt.

We lived in this house; we started a new school that was across the street, and I made friends with a girl a few doors down from us with whom I tried to spend a lot of time at her house, just to avoid the chaos of mine. Why did we have this house, but my mom drove a beat-up old green manual Volkswagen Bug with holes in the floor? What was this situation we were living in? I wanted to go home. Home to safety, home to my Grams. The next-door neighbors had three teenage girls. They were clearly much older than us and their family always looked happy or at least content. I was in complete awe of this and longed for that place where I wasn't scared to just be at home. The girls took a liking to us and were always pleasant and waved when they saw us. But when the new school year was fast approaching and our parents had made zero mention of new school clothes, and we'd worn a uniform to school all our lives, we must shame ourselves to knock on the neighbor's door, hoping one of the girls would answer, and they did. I had no choice but to be honest and ask if they had anything that perhaps no longer fit them that we could wear. They were good people, especially the youngest. She was the one who'd come sit for us when my mom worked nights, so to protect us from my dad who was in fact there, and by that sheer fact, I'm pretty sure she knew how bad it was for us. She packed up an entire trash bag full of clothes, shirts, pants, all the latest styles and trends, or maybe they were last year's, but they were new to me. Instead of shame, she made me feel empowered, like I was going to be the best-dressed kid in school. She was so kind and sweet to help. I took the bags home, and Sam and I called dibs on what we discovered. No one was happy about that, especially my dad. "Where'd that shirt come from? Where'd you get those ugly red pants?" as he glowered at me. I just told him the neighbor had some clothes they were going to give away and thought we could use them. "What are we, charity now?" he barked. Well, yeah, Dad, we kind of are. All the money goes towards your drinking habit. So much so that we had no clothes to wear for a new school, all thanks to you. Mom's driving a car with holes in the floor! Why are you like this? That's what I wanted to say but didn't. I just hoped he'd leave it alone and go about his way to the basement to watch baseball, like he always did. This meant he wasn't coming to attack me for anything or about anything, even if just for a little while.

Even today, every time I hear even a soda can opening, I associate that with the crack of a beer being opened. Or how every time I hear a baseball announcer, all I associate that

with is how my dad would be so consumed in a game that would ultimately render him unconscious from the copious amounts of beer he drank. But when he came to, I was his target. It's a vicious cycle of reminders that haunt me daily. The one place my brain didn't turn off from all reminders from was my Grams. And she now seemed so far away. A car ride over the Walt Whitman Bridge felt like an eternity. I needed her now more than ever and to be shielded by the big green steel door.

Chapter Three

My Gram's house on the surface looked sort of like a museum. The big green steel front door opened into a small foyer with the staircase rising straight ahead—a classic South Philly row home layout that anyone from the neighborhood would recognize instantly. In the same small foyer was a corner "lighted" decorative piece affixed halfway down the wall with a mirror, a dim light underneath, and cast iron surrounding the bottom as a sort of border. It had on top what appeared to be a naked woman. I didn't ask questions, perhaps it was a famous statue, it was just always there. I eventually found out it was basically the nightlight that was always on no matter what time of day. The staircase seemed so grand with its golden iron banister that curved in a spiral at the bottom as to say, "see how fancy this railing is, it was expensive." The rug was a light green shag carpeting, lacking the shag from the wear and tear of raising her own family, I'm sure. And it was covered with an oriental area rug to probably cover the bad areas, but even that too was worn. Gram used to tell me stories about when she was young and how she met my Grandpop while he was in the military and he'd send her boxes of chewing gum, and little things he knew she liked to eat to try to win her over. Well, it worked because four kids later, three girls, the youngest a boy, and a new house in the best neighborhood in South Philly; my Gram was surely something special and clearly *not* just to me. My grandparents ran the Marlow, a local motel and bar that became the go-to spot for anyone who was anyone in South Philly during those years. Gram worked there hosting, and my Pop ran the joint. No one really talked about it in detail, I just got pieces of information I've put together over time. They had purchased it with my Pop's family and, well, anytime you do anything business-related with family, it usually falls out, just like this did. I always thought it was so elegant in the photos I'd seen, and everyone dressed as if it were a black-tie affair. But growing up it was a sore spot that no one ever wanted to talk about. But I knew by the loads of liquor, whiskey, and everything in between stocked in the bottom of the dining room hutch that there was clearly a bar somewhere in the past.

In the living room, stood a crushed black velvet love seat with gold embroidered flowers that was draped with a multicolored Afghan blanket over the top of it that my grandmother knitted herself. She knitted blankets for every-thing and everyone. And every grandchild that was born had a specific baby blanket, and no two were the same. She had an object that looked like an end table next to the love seat, but it wasn't. It had a cloth top that opened like a treasure chest, revealing a rainbow of yarn skeins and silver knitting needles of various sizes, a collection I couldn't properly name but knew was the source of every blanket that had ever warmed me. And that was where the multicolored Afghan came from, her very own weathered but beautiful hands. There were black and white Italian marble "coffee tables" that were never used for any beverages, neither hot nor cold. The tables held random things like Italian sculptures that were a clear hazard for a small child, and even some adults. There was a round gold container that held Grams glasses; sunglasses, reading glasses, glasses she probably never used, but she'd let me try on, especially when I was little. There was a red pair of sunglasses, with lenses that were rose-colored that covered your entire eyebrow; they were so big and those were my absolute favorite. Everything I saw through those lenses was pink and beautiful. I'd wear them and carry her giant purse around that seemed extremely heavy for a petite woman who never went anywhere, all while pretending I was fancy or someone special. I'd dig through the purse and find a compact of powder or some random lipstick she'd kept in it and put it on, and she never stopped me but got the biggest kick out of it. I don't have the giant handbag, but I do have those red glasses even to this day. I don't wear them; I just keep them in the sleeve they were always in as a reminder that no matter how bad it seems, we can look through rose-colored glasses and see the good sometimes, if we just look hard enough. But sometimes, taking them off is even harder than looking through them. Directly behind the tables were two sets of gold, and I do mean gold, velvet couches covered in plastic. In case you're unfamiliar and asking about the plastic, this was a very typical Italian family thing to do. This prevented any spills and protected what was now at least 30-year-old furniture from damage. But despite the plastic and the velvet, these weren't any normal couches. These were designed in a way that unless you were a contortionist, the comfortability factor was zero. They were sort of curved like a partial "S shape" with a very low, almost non-existent back so no person could sit comfortably. As if that wasn't Italian enough, the walls behind the couches were all mirrors from floor to ceiling. As kids, we were always in the mirror trying to see our breath or making funny faces at one another. We were constantly yelled at by Gram, "Do not touch the mirrors! I can see your fingerprints!". Even though we knew what she'd say every single time, it was still fun to see how much fun a giant mirror could be. My Gram's voice filled every corner of that house. At four-foot-eleven, what she lacked in height, she made up for in volume, a trait I'd later recognize in every Italian family. And her words didn't just reach you; they found you, wherever you were hiding. All us kids, cousins included, just complied, and stayed away from the mirrors, the tables, the couches, and went to the areas we were allowed to be, like the floor or outside. Between the couches was a giant light. The base was gold velvet, just like the couches that sat on the same black marble to match the "don't ever touch tables". The lampshade was a giant black cylinder. I've never seen a lampshade quite this big. Maybe it was custom-made. And now that I think about it, could everything have been custom-made? Or was there a secret store that sold only gaudy Italian furniture in matching sets? This light was never turned on, ever. Probably for fear that all the velvet and plastic would ignite simultaneously. But the same area was used for the Christmas tree. The lamp was removed, to which I have no idea where a six-foot lamp gets placed for a season. Then, in its place each year, there was an artificial huge white tree that was elevated atop this middle table somehow, with red lights, red garland, and red ornaments. With the giant lamp that never got turned on, now there was light, and it gave a warm feeling to the sheer menagerie feel that the room had. Plus, it was Christmas and that was the best time at my Gram's as a kid. Cookies, pies, seven fishes on Christmas Eve, homemade gravy, meatballs, braciola, manicotti; the food is endless on not just Christmas but any holiday, really. But as gaudy as it was, I confess, I did love the tree. I even took the ornaments as an adult and created the same white tree as an homage to Christmas at my Grams. I even make the same foods each year and keep the traditions that she ensured to do that made my life somewhat bearable. There was a giant entertainment unit that stretched from one end of the wall to the other end. It housed a record player, a fancy TV that you could hide with a cover that slid over it, and speakers on each end. This is not something we'd ever see today, but it was never used, at least not while I was there. My gram had a 27-inch TV on top of this beautiful entertainment center so she could see it and hear it while she sat in her love seat. She sat in the love seat because that's where my Pop sat. I think it's safe to say this giant entertainment unit was in fact a functioning piece of equipment at one time, but once my Pop died, it was like a part of her did too. So, she never used anything that may have been something they did together. Maybe they danced to records they'd put on or watched old TV shows together. She didn't even sleep in the bedroom they shared, which was so beautiful and so perfect. Suits hung in the closet, dresses, and hat boxes, with shoes and gloves to match each one. It was like a moment in time had stopped and the door was shut and never opened again. On the other end of the room atop the never-used entertainment center, and now just a catch-all, was this giant golden Buddha. It was beautiful with a red stone between its eyes. It was truly lifelike and sat about

3 feet high in a cross-legged position with its eyes closed but was only there for decoration and eventually was just used to hold the mail. My Gram was a devout Catholic and even said the rosary every night; so, this was strictly to be bold and decorative like the rest of the golden room. I'd sit next to her on this love seat, and you could feel the warmth and comfort in this huge sterile room of furniture and artifacts that no one could enjoy. But I figured out very young why this love seat was so important. It would go on to heal many a day for me sitting in that spot with her, and even allowed me to help heal her on the difficult days that lay ahead.

Chapter Four

Everyone has a place they love to run to when things get difficult, or when they have a bad day. Some kids and teens might hunker in front of the television, eat junk food, and scroll through whatever social media is most popular in that moment, or even just get lost in a video game. Even some adults will in fact do those things as well. Others perhaps will call someone to help, others maybe will go to a bar and drink, some eat their feelings, and some will shop till they drop. Adult, teen, or kid, you'll do whatever you can to numb whatever pain or frustration caused that difficult or abysmal day. Unfortunately for me, I had nowhere to run, nowhere to hide, all because I lived with a man who stole my innocence to ever be a child or a young girl. I was never the kid who could find those pockets of time to deal with my difficult, no-good, very-bad day. I'd have traded lives with anyone to not have to live in the rollercoaster of torment and abuse I was consistently on. When my parents met, they were both working at a restaurant in Center City, Philadelphia. My dad was a cook, and my mom was a waitress. They moved in together in an apartment in said city, and it all seems like the start of a Hollywood romcom, right? Whereas I don't know all the details of their dating period or even their marriage, but I'm sure neither of them told the other about the secret past they'd lived up to that point. The past of fighting in Vietnam. A severe drinking problem. And a previous marriage. Well, there goes your romcom-turned-mystery, perhaps thriller, and no longer a romance nor a comedy.

My mom had been married before, at 19. She was married to him for only a short while, and he was abusive, go figure. My Gram had this large rectangular frame in her kitchen that covered the whole wall upon entering and it was the first thing you saw. The background in the frame was the sheet music to Frank Sinatra's "My Way." It was Pop's favorite song, and it was covered in a collage of photos of family, kids, grandkids, and the like. It was creative and amazing, and each time I'd look at it, I'd find something new: a new photo I wasn't tall enough to see before, a new face I'd learn about, but unfortunately, I wasn't born yet, so I never made the cut. But the many people who protected me along the way were in this collage, and it brought me comfort seeing it. But, through all the photos I saw, each time one always stood out to me that I didn't know the detail of and was afraid to ask. It was still a collage photo like the rest, except this one my mom was wearing a wedding veil, and she was clearly the bride. She looked so pretty, like a vintage 60s bride from a magazine. There was no groom, and no other photos to piece this event together like the others. It wasn't until I was a teenager that I found out my mom had been married for less than a year to this abusive man. She's never spoken of it to me. I've only found out through others that it didn't end well. Yet here I am doing the math thinking, "wait, am I actually someone else's kid?" But it was impossible; I was in fact the daughter of the second man my mom married, who was also abusive. I noticed a pattern, and I'm sure everyone else did too.

My dad was one of four kids and had two alcoholic parents-shocker. I know nothing of how he grew up, never heard any stories of what he did for fun, his siblings, his parents, nothing. I just knew him as the man who would get angry, blackout drunk, and if I was anywhere in the vicinity of his target, I'd be where his temper landed. He was, in fact, an Army veteran and fought in Vietnam, and I know that had to have a huge impact on his psyche and probably lived with undiagnosed PTSD. My mom would make excuses for how he was and why he was the "way he was". She said it was because when he arrived back from the war, no one came to meet him or greet his return. I'm sure this had a severe, lasting impact, but making excuses for a man who came from a line of alcoholics and now abuses his wife and kids is no excuse for the severe, lasting impact I must deal with because of his actions. I don't know how long it took until the darkness of their pasts came to light. It appears my mom was in denial, and my dad was a severe alcoholic. I'm certain this was not something either of them knew of the other when they had decided to create, me. I don't know if I was planned or just created in a moment in time where perhaps my parents were hoping a child would conceal the pasts that they both faced in a lonely state of solo isolation. It wouldn't be long before my grandparents knew my dad was not the one for my mom. I don't know what he did to put them off so soon, or maybe just the parental instinct we all "should" have. I don't know how my parents were married, or where, or even when; was there some magical proposal that sucked my mom into his world? But I suppose being already pregnant with me didn't help the cause with my grandparents, because remember...I was the "miracle of joy" that everyone needed at such a bad time, right? Right. It would only be a few months before my Pop's heart couldn't beat another day, and five days later here comes the creation from the couple who couldn't see past the other one's shortcomings or distant past. Then I arrived just in time to be present for the most epic failure a marriage has ever seen, and a past I cannot run away from. Neither of my parents went to college, so they just worked whatever job was available to support the now three children they thought would cure their chaotic relationship. My mom would take part-time jobs at the local mall at night, and one of the girls from next door would stay with us. Probably to make sure nothing happened to us while she was gone. I don't even think my mom paid them. She even worked handing out flyers for Barbizon Modeling School on random street corners in Center City Philadelphia. My Aunt Gio worked as the director of the school, so she'd always have random jobs for people to do. Hand out flyers to attempt to gain students, stuff mailers with a stack of brochures about how you can be the next top model. She even had odd jobs as far as cleaning the make-up brushes that were used to make the students camera-ready. There was no internet for advertising in this case of the flyer push my mom graciously signed up for. So, she'd make up my mom's face with the heavy 80's makeup; you know the heavy blush, eyeliner of a raccoon, and awful red lipstick. She'd dress her up in stuff she'd never wear, all to draw attention to the pretty woman handing out flyers for people to inquire about the school. It was a job, I guess. It felt sort of exploitative, but I guess you do what you've got to do to feed three kids and, again, feeding an addiction to a man she decided was her ride or die. Quite possibly the die part was valid as she lived in fear daily for her life. My dad always worked weird hours. Like a job that he'd have to get up at 2 am to go to and work till 2 pm the next day. I have no idea what he did, but it was always blue-collar work, and he was always tired with bloodshot eyes. Not the blue-collar work you think of like union work, or construction or even landscaping. None of that was my dad in any capacity. He was the one who had seemed like a jack of all trades with no "trade." He worked in a deli for a long time, did odd jobs in between, and was a delivery driver to distribute ice cream products to various stores and grocery chains, which was the last one I knew of. His work ethic was something he had an undeniable strength in. I mean, who gets up at 2 am unless you're a doctor or rushing to a fire? Even though I knew he got up early and came home 12 or so hours later, once I had figured out why, the one thing I was certain of about my dad is that he worked to drink. He'd work, he'd come home, drink, and find some way to ruin my childhood, or lack thereof. He'd get pissed off just because the Phillies lost or because I was just in the way. No matter how hard I tried, he'd find a way to take that long day of work out on me. He'd backhand me for something I did, or for laughing with my mom. He thought it was about him. He'd grab my arm and yell, "How dare you talk and laugh about me!" Then came another slam against the wall or a hit to the face. I'd walk upstairs to my room, completely clouded in shame. I only knew a few things about my dad and his routines, but one thing I was certain of, he was the textbook case of an abusive alcoholic. Morning would eventually come, and my nightmare would start all over again. I was thankful he left when I was sleeping, or whatever you call knowing it's 2 a.m. and I can't wait to hear the front door shut so I can get some semblance of peaceful sleep. From what I could see, the bar for my life was set very low if it was any indication of the example that was being set before me. There was never, and I mean never, talk of college, or even what we wanted to be when we grew up, absolutely nothing. And when you're living paycheck to paycheck to feed three kids, and feeding an alcohol addiction, I'm sure weighed on them like a ton of bricks. But they made the choices that they had to live with. Us kids, well, we were just innocent bystanders in the destruction that was erupting each day inside that little yellow house. Little did they know the collateral damage would far exceed childhood.

Chapter Five

My Gram was the epitome of protection to me; yet there was one person who, amongst the unfortunate tragedy that was my existence, saw me. I mean truly saw *me*, recognized my worth when no one else did, and moved mountains to bring even small moments of joy into my life. She was my Aunt Giovanna, Aunt Gio for short. Since she was my mom's oldest sister, again like Aunt Franny, I think she felt some sort of obligation to protect us. But her way of doing it was far better than the obligatory take us in and let us stay for a few days till the dust settled. She was the epitome of fun and exposed me to things that would change the trajectory of my life as I knew it. She wasn't only fun, but also crazily creative. She knew I was in a new school, a new town, only knew the few kids in my class, but she knew exactly what was needed. She knew how to throw a birthday party everyone would remember. My birthday is in February, so I'm always forced indoors to do anything, if at all. I don't have a birthday in the summer where you invite everyone over for a BBQ and kids swim until their feet wrinkle. I surely didn't have that, but I had an Aunt Gio. For my birthday, she made a backdrop in all neon colors reading "Happy Birthday Nicole!" The backdrop covered the entire wall; did she use a tarp or a large plastic tablecloth? Either way, it was a Jackson Pollock of happy birthday to me in every color imaginable. It was the '80s, so everything was neon and pop culture was present in the form of what I call the "original" Madonna, where everyone had lace gloves, black rubber bracelets that climbed your entire forearm, and yes, neon everything. Some of the kids in my class came, probably unsure and curious about what type of world they were about to enter in that little yellow house. But Aunt Gio was the life of the party. Remember my Michael Jackson poster on the wall at my Grams? The Human Nature suit of yellow and white? No, the poster didn't make an appearance, but something even better! Mattel had come out with Michael Jackson dolls during his heightened fame, and my aunt found the one with him in the yellow and white suit and put him standing *ON MY CAKE*! He wasn't the only one there, but a gal by the name of Cyndi Lauper also accompanied him! I thought she was the best and so part of the pop culture I knew at that time. But this doll wasn't sold in stores like Michael was. Aunt Gio took a Barbie doll, dyed, and cut her hair, found material to make clothes that looked just like hers, with a big blue and white skirt and a top to match. She even had earrings!

At the time Cyndi Lauper had shaved the side of her head and the other draped long bright red hair, cause, well, she was different, and different made me feel comfort. This doll had *THAT* hair. I couldn't believe it, she had Michael Jackson and Cyndi Lauper on doll stands atop my cake, just hanging out like that was a normal kid's birthday cake. She took pictures with the camera that had those giant flash bulbs of all of us standing in front of the giant sign and once-in-a-lifetime cake. She also made sure there was a microphone, a speaker, and music so we could all have our own version of karaoke. Everyone wanted a turn, and we played and acted goofy together, singing our hearts out to every pop artist out at that time. Because of one person not caring what anyone thought I deserved and looking past all the shame I carried, it turned out to be the one day I felt like I was the most important kid in the world. And my dad hated every second of it. We disrupted his basement quiet time of drinking until blackout drunk. But on this day, I didn't care.

Aunt Gio worked at Barbizon Modeling School as the director, as mentioned before with the flyer fiasco and my mom's side gig, and she was there for quite a few years. She even worked under a fake name, which confused me for a long time, seeing her desk nameplate knowing that it was not her actual name. But it was to keep her personal life separate, so she went by sort of a professional pseudonym among the students. Aunt Gio introduced me to so many things I never knew existed. Starting at a young age, I went to dancing school. I'm sure she or my Gram paid for it because no one with an addiction uses any disposable income to help their child succeed in life, and we were as poor as it got. I absolutely loved to dance. I loved it so much that Aunt Gio would do my makeup, dress me up in whatever recital costume we were assigned that season, and let me walk the runway and dance my heart out at the school. She saw something in me and cultivated it. She made sure I continued with dance and even introduced me to the theatre. Broadway musicals specifically: shows like Phantom of the Opera, Les Misérables, Cats, West Side Story; all the classics, and many more. I was hooked, and that's an understatement. I wanted to be on stage just like that and sing and dance and get lost in a world where any character or song you could dream up could be a smash Broadway hit. She'd max out her credit cards just to take me to see these magnificent shows I never knew existed. It was an entire world I never knew was so accessible and she told me I could be anything I could ever dream of. No one told me I could dream, let alone what I could dream of being when I grew up. I wasn't allowed to have dreams, but according to her, I could do anything. Because of this new hunger for all things performance and stage, I set my eyes on every talent show and platform I could get on just to see what I had outside of dance that might be lying dormant inside me. I admired each performer I saw on stage and couldn't wait to take my mark on one myself. There were things held in the "all-purpose" room of the school, which, as we all know, served as a gym, a cafeteria, and had a stage for school assemblies, or in this case, a talent show. They'd fold up the white tables we'd eat lunch on and put out metal folding chairs for family and friends to see the hard practiced performances. All while trying to overcome the stench of food served that day and the odor of prepubescent boys who always played too rough during gym for a room that had concrete floors. I was in an ensemble group with a bunch of girls from 4th- 6th grade dancing to Footloose. The ironic thing is that in the movie Footloose, it was forbidden to dance in the town. And here we were about 15 girls deep dancing our hearts out on that all-purpose room stage. That was all I needed to know I had zero fear of this whole stage business. I had been in dance recitals, but I was too young to even understand what being on stage meant. And why it was so dark in the audience and why the light was only on all of us. You didn't need to know any of that. Just that the dance teacher was happy you didn't make a total fool of yourself for all the work she put in over nine months teaching you this two-minute routine. I confirmed I had zero fear of being on stage because you'd showcase the whole talent show of performances in front of your school peers during the school day as "an assembly". A bunch of bratty elementary school kids who would make fun of anything if given the chance. The thing is with assemblies, they left the lights on, so you could see everyone staring back at you. However, once the music came on, I couldn't care less; I was blind to all of them. I danced my heart out for both those kids and the adults at night. And I knew that this very simple thing called a stage transported me from a life I struggled to be in, into a world of endless possibility where I could feel alive and dream and be anyone I wanted to be. I was still friends with the girl down the street; she was a year older than me. But even so, we had a connection. She was friends with another girl in her grade, and we all eventually became friends and, well, did what girls do in 5th and 6th grade: listen to music, make up dances, and eat endless boxes of Kraft Mac and Cheese, just to name a few.

In enters Aunt Gio, yet again, with her larger-than-life charisma and presence. Knowing how much I have grown to love the stage and performing, and all things theatre, she had an idea for that year's upcoming talent show. I don't just mean any idea. I mean this idea would take work, time, and a complete makeover. You see, Aunt Gio was a master make-up artist and the creativity she exuded was impermeable. She was going to not only dress us up in full Broadway makeup and costume, but also for the show of Andrew Lloyd Webber's infamous CATS! We, and by "we," I mean me and my only two friends, were going to be transformed head to toe into Jellicle Cats. If you've never seen the show, trust me when I say the make-up alone was a very ambitious feat to attempt. Head to toe bodysuit, full face make-up, wigs with ears, and even a furry tail. Let's not leave out the entire four-and-a-half-minute song of a spectacle of Cats choreography like no one has seen before, at least not in this town. Aunt Gio was very persuasive; I mean she had me at theater and dance, but it wasn't me she had to convince. My friends thought my aunt was larger than life and even as crazy as her idea sounded, even their parents agreed to let them do it! Aunt Gio wore a long denim skirt, black tie-up combat boots that resemble Doc Martens, and a button-down denim shirt of sorts. She wore a Mickey Mouse pocket watch on a long black shoelace string around her neck and had reddish-blonde hair and exuded funky cool aunt-ness. She was a model when she was young, stunningly beautiful with long dark red hair, probably why she took the route of running a modeling school. She was always beautiful to me and was awe-inspiring; and I wanted to be just like her. And she had a "Louis". Louis was with her as her companion even as far back as when I was born. They've never married, but she said she doesn't need a piece of paper to say they are together forever. He was always so nice to me, a quiet man with salt-and-pepper hair that eventually turned full gray earlier than I thought possible. They drove a green Volkswagen bus like two hippies stuck in a part of life they would like to preserve and live in for their duration together.

When we started practicing for the talent show, we watched her in awe in front of us, like she was a seasoned choreographer with the likes of Debbie Allen in Fame. All she needed was a long wooden stick to bang the floor with. We picked up the steps quickly because every chance we got was Aunt Gio driving over in her bus so we could get to work.

We found out that this year's show was not going to be held in the school's all-purpose room, but the middle school auditorium! Wait, that's an actual giant stage, and a room full of cushioned seats for an audience to sit and judge your performance. And here we are, three girls who were about to dress up like cats and perform a choreographed dance by a woman who probably should have highly considered that life for herself. We rehearsed in driveways, sidewalks, the grass, anywhere we could have room to move. We even had full dress rehearsals like this was an actual Broadway performance. Many hours were spent perfecting our routine, and with one day to go before the big shows. Except this time, the school administration told us last minute that there was no daytime show for your peers, all nighttime, no ticket needed, free of charge, and anyone was welcome. Um, ok, well one shot is all we have. Aunt Gio spent hours putting on our wigs with some type of face glue around our foreheads, so it looked like actual fur with ears. She painted our faces to where we didn't even recognize ourselves. It was sheer perfection. We got dressed in all black leotards, leg warmers that she glued fur to that covered our black ballet shoes. And to top it off, a long black fuzzy tail pinned to the back. She marveled at her creation. Even adding glitter to our wigs at the end so we'd sparkle on stage. Our pitiful excuse for a "dining room table" was a long folding table with a tablecloth on it that had turned into a special effects makeup room. This was surely not a place for those who didn't understand or care. My dad walked by several times, teeming at the mess, asking when it would be done. She just ignored him and shooed him away with her hand and said this was our day and that's what mattered. He'd never argue with her. She's the big sister and she wasn't afraid of anything, especially him. Nothing else mattered in that moment because it was time to go. Once we got there, some classrooms were set up to hold the acts until it was their time to perform. No one could tell who we were or what to expect. Just that no one else could even put a flame to what was about to happen on that stage. The middle school auditorium looked and felt so big. But not unfamiliar because I had sat in seats very similar with Aunt Gio and watched regular people turn into beautiful characters on stage and was in awe of each breath they took. It was our turn. Showtime! We took the stage, and it was black and eerily quiet. Each one of us, as the song started, got a spotlight put on us for the dramatics I'm assuming. But it worked because as soon as the full music came on, the stage lights came on, and here we were, straight out of a Broadway show. I danced my heart out and made every move as if I were a famous professional dancer. The crowd cheered and clapped loudly when we were through, but I will never forget Aunt Gio standing there stage right applauding and beaming so proud of how well we did. But especially proud of watching me become something I had only dreamed of. And this was just the beginning...

Chapter Six

According to the National Institutes of Health, an alcohol use disorder is defined as a "chronic relapsing brain disease" that causes a person to drink compulsively despite adverse consequences to daily life and overall health. You could have added a photo of my dad next to the definition as an example. This is not something I would have understood or even agreed with you about, knowing my dad or at least the version he conveyed to me. It's not until you're older that you understand a statement like that pertaining to someone who had a direct impact in causing so much destruction to your life. According to the definition, Bill had a supposed "disease" of his brain which caused him to have nothing but adverse consequences. He never admitted he had a "real" problem, nor would he have ever gotten help on his own for... at least until it was too late. My dad was about five feet ten inches tall; he had dirty blonde combed-back hair and sea-blue eyes. He had a mustache on and off, but never a beard. He had rough, calloused hands from working so much in whatever blue-collar job he was in at the time, and he always had a pensive look on his face, as if he were permanently angry about something. He was just average in appearance and height, nothing that made him stand out from a crowd. But to me, he looked like my all-time biggest fear.

Bill loved the Philadelphia Phillies. The team at the time was by far the best the league had ever seen, with the likes of Pete Rose, Steve Carlton, and Mike Schmidt. He wasn't just a fan; he was a huge collector of Phillies memorabilia. He had team player jerseys in plastic hanging in the closet, signed baseballs in plexiglass square boxes that held and displayed the balls, signed baseball cards, and everything in between. I'd never known him to go to an actual game, only to sit and watch every single game with at least a twelve-pack of beer. If they lost, you knew by the sound of his footsteps to get out of dodge. I never knew where or when this obsession started or the collecting of all things Phillies. Perhaps he started this collection before I was born? Maybe he started it hoping to trade and make some money off his now treasured items? Neither of those was in his mind. Remember, he worked whatever odd jobs he could, and my mom also was forced to work meaningless part-time jobs at night. All disposable income went to feed his addiction, and it seemed like he not only had one to feed, but two. He was practically sitting on thousands, quite possibly tens of thousands by way of this "memorabilia".

This was well before the days of eBay, Amazon, Craig's List, hell, even the internet, so where did all this stuff come from? Did he have a baseball *dealer*? Well, wherever it came from, he was taking what he knew should go to support his family and spending it on things he stored in the closet and locked up so no one could find them. That's not how a collection works, Bill; that's called hoarding. That's called the Phillies being his god, and he treated his collectibles with greater care than he ever treated his wife or his children. And by children, I mean mainly me. But wait…we were poor, had to get secondhand clothes from the neighbor, our car has a hole in the floor, but hey Bill, good thing you have your Phillies stuff. Again, it must be the "brain disease," right? Seems like that is an excuse for people to act however they want, and they get to blame something or someone rather than themselves. Bill blamed me for everything. It could be a rainy day and he'd have blamed me as if I put the clouds in the sky. He wasn't interested in anything regarding me or my well-being. Probably no concern even if I lived or died. I somehow contracted mononucleosis in sixth grade. It's coined the "kissing disease"; it comes from the Epstein-Barr virus, which doesn't go away fully after having it despite feeling better. So, I'm now the proud recipient of this virus lying dormant in my system forever. This virus can present itself through saliva or a carrier just sneezes near you. I had never kissed anyone, so I know it wasn't through that saliva. You get this through a weakened immune system, and stress causes just that and germs and bacteria to invade your cells, and they don't care if you're young or old. They just hold on to their job to wreak havoc. I was a kid with enough stress to cause a month-long virus to take an incubation spot in my body. It was Christmas time, and I was already on break from school, but I was so tired and sick that I slept straight through Christmas all the way till New Year's Day. I remember waking up and the Mummer's parade was on. This is a Philly tradition where grown men (and women & little kids at times) create particularly themed parade floats and dress up in extravagant costumes that match. They even put on a performance of sorts in their assigned category. You have the fancy brigade all the way down to just some silly clowns. I have no idea how you convince a bunch of grown men who are usually blue-collar union workers to spend a year building a float and dress up like Sir Elton John. All while putting a choreographed dance routine together in hopes of winning some acclaim in the small borough in their part of Philly. Aunt Gio was a judge at one point for the Fancy Brigade, but why was I not surprised? The parade went right past my Gram's house on Broad Street for many decades and still does. Everyone from the tri-state area, not even just Philly, makes their way to the Mummers Parade after their New Year's Eve hangover subsides and starts the drink fest all over again from mid- morning until dark when the parade is over. And then they'd make their way to 2nd Street as the after party. I can appreciate the city's tradition, but to me, it was and will always be a little bit obnoxious. I was 11. Eleven years old, and to think I was so sick that I slept through a holiday to which I later found out Aunt Gio funded most of it anyhow. I'm sure this was so we didn't go without opening presents or the thought that Santa Claus forgot us or even worse, we weren't good that year to even get anything left for us. She always came through in the clutch, and that drove Bill mad. If he had it his way, we'd have nothing to open on Christmas, or birthdays, or any day for that matter, because according to him, we didn't deserve anything. To me, Bill was neither a good father nor a good husband. He was physically, mentally, and verbally abusive. He drank his weight in beer and beat me until I cried and begged for him to stop. This is how I identified the man who was my father. I do think, deep down, he resented me and very well might have hated me. It didn't matter, though, because the feeling was fiercely mutual. This label of a "relapsing brain disease" just allowed me to be the collateral damage of his too-many-to-count adverse actions.

Chapter Seven

My mom got a job working at Jefferson Hospital in Philly as a secretary in the Radiology department. It was a temp job but better because it was during regular business hours and much better than the night jobs at the mall. Aunt Franny, with the three boys who saved us many a night from my dad when we were little, got her the job. They called it a secretary then, but today you'd call her the Executive Administrative Assistant. She oversaw ensuring many doctors and staff had what they needed, and I'm sure a litany of other responsibilities that required much detail. She must have been doing a good job because they eventually made her a permanent part of the team. This meant no more standing on street corners handing out flyers, and no more multiple jobs that caused our neighbors to have to watch us late at night. But it especially meant I wasn't going to be home alone with the monster that awaited me every day. She must have achieved some camaraderie and felt like she belonged at this job because some confidence came out of her that I'd never seen the likes of in her before. So much confidence that she told Bill he needed to leave. I guess after 11 years she was tired of those "adverse consequences" from his relapsing alcohol brain, too. I know there were conversations behind closed doors, lots of yelling, and us kids sitting in fear at the bottom of the steps. There was probably some begging from my dad that *he'd change*, and whatever other false promises he claimed to make to us to stay in that little yellow house and ultimately torment the people in it. There was a deafening silence that came over the house, no more yelling, no slamming of doors. Just us kids knowing something was looming, and we scurried as far away from the scene as we could. I senselessly ran into the kitchen and sat in the "nook," my back facing the wall in hopes that no one would find me there. I was an avid reader, so no one thought anything when I had my face in a book. I figured this would be one of those times. I had "Are You There, God? It's Me, Margaret" written by Judy Blume by sheer happenstance on the bench next to me. I had probably read the book a dozen times or more, so what's one more time if it will avoid any exchanges with anyone about my mom's newfound confidence or her newly established demands on ending her marriage. Just as I thought I was in the clear and enveloped in Margaret and her pleading with asking God if He was there, Bill walked into the kitchen. I no longer saw the words on the page but the backs of my eyelids from shutting them in fear. I immediately felt my shoulders creep toward my ears. My fingers pinched the pages so hard they crinkled. The familiar thud of his boots against the linoleum grew louder, closer. He found me, damn.

I looked up from my book, Margaret's problems suddenly insignificant, to find his bloodshot eyes fixed on mine, his breath carrying the sour-sweet smell of beer. But had a perplexed expression of someone who saw their life just flash before them. He said, "Your mother gave me an ultimatum. Either I quit drinking, or I need to leave." Now considering I was his primary target, and he didn't like me all that much, why was he telling *me* this? I didn't care, nor even understand the capacity of what he was telling me. All I knew was he was the family villain, and he was now facing his "adverse consequences from his brain disease" that he single-handedly created. I think he was waiting for me to respond, but all I wanted to do was just disappear. He came towards me, and I closed my eyes in hopes he wasn't about to hurl me into a wall in his typical angered fashion. Instead, he drug me from the bench and threw my book on the table. He picked me up as if I were a small child and sat me on the counter next to the sink. The cold Formica bit into my thighs. This was forbidden territory—we were never allowed on the counters. The house had gone silent, no footsteps, no voices. Just me and him. My chest tightened as I realized Mom wasn't coming to rescue me, despite her newfound backbone at work. Where had that strength vanished to know when I needed it most?

I was big enough to jump down from the counter and run, but I was frozen with fear.

Like I had turned into cement. He walked over to the end of the counter and proceeded to plop down what was left of his beer and started opening each can and pouring it down the drain. He asked me if I wanted to help. Help you do what? Pour your beer down the sink in some symbolic motion to show Mom you will stop drinking? HA! What a crock. But nevertheless, I took the cans and opened them faster than they'd drain in the sink. Once the last one was trashed, I believe he thought that was enough of a dramatic moment to showcase to my mom he'd "stop drinking". A cancer patient doesn't just not have cancer after someone tells them to stop being sick. A dying parent doesn't just stop dying because you said to stop dying. And you don't stop being an alcoholic just because you pour some beer down the drain. Sometimes actions mean nothing when you've spent years acting one way and now saying you'll act another. Holding my breath to see what was going to happen next, like I did most days, had me questioning the eerie silence that was surrounding the house that day. I had just helped dump a case of beer down the drain, so I was expecting some yelling and replenishing of the precious liquid that was now in the far sewers, well beyond that little yellow house. I peeked into my parent's room, which was right off the kitchen, to find Bill, with a small brown wicker suitcase open on his dresser. He was packing. The monster was leaving. Finally.

Chapter Eight

I don't know where Bill went initially, but eventually he moved about a mile down the road into a small complex of apartments that faced the high-speed line train tracks. That train ran every twenty minutes, which meant it was probably a cheap place to live…and loud. What this told me was my dad had an entirely different place to live, which meant this wasn't just a separation. All his stuff was gone. Even down to the last baseball card hidden in the closet. Gone, just like that. It took my mom getting a job and finally getting some guts in her for this to happen…or so I thought. Being the oldest, I had a lot of responsibility when it came to my younger siblings just in general, and I did what I could to shield them from the torment I was enduring. But this time I didn't know what to tell them. I don't recall a moment when my mom *officially* told me they were getting a divorce, as if I hadn't lived a short now 12 years in utter hell and the man who caused it just left. Did she think I was too young to understand? Too fragile to comprehend what this would mean for the future? Well, I sure wasn't too young to get beaten to set the example most days by the monster in question. I know for sure there wasn't a sit-down with all us kids with both parents letting us know what was going on and making sure to tell us, "We love you very much and you did nothing wrong" garbage that you see on TV or in movies. There wasn't a conversation about any of it. As if we were left to figure it all out by the actions being taken that we had to be subjected to. Like the far too many visits we had to go to family court and talk to people whom I'm assuming were lawyers, social workers, CPS, and the like. They talked to each of us kids separately most times, I guess to see if our stories lined up. Why did it seem like we were the ones on trial? Aren't we the victims here? Isn't Bill the defendant? Like I said, I had no idea of their divorce process, but apparently, we were just pawns in their dumb game of cat and mouse. Somehow, people who didn't know me or what our life had been up to this point, besides a few interrogations of small children, were the ones who were going to decide who was the better parent, or who could provide a better life. Now I'm no professional lawyer, or a psychologist, but from this and my own adult experiences, the list is endless in court when kids are involved. Especially kids coming from a family that was now exposed for having an abusive father that they were fighting over, but also a mother who stood idly by and let it happen. If I were the judge, I'd have asked if there was anyone else who could take us. I had my Gram, Aunt Gio, any one of the people who took us in over the years would suffice. But that's not what happened, unfortunately. Mom gained full, sole, and residential custody of me, Sam, and Luke. And two visits with Bill for only a few hours at most at a time every other weekend…I guess our stories lined up well. Either that or the judge just felt pity for my mom and saw she was also a victim of a situation she couldn't get out of. At least we didn't have to talk to these strangers anymore and tell them the awful things that occurred to us at the hands of our father and by happenstance, our mother. Reluctantly, the first time we had to visit with Bill, we were all filled with an unrelenting dread, rightfully so. We went from being questioned by a crew of "child protective services" and their brain-probing entourage to the home of the man who caused the mess to begin with. I didn't feel very protected, to say the least. No one prepared us for what we might encounter or what state of mind Bill might be in, all things considered. Was he still drinking? What would happen if he hit me (again) or my siblings? How would I fight back? How would we call for help if we felt unsafe? Could we just make a run for it without him chasing us? And if he did catch us, would I get an even worse beating for running? Because I was the oldest, or probably because I always lived in this survival mode when it came to Bill, I had to cover every scenario that could possibly happen to get us to safety should he snap. His apartment was on the second floor, and not much in it. He had a bed in his room, a small couch in the living area, a fold-out food table, and a small TV. There was no exploration of the nooks and crannies of the 300 square feet that encapsulated the walls I felt so closed in to. I stared at the digital clock that was sitting atop the table, praying it would move faster while Bill made small talk with Sam and Luke. My brain could not recall what was said or what was done in the two-hour window we were forced to be there, except scouring every spot I could see without moving for the trace of a beer can. The clock hit the hour mark, and I got up so fast, like a runner starting a race hearing the horn at the start line. I grabbed the kids and said, "Okay, we have to go now". There were no hugs or "I love you" or even a "see you later". I bolted down the steps as I heard his footsteps following behind us. Please hurry; why does it feel like there are a million steps and the front door is so far away? I opened the door and walked outside, taking in a huge breath of air as if I had been smothered or suffocated and finally broken through as my lungs begged for oxygen. I held the kid's hands, and they said goodbye, and he just put his hand up and waved. I said nothing, and I never looked back to see if he was standing and watching us walk away until we were out of sight. Our house wasn't that far away, which meant he was still too close for comfort. In two more weeks for two hours, I dreaded it, and we weren't even home yet. Back to the little yellow house of hell. I wasn't aware, as no child should be, of the dealings and finalization of their parent's divorce. I went about my life just knowing that at least for two weeks I didn't have to fear being beaten or sleep in a closet with my little sister, fearing for my life. My mom worked a lot now at her "new job". Granted it was in Philly and she did take the train over, but why were the girls from next door watching us so much at night again then? Don't normal jobs end at normal hours? As a kid, I was always observant and always tried to put things together to make sense. Even as an adult, I'm still this way. Everything needs to line up, be linear in thought, and have a cause and effect. It isn't to point blame; it's so I can wrap my head around the various pieces of the puzzle laid before me. I probably would have made a good detective or an even better lawyer. Something was amiss, and I was determined to figure it out. Two weeks came and went, another dreadful forced visit for two hours which seemed like an eternity. Except this time, we just sat close together on the tiny couch while Bill watched the Phillies game from his small TV. Are the Phillies *never not on*? Why are we even here? Did my mom consider this a break for her from us? Not that she was ever home anyhow. I know it was killing him not to crack open a beer. It was probably a legality in their visitation agreement that he could no longer drink around us. Maybe that's why they are only two hours. He perpetuated anger. Time to go. I'm not waiting for him to see us out; we head out as if we are an army of kids on a mission to escape.

Some time passed, and school was the only safe place I felt. The doors were automatically locked, and there was a camera and a buzzer to ask why that visitor was there. It made sure to keep the people who weren't supposed to be there out. I prayed Bill never came to school. Because the kids all lived within walking distance of the school, there were no school buses, only the safety patrol. They were like little crossing guards assigned to the different streets where kids walked from. Some were far, and that sucked. Others were so close you could see the kids walking into school. No matter what, you crossed at the main crosswalk with an actual crossing guard. I manned all those crappy posts, so much so that when it was time for the naming of the new squad, I was made lieutenant. Of course, Megan, who just happened to be the mayor's daughter, was named captain. Some things never change as an adult either; it's who you know not if you truly deserve it. We had to wear orange safety belts that strapped to our chests and over our arms, but this time, I got a badge. An official badge naming me as rank saying I never had to stand on that far corner crossing these kids who didn't listen anyhow. I got to stand on the front steps of the school and make sure all things start and end of school were done in an orderly fashion. It was sort of a big leadership responsibility for a kid, but all things considered this was cake. Even though this was a good thing I felt proud of, no one truly cared. My mom was so preoccupied with her new job, and I sure as hell wasn't telling Bill, no way no how. I'd rather give up the role entirely than have him show up one day drunk at the school knowing I was fully accessible to him. Outside of this, I was preparing for the 6th grade graduation. The school was K-6th, and even though I was only there a few years, I did dress up as a cat and killed it in the talent show and every performance, they'd allow me in since; and this was no different...I was asked by my music teacher if I'd sing "I've had the time of my life" by Jennifer Warnes and Bill Medley. Better known as the last song from Dirty Dancing when Baby finally nailed the lift. The only thing was it wasn't a solo song; it was a duet, so a kid named Tim was my counterpart. Tim was timid. Timid Tim. Was there no other who could complement my newly found Broadway style of singing? Nope, I was stuck with Timid Tim. The teacher worked tirelessly as it would be the song we'd sing as a wrap to the graduation ceremony. After many rehearsals and hoping Tim didn't forget the words or be trampled by me, it was time for that long-awaited day. We had to dress nice. I didn't have anything nice, (being poor sucked), so I wore some red dress my mom had gotten for her new job that she let me wear. It was a grown-up dress and had a belt and was far too big for me, and I looked ridiculous. Even so, the show must go on. I sang my heart out and even Jennifer Warren herself would have been proud. That's where I felt the most alive, the most joyful, and the freest...on stage. I was transported into someone else entirely. Not very many things made me happy, but this...this caused me pure elation. My mom might have been there, but I don't remember seeing her. And I know for certain Bill wasn't there. All I could see was the oversized red dress I couldn't wait to get out of. So, that was it; no more all-purpose room, no more safety patrol, and no more makeshift performances to transport me to another world. Middle School seemed big, but it also had a big official auditorium with a giant stage. They had their own theater program that I'd jump into the deep end if I were asked. But there was this strange feeling in the air. Like the feeling right before it snows and not in the I'm getting a snow day kind of feeling. This felt more like a storm approaching. And one that I could have never seen coming.

Chapter Nine

A storm can be considered many things. It can be a physical storm where there is rain, hail, snow; and some are worse like hurricanes and tornadoes. Others are the ones we experience in our life that come in an array of various circumstances that we directly cause ourselves, or even indirectly involving us. But nonetheless, we're still sucked into the eye of it. Even at times dealing with the collateral damage it caused. No matter what kind of storm you are in, its essence is a violent disturbance in the atmosphere. I think up to this point you can say I've been through a few of these, as a matter of fact one would think I have a black cloud that follows me just waiting for the exact moment of centripetal force that wants to take me into its path. The storm I was about to experience would have a direct impact on my adolescence and adult life, the decisions that were made on my behalf, and even the ones I could and would eventually make on my own. Despite a pending divorce, a full-time job, and three kids, I'd assumed my mom wasn't trying to mess up any further. She seemed to be handling things well up to this point, all things considered. What I didn't know was that my next storm was coming in by way of a 20-something-year-old radiology medical resident from Brazil named Tiago. Yep, I got a direct storm, all the way from another country; make that continent. You see, her "new job" created "new relationships" that would eventually be detrimental not only to her, but to me and my siblings as well. This wasn't a meaningful relationship that was formed post-finalization of her divorce from Bill. This was formed because of her finding someone who was smitten with her when she was at her most vulnerable and acting on it. That's not being smitten that's called a rebound, mom. I'm sure he had no idea what he was in for when he met her, that much I do know. A woman who is 12 years his senior with three emotionally and physically abused kids and going through a messy divorce from a lunatic absolutely sounds like a situation a guy in his mid-20's would avoid at all costs! But even with the baggage she carried, somehow this *man child* was now the replacement for Bill, as if the terrorizing marriage to him wasn't enough for her, or for me. I don't recall meeting him, or him being some amazing guy. He just showed up on the scene one day and started marking his territory in the little yellow house of hell. While this was all happening, I had to adapt, again, but this time to middle school. And I'm sure anyone who had lived in the United States and gone to public school can attest that middle school just sucks. You're not old enough to make decisions for yourself, but old enough for people to hold you responsible for things like the combination to your locker or getting to your next class that's on the other side of the building from said locker in 3 minutes flat before the bell rang. We lived about 10 minutes from the hood, so you had everyone and anyone coming to this school since it was regional. Rich kids, poor kids, and everything in-between. I had so much chaos happening in my own world I couldn't even comprehend who was who, nor did I care. I didn't care who thought they were "tough," who were the "jocks," or the "mean girls" that somehow thought they now ran the school. For as small as this school was, it felt so far away from the small yellow house, and there were no school buses. So, walking to school each day was exhausting even before I started it. I walked at least a mile to the park that sits in the center of the town, then through it, which was about another mile. The Park, which is its name, *how original*...was big enough for soccer games, softball games, picnics, and whatever other nonsense sports this town held, so it was a far way to go since school was now on the other side of town. No matter if in the dead of 90-degree heat or the freezing cold of winter, I walked there and home. Other kids got dropped off by their parents like normal families. Not me. I had a mom who was getting herself to Philly each morning to see her now-boy toy and a dad who was an abusive drunk I avoided at all costs, so walking it was. I was just hoping not to run into anyone who might know me, or what I was living through, and tell the school so I could avoid a trip to the guidance counselor's office to question my sanity. I had seen enough counselors, social workers, and people in that field being dragged through family court to last a lifetime. I avoided the office and guidance hallway at all costs. A lot of the school itself was and is still a blur to me. I don't recall any teachers that stood out or made some difference in my life. I remember simple things like seeing the people from my elementary school that I'd pass in the hall, or which outside door I could go into that avoided the coming and going crowd. One thing I can recall is a girl who was in 8th grade, well-liked, into sports, and very pretty with long blonde hair. She got severely burned by the Bunsen burners they were using that day in science lab. The fire caught onto her shirt, and she had a lot of hairspray in her hair (this was the late 80's, so big hair was a cultural prerequisite), so she tried to take it off as the fire was spreading and caught that hairspray as if it were gasoline. After her recovery, she wore long gloves to cover the scars left from the burns on her hands and arms for a long time, and her hair was never the beautiful blonde it used to be. I can recall things like that but not actually sitting in class, or even where the cafeteria was. It's funny how the brain will block out trauma in some sort of protective fashion for you, as if you ever remember you will somehow become certifiably crazy. You really don't need memories to do that. What I know is not crazy, at least for me, is that every time I passed the auditorium, I tried to peek in to see if anything was happening that I might be able to find my way into. There was never anything going on in there during the school day unless it was a dumb assembly about not doing drugs or some other nonsense about whatever sports were happening; this was a big sports town, especially wrestling. I think someone eventually went on to compete in the Olympics. But guys rolling around on a sweaty mat hardly seems like a sport in my opinion. They did mention the upcoming fall musical and my ears immediately perked up. Little Shop of Horrors. You know, the show about the nerdy guy who loves the pretty girl he fawns over but thinks he'll never get; oh, and the giant human-eating plant. Wait? What did they say? You must audition? Ok, how many people really are involved in this theater world besides me? Isn't it all football and wrestling? As I waited in the crowd to leave the auditorium, I looked back at the stage. I'm doing it. What do I have to lose? Worst they can do is put me in the back as the chorus. At least I'm on stage as someone else, far removed from the existence I was living. Over the next two years, some good, some bad, and some disturbing things would happen. I got the lead as Audrey in Little Shop; I met some good friends that would cheer me on through the parts I didn't think I was good for; and not all of them were. But Jen King was. She was the lead in the Spring musical Funny Girl, and I knew she'd go on to do big things with a voice like that. It was big, like Broadway big. I was in awe of her range and how it came so easily. But that's where it stopped for her, her voice. I was able to become someone else on the stage entirely. You need me to sing, I can do that. Dance, I can absolutely do that. Act, well if you only knew. I went on to be in fall and spring ensembles, like Les Misérables, where we all dressed the part and sang solos of our choice. The music director was great, Miss Iyello would challenge you till you hit the note you never thought was in you. I had a talent show to prepare for; this was the last one of my times at the school. I was preparing to sing "The Rose" by Bette Midler. Again, Miss Iyello gave me the confidence to do it solo and partly a cappella, and I practiced and practiced wanting to make this my debut for any drama teacher watching from the high school. But my life had other plans. Bill started questioning me about Tiago. How long has your mom known him, how long have you known him, how old is he, is he living in the house… frankly I don't know, and I don't care, Bill. And *why do you care?* You had your chance and blew it. Quit grilling me like your personal sandwich. I didn't have the information he was hoping for, to possibly use against her in court I presume, so he went on his own private investigator search. And by search, I mean stalking. He started watching my mom and Tiago through the windows of the house, unbeknownst to everyone. What was he looking for? Isn't this some sort of crime? The next visit he'd tell me what he saw, which I assure you wasn't us and Tiago playing board games or acting like some happy family, but Bill wasn't having it. He told me if I said anything, it would be my last...my last? What does that threat entail exactly, *Bill*? He wasn't in a position of power anymore and he knew it, so he tried to scare me like he had many times before but this time it was only empty words. Tiago didn't live there; he came occasionally, and I barely spoke to him. My focus was rehearsing for my big moment, and I wasn't about to let this real-life drama hinder my on-stage moment. Yet, I came home from school one day to find a 45 record in its sleeve on the steps...creepy. It was Foreigner's "I Want to Know What Love Is." I gave it to my mom when she got home and said it was on the steps; she held it as if it was burning her skin and immediately threw it away. Hmmm, ok well it obviously wasn't from Tiago, so it had to be from the stalker who was watching her every move. Mom, say something! Tell the police! Nope, she went about her life, I'm sure keeping this in her back pocket. The records kept coming. I don't remember the names or artists; I just know there was a crazy man again in our midst. I told her what he told me, that he'd been watching her and asking questions about this new man he'd apparently seen through *windows*?! Oh, and if I said anything, it would be 'my last'. Um, mom this is scary, he's watching your every move. Well, she finally did something about it and got a restraining order, no more than 500 feet from her or the house, or us. But here I am trying to prepare for the big solo that awaited me and here is the domestic violence king starting his nonsense yet again. My mom was taking the High Speedline to work, which is just like an above-ground subway from New Jersey to Philly, but deemed it unsafe, so she now drives to work, or Tiago drives her to work in his blue Volkswagen Gulf, ugh typical. But Bill doesn't miss a beat. He follows them, unbeknownst to them. But what I can only assume to be the rage that overtook him every night before blackout drunk, he sees them on the highway and attempts to run them off the road! Was he trying to kill them? If I can't have her, no one can…but he'd prefer to go to jail should his plan work. He went and did this on many occasions, followed them to the parking garage, and watched them together, and followed them and just stood there like some psycho in the dark. The brain is a powerful thing, but when led by emotions, especially past ones you haven't dealt with, it is like walking in a minefield. My dad saw himself at war with an enemy and did what he thought was the way to kill it, but it was only his own demons he never faced. I understood my mom not wanting to look over her shoulder anymore and not live in constant fear for her or for us. Then you can ask, well, what stopped her the entire time she was married to him then? I don't know when their divorce was finalized; maybe it already was. But my mom had one foot out the door. Whomever she talked to, whatever the lawyers and police recommended, she was upheaving our lives yet again. Why is the house for sale? Where are we going *now*? These are the questions I asked myself because I was just starting to find my place in this town I was reluctantly dragged to. I don't remember a conversation about where we would go, when we would leave, what the house looks like, or any of the questions that normal families have about moving, especially when the main impact is the kids involved in it. I don't remember packing, loading a truck with all our belongings; I don't even remember what time of year it was. It's like most of my life was spent with Doc Brown in the Delorean going from place to place, and my time there was always limited. Unfortunately, my life wasn't a movie, and the way this time machine worked, I wasn't trying to go back in time to prevent anything from happening. This was a constant forward motion of adaptation. I was thrust into a future I had no choice in, and my time-traveled mind cannot recollect the bits and pieces of critical moments, just the collateral damage. We were given limited news that we were moving south, about 40 minutes away. We'd finish out school and then we were headed out to start a new school yet again. Well, since this was my last year here, I had made this performance count. Up until now, I was on point, every step taken, every song sung, and every scene acted as if I were already on my way to Juilliard, but this time was vastly different. I was known and heard so many times I would "knock it out of the park," so...no pressure there. My brain hadn't processed the next change coming, and I was so clouded with what was happening, but I still practiced until I knew the words in my sleep as it was the only thing keeping me remotely sane. During the school day assembly, I got up in front of the entire student body on the stage ready to sing my heart out. I heard the music starting to play, and nothing came out of my mouth. Absolutely nothing, not even so much as a humming. As much as I knew what to say, my mouth would not budge, just the music and simultaneous silence. The audience holding their breath and I'm sure some snarky comments, I just walked off the stage. Thankfully the MC was a friend and he covered for me, saying there was a technical difficulty with the mic. I ran down the hall and slid down the wall in typical teen fashion and cried. I don't recall what happened next, but I knew I had to use this anger and sadness so I could come back for the night performance. My family never showed up for these things, so how appropriate it was to find my emotions in the exact part of the song they needed. *"When the night has been too lonely, and the road has been too long. And you think that love is only for the lucky and the strong. Just remember in the winter, far beneath the bitter snow lies the seed that with the sun's love in the spring becomes the rose."*

That night, I was dressed and ready. I was a couple acts up, and the MC pulled me aside and said words I'll never forget: "So, are you going to be able to remember the words tonight? No matter what you have going on, you go out there and use whatever it is you're carrying right now. Because I can't say the mics don't work again," as he chuckled and walked away to announce the next act. He was a jock, and I was a smart, damaged drama nerd, but he was always friendly and nice to me. Ironically, his name was "Cliff." You'll meet another Cliff later in the story who had an even greater impact not just on being my supporter, but so much more. I didn't forget the words this time. I belted them out; I pulled out a range I didn't even know I had in me. I finished with my heart pounding and tears just starting to well in my eyes. The entire auditorium roared in applause. I closed my eyes briefly as I felt the tears trickle down my cheeks. I even though there was no one there to support me, it didn't matter. I did what I came to do, and I left the stage with Cliff smiling at me, holding his mic under his arm, applauding, and nodding his head at me. Once I walked off the stage, he patted me on the back and said, "See, you *did know* the words!" and laughed as if I were one of his football buddies as he headed back to the stage to introduce the next act. I walked home in the cold. In the dark, alone, through The Park. That's the thing about darkness; it eliminates the light but shines on the negativity and sadness and amplifies your trauma and shame. It creeps up and tightens you in; it grips like a vice both in the present and the future. If this was any indication of what awaited me, I didn't want any part of it.

Chapter Ten

It was now spring, which meant the school year would be coming to an end soon. Bill was told we were leaving, so he conveniently introduced us to his "friend" Judy at one of our obligatory visits. How quickly he replaced stalking someone who was fearing for their life with a relationship with a woman who had absolutely no idea the man she was getting involved with. She was nice, with short blonde hair, thin lips, and smoked long Vantage cigarettes, and met at work. Judy was around occasionally; she lived in the suburbs outside of Philly, which was about an hour one way. Being the detective that I was, I asked why she lived so far away. She told me she was recently divorced...from an alcoholic. WHAT. Bill *is an alcoholic!* He just replaced his 12-pack of Schmidt's with a 12-pack of diet Pepsi when she was around. This can't be real. What kind of lies is Bill feeding this woman? She had two children, a boy, and a girl. I didn't meet them till much later, but they too didn't find my dad the upstanding man they'd hoped to gain. He stopped and left my mom alone temporarily, only because he was preoccupied with another woman, he wasn't worried about a legal restraining order, which I'm sure Judy knew nothing about. Time was ticking. I was ticking. Like a bomb that would detonate at any moment.

Now in a place where I was stricken with rebellion. It felt like a sickness that was rising inside me as time grew closer to leaving yet again. But still, I pushed it down, as usual. I don't recall my mom packing up the house, or even the slightest memory of a life being boxed up yet to start over once again. I understood my mom's fear of my dad and wanting to be as far away from him as possible, but this time it was different. As if I or my siblings didn't endure enough up to this point, the bomb-or shall I say bombs-dropped. My mom was marrying Tiago. And Bill was buying my mom out of the little yellow house. I was convinced this house was cursed as the perfect storm I knew was coming had arrived, and I was in the middle of it. It wasn't long before Mom and Tiago married in Philly at some fancy hotel; she wore a cream-colored suit, and I had no idea what he wore. I know I had nothing to wear to a sudden wedding, so I wore some oversized business casual jumpsuit of Mom's; just like my graduation in the red dress, I looked ridiculous, and the entire day was bizarre. I don't even remember the ceremony. Then I was asked to pose for family pictures...pictures? This isn't my family, well three of you are. This guy is young enough to be my brother. No, I won't partake in your counterfeit idea of what you think is a family, *Mom*. I remember walking in the large hallways of the event space avoiding all contact with anyone just trying to escape to anywhere but here. The Miss America pageant was being held at the same hotel, so they were randomly walking throughout the halls smiling and scurrying off to this event or that. I didn't care about their sashes or what state they represented, or even if they smiled at me with their fake Vaseline teeth. I just slouched down the wall till my butt hit the floor as I had so recently done weeks before, now sunken in a space of uncertainty and doubt that things were going to be anything but normal. I sat there and watched my uncle clutching a full plate of food talk to any Miss America contestant that crossed his path and hit on them like he was 24 and not married with three kids. All I could think was *"there's food?"* I was crawling in my skin and the only person there who saw me was my Gram. She didn't need to say anything to know how I felt. Because I'm sure she felt the same way.

The moving ultimately happened, and my mom and Tiago moved into a development in the suburbs of South Jersey, into a cookie-cutter house with a lawn and a yard. I guess this was mom's dream life; I mean, she had endured a lot. But what was the motive in such a fast marriage? Wasn't he from another country? That thought rose in me daily, always wondering why the rush. But this is before Google and the internet, so I had to investigate and do my own research. Was this so he could be, by default, a U.S. citizen by marrying someone who already was? Was he supposed to go back on a work visa? Eventually, I stopped caring because I had no control over this, and no one cared about anything I had to say anyway, but I had to shift and adapt again. Then, shortly after, Bill took over the little yellow house; except this time, it was with Judy. I know this because we're still required to "visit" with him despite the restraining order; some loophole I assumed. They got married too, *in the house*. The house we were moved into years before and taken away from everyone I loved, the house my mom lived in and worked 3 jobs to support us, the house I was beaten in, the house I was abused in, the house where I would hide my sister and I in closets until Bill was blacked out from his drunken rages. This is the house where my mom told Bill himself to leave our lives and never return. But this is the house Bill decided to start a life with a woman who didn't know who he truly was and didn't know the life that haunted the walls of the little yellow house.

The summer was a blur, like much of my life where I've disassociated from so much of who I am because of the circumstances I was living in, or rather living through based on someone else's decisions. I started another new school; except this time, I was a freshman in high school. I didn't know anyone but was told where my bus stop was and what time to be there. I'd never been on a school bus *in my life*. I didn't know what to expect, only what I'd seen in movies or TV of kids yelling and throwing things and the awkward group sitting in the front and the cool kids in the back. My life was playing out in the same way, always feeling like I had the front of a cool kid with the awkwardness of the space that surrounded me. When I got on the bus, a girl spoke to me that I sat in front of; her name was Dani, and she said she lived down the street. I hope she doesn't want to be friends; I can't endure telling her the mess of a life I was living. Even so, I smiled, and we were then just two kids in a new school trying to find our homerooms. I don't remember finding that homeroom; I don't remember any of my classes, even feeling "new" at all, or it is just a hidden memory that will come bubbling up to the surface later in life. I heard there was a choir and a theater program, and I was determined to find out about both. I snuck my way around the first floor of the school between classes; I wasn't interested in this school for who I could be friends with, for what I could learn, I was only there for where I could lose myself into what kept me from complete self-destruction. Music vocal room found! There's the bell, too much time has passed; I'd have to do some digging later, but just like the last school, now I had a mission to accomplish. I think my mom knew she had to do something to redeem this enormous change she asked us to endure, yet again, so what better way than to get away from this new round of domestic trauma than for me to be forced to start dance classes again. I say again because our world was constantly changing, and I was never in one place too long. I'd get attached to a studio, a teacher, and we'd be on to the next change. But dance was like a drug for me, and she knew that. Enter Miss Kathy. Dancing was something I did as a little kid, probably just to put me into an activity to keep me away from the chaos that I had called home. But what I didn't know and what I'm sure no one else knew is what it would do on the inside of me. This was it; this was the thing in my blood that fueled all the other things like gasoline. I got lost in it and there was no world I was struggling to tolerate each day that this wasn't a cure for. Dancing was in my DNA, and this went on for years as the small piece to release the anger I had ravaging inside of me was released somewhere. Performing was a part of me. I'd dance so hard until sweat covered my entire boy, or my shoes even needed to be replaced. And instead of asking for new ones, I'd borrow the loaners Miss Kathy had on hand. She wasn't only a teacher and choreographer, but she saw something I had in me that I didn't know I had and showed me how to harness it. She challenged me. And in the moments where it all came to the surface and I'd feel shame or fear, I'd push it all back down and find a way to dance until the sweat covered my tears. She saw this and put me in solos and in the front as a leader to the others because she saw *me*. My abilities heightened and my skill was starting to be perfected. I was now a lead in the school choir, and I was involved in the theater even if I was only in the chorus. I had recitals to practice for and perfect my craft for dance, so in this moment in time, I didn't care what was happening in the life I was forced to live outside of this. While waiting stage left in dress rehearsal for my final solo of the performance, I knew a few things in this very moment. I had people, like Miss Kathy, believing in me as a dancer; I had Aunt Gio and Gram, who always knew I was a world apart. But the clarity I felt in that instant showed I'd eventually get out of this life, move to New York, go to Juilliard, and dance on Broadway. I was never so confident of what I could do in my life, but just like a tornado you don't see coming to destroy everything in its path, one came into my world and did exactly what it was designed to do: destroy. My mom was now *moving to Brazil.* Yes, I too gasped just like you did reading that. It was so surreal to me. How could this be? How? Why? When? I had so. many. questions. And again, because of someone else's decisions about what my future would now look like, I was ultimately left with nothing but the broken pieces of myself to pick up and figure out how to live among the destruction. I left all I had on the stage that final performance, with every ounce of who I was, and I've never, ever gone back, and my dreams were crushed by the very weight of that decision someone else made..

Chapter Eleven

I found myself in my Gram's bedroom, sweating, just lying there unable to move, as my my body felt hot with anger yet cold with abandonment. Tears streaming down my face even as I clenched my jaw against them. Part of me wanted to scream, part of me wanted to disappear into the mattress and never emerge. Today was the day my mom left for Brazil. Again, I found myself in a place where I didn't remember packing, moving, or even how I found myself in the very room I was in. I remember that I contended because I was in high school, at the end of my sophomore year, and I didn't want to move to another home, let alone another country. And in saving grace, as always, my Gram said I could stay and live with her. Except Sam and Luke were forced to go as they were too young, and my Gram couldn't manage all of us. My mom didn't think much about it, I'm sure, as she was too concerned about the wealthy life she'd be living now to wonder if her choices meant destruction for her kids in any way. I call it being abandoned and selfish; she calls it giving a better life to her kids. Funny how when we ask God to bless the plans we make for ourselves, it eventually becomes hard because that's not what He has called us to do. He didn't call her to Brazil; a rich doctor did, who was still just a man.

She was saying her goodbyes to her sisters and to my Gram, but I didn't want to be a part of the phony depiction of a life she was chasing after. It was an easy decision to leave me behind because I caused her difficulties, and I reminded her too much of what she was running away from. I also called out the sham of a life she was living with a man half her age, and I was problematic for a newly married couple trying to live their best life. Whatever. I'd seen her true colors long before this moment. I'm not saying we don't all deserve to have better and live a full life; of course, we do. I'm saying that she didn't get to interrupt my life again based on the bad choices she made, not this time. I'm sure she felt she could escape the man whom she feared and who had abused her and her daughter for well over a decade and go live a life that someone was promising her could be better elsewhere. Who do you think won in this scenario? The empty promises did...the promises of wealth and riches and a new life for her. The grown woman was leaving that 15-year-old abused daughter that she saw every moment of struggle and pain. Just leaving her there...abandoned, like an old toy. Only to let her survive another day, get kicked around, and fight for her life. The contingency was I still had to adjust to a new school yet again. I didn't care because I was safe and once again this woman, my Gram. She chose *me* when no one else did. My Gram's room seemed completely untouched, ever since my Pop died. It was still like stepping into a movie set that was in the 1950s in complete continuity with the period it held meticulously intact. Every article of clothing, Pop's night table knickknacks, furniture, a vanity with a little stool and a neat, mirrored tray of old make-up and lipstick, photos, bedding, even down to the glass perfume atomizers. The drapes were pulled as if to not let the sun cause any damage to what was being preserved in that room; things, treasures, love, an era, and a marriage that ended far too soon. It was a moment in time that stood completely still. No one dared to go into this room, but I didn't care, it was peaceful, had an air-conditioner, and it was the middle of summer. I clicked the unit on and felt the cold air pour out in the thickness of the dark room. It was the most comforting place for me that day and not because of the cool air. But because the room was off limits, and no one would dare go in but me, or so I thought. As I lay on the bed in a fetal position contemplating every 'why' there was to ask, my Aunt Franny peeked her head in past the accordion door that I forgot to lock. So many times, she provided shelter to us when we left in one of my dad's drunken rages. Many nights she protected us, and I played with my cousins wearing their airplane or train pj's, sheltered from the darkness outside that seemed so big at the time. She wanted to protect me now, but this time it was too big even for her. She sat on the edge of the bed not knowing what to say to me but knowing how incredibly discarded and sad I felt. She told me my mom left and wanted her to say goodbye to me for her. Coward...

My heart was too broken to care and my eyes too swollen to shed any more tears. It was starting to cool off in the room and I had no idea what time it was as the room was always dark and I only had a little light on the dresser. She asked me if I was hungry; I just glanced at her as if completely offended that anyone would ask me that in this moment. I just nodded my head no, and she said there was food if I got hungry on the stove. I wasn't planning on leaving the room any time soon if I could at all help it. There was a bed, air conditioning, a full bathroom that clearly no one had used in a long time, so I had what I needed for now. She wanted to help but has never had a daughter so I think she was a bit stuck for what to say except "I would have you live with me, but I don't have the room with the boys. They are teenagers now and take up every bit of space. I would if I could". Right, thanks. She gently tapped on my ankle and told me it would all be okay and she's there if I need her. I just blinked away the tear that tried to escape and turned over as if to convey to please leave me alone, but I was so desperate to not be. I lay there wondering if Sam and Luke were okay and if they were safe. I had assumed by that time they were already on a plane high above the clouds completely untouchable from the darkness that lurked below. I eventually fell asleep and woke up a few hours later because I was cold. I looked around and got my bearings, feeling entirely disoriented from where I was. Oh right. I remember now, discarded. The little clock on the nightstand ticked so loudly and I saw it was only 7p.m. and I sat up thinking anyone that may have been here can't possibly still be here; perhaps it's safe to move about. I peeked out the heavy black drapes to see if I saw any cars, but only to see it was still daylight and a beam of sunlight blinded me as I closed the drapes in anger. How is it still TODAY? What do I do now? How do I do this? I started to panic. I went to the bathroom and splashed water on my red swollen face and bloodshot eyes. I had never felt so alone. I sat on the bed looking at a statue of the Blessed Mother that Gram had on her high dresser, along with a black and white photo of when she was around my age, in a crinoline rounded dress sitting on the grass, smiling. She was so beautiful. I gazed at the items that enveloped this room that allowed my brain to be occupied and transported into my very own time warp. I heard the hallway floor creak; I knew someone was trying to see if I was okay, or to just see if I was still in the state of shock I was left in. I heard the accordion door slide slightly open, *"Grandmom...?"*. This is what my Gram would call me as if I were still a little kid going through her purse looking for makeup. This was an endearing term to me as this was only said when I was small and vulnerable; it carried a sweetness to it that only she could pull off. My torso was now slumped over to the side while my feet hung over the bed as if moving my whole body back to its fetal position required far too much effort. She came and sat on the edge of the bed next to me as she placed her hand on my knee, gently rubbing and tapping it as if to somehow tell me telepathically it's all going to be okay. "Are you hungry?" she asked. "Not much of an appetite, Gram, but thanks." Being she was a little Italian woman; she was always asking if I was hungry. Wait, when was the last time *she* was in this room ran past my thoughts...was she sad to be in here, was it hard for her to even open the door to a world she once lived in? But I was brought back to the present moment abruptly with her comforting tapping on my leg waiting for me to give her the answer she wanted, not the one I gave her. If I said yes or no, she would wind up making an entire pound of pasta because Italian mothers don't know how to make anything on a small scale. "Come and eat, Grandmom." Her hand never left me, and I could smell the scent of her perfume lingering as the heat from the hallway made its way into the bedroom, mixing with the cool air in the time machine bedroom. Her nails were always long and manicured, painted in fire engine red, and I placed my hand onto hers. A few tears fell down my cheeks because I knew she loved me. I knew she always welcomed me and provided a safe place for me. I sat up, and she wiped my lingering tears with her soft, weathered hands. Her hands held so much love, so much sacrifice, and they were one of my favorite parts of her. I followed her out of the room as the stuffiness and heat of the upstairs rowhome hallway hit me as if I were entering another dimension. I hadn't left this room in almost 24 hours. The stillness of it and the memories that were frozen in time were comforting to me as I became one of those moments frozen and now buried in it. I slid the door closed while my Gram waited at the top of the steps for me. I followed her down, starting to feel the coolness of the giant air-conditioning unit housed in the dining room come over me, all while the smell of gravy and meatballs intrigued my barely-there appetite. I was in a haze until I hit the last step. I know that God likes to make sure we know He's with us, even in the moments where He couldn't seem further away. I know this because as I lifted my head, I saw a light coming from the kitchen. Everything seemed bright as my eyes tried to adjust because I had been hunkered down in a dimly lit room for what seemed like days. Gram had put on the big light. The same big light that was put on for me when I came home many years prior, eating Kraft mac and cheese in that very kitchen straight out of the pot. That light meant you were loved. That light meant you were wanted. That light meant you were home. But *she* was the biggest light of all.

Chapter Twelve

A navy-blue polyester one-piece jumper, a white long-sleeved blouse with a Peter Pan collar, white tights, and blue and white saddle shoes to match. This was the painful dress code that was required for me to wear to enter my new school, St. Mary's All Girls' Catholic High School. The very same one from elementary school, just now in a larger size. Not only was I trying to figure out how I was left by the very person who, too, went to the same high school many years prior, but now I had to figure out how I was supposed to understand a new place and adjust yet again to another situation based on someone else's poor decision making. My uniform was neatly pressed with the hem just as the rule says, no more than 2 inches above the knee. What I'd later find out is girls in this school didn't care about regulations. They hiked their uniforms up and tucked them into the shorts they'd wear underneath and pulled them down right when the nuns would come in with their rulers for hem checks during our lunch period. My Gram made sure to iron that uniform as if I was going to a queen's coronation each day. I took up residence in the back brown bedroom and it was just as I left it. Michael was still hanging on the wall, the little black-and-white TV took up most of the dresser, but still, no air conditioning. A box fan was my only source of coolant, and September in a row home in the city meant that any fan you had would only circulate the already stagnant hot air that was in the room. I spent most nights downstairs lying on the gold velvet S-shaped couches that by this time barely fit me in a reclined position. But every morning the phone would ring once at 4 am, and this call was Gram's cue to go next door to her friend's house to have coffee. She'd get her keys and open the big green door that would rub against the plastic mat she had put in front of it, and I'd hear the door close behind her. She'd come in an hour later, and by this time I was back up in the bedroom trying to muster the energy and courage to go to school. Before she'd have a chance to yell up the stairs, I'd just barely speak loud enough, "I'm up". I'd sit on the bed every day and look at the neatly hung uniform, desperately trying to understand what was happening in my existence. I looked like something out of the 1960's. My mom and my aunts went to this same school, and nothing evolved whatsoever. Even down to the patch on the left side of my chest that needed to be ironed on with the "crest" of the school. The very same uniform and crest that were seen as they all stood in those horrible school photos strewn about the house. I bravely endured this rerun of a Twilight Zone episode every single day from that point forward. I had to take public transportation to school. The city bus that ran down Broad Street, where I now lived, had a bus stop that was in eye shot of the front door. But far enough away that once you left, there was no time to go back in for anything you might have forgotten. Gram would pack my lunch each day: ham, cheese, and whatever else. The cheese would always be congealed as it was just the prepackaged slices you had to take the plastic cover off. I didn't have any money to buy lunch, so congealed cheese it was. I'd get on the bus and take out the tokens the kids in school were given to buy as it was cheaper than paying bus fare every day. I'd clink the token in and find a seat close enough to the front but near a window. I grew up here, and I knew my way around the city, but never alone. I looked out the window so I could count the streets and look for the cross street of my stop to get off. This was the main bus, so it made a lot of stops. I figured if I missed my stop, they'd go to the next block anyway. City blocks aren't too long, but if you don't know where you are, it can twist you around a bit. There were no cell phones or GPS, so I was relying on my already clouded memory to get me where I needed to go. My stop, Moore Street. I'd walk to the front, and the driver knew my stop by now, even though I couldn't tell you what he looked like; he knew I was only a kid, and I like to think he looked out for me. I'd walk about 10 blocks to where you couldn't go any further to be met with a brick building caged in by a giant chain-link fence with a giant statue of the Blessed Mother perched upon a stone block. It seemed a little excessive to keep the mother of Jesus encased behind a steel fence while seemingly protecting the school, but who was I to argue with the Catholic religion. I had eventually found all my classes, most of which were taught by nuns, and was told I didn't need to take a PE class as I had had more than enough credits to cover the entire rest of the time I was there. So, I called that a win because PE sucks no matter what school you are in. We didn't have combination locks on the lockers; we had to open them with an actual key. And this key was sewn into the armpit of my uniform tied on a long ribbon that corresponded to the

86

year you were in. This was my junior year, and they were yellow. I'm 16 years old, lived about 3 lifetimes already, now opening my high school locker with a key attached to a ribbon that's attached to *me*. Let me say that again, no one trusted the girls enough to carry the keys, so they made sure they were affixed *to* you.

I felt this didn't teach responsibility as I'd been taking care of myself and my siblings for as long as I could remember. If I could use a stove, know how to do laundry, watch my little sister, and brother, and fend off a drunk parent all at the ripe age of 8; I think I can remember where I'd put a key to a locker. Still, I was already very dissociated, so I did what I was told to not cause trouble for myself. I don't remember any classes, nor do I remember anything short of lunchtime hem checks but remember the occasional girl smoking on the corner with her hiked-up uniform while I walked the 10 blocks back to catch the bus home. I'd arrive well after 4 p.m., and every day like clockwork Gram was standing, looking out the screen door waiting for my return from the pit of hell I had just endured. She'd open the door and say "yeah?". That was her way of saying hello and how was your day. It took me over an hour to get home each day, so I'd throw my backpack down and throw off my shoes and the white tights that seemed to just take on the navy color of the inside of the shoes at this point. Gram always had something cooking for dinner; I could smell it as soon as I walked in. Italian Grandmothers have no idea how to not cook, or even just order a pizza. It's in their blood that whatever is wrong, or right, food is the answer. She had meat delivered by the butcher, so anything she made I knew was fresh and never frozen. She made everything from scratch; even her mashed potatoes were so creamy and even tinged with yellow from all the butter she used. To this day, I have no idea how she did that, but don't think I don't try every time. That night, in fact, she did serve her mashed potatoes, Italian green beans, and pork chops that she had simmering probably all day in a small pan, one for me and one for her. Anything she made was melt-in-your-mouth delicious and didn't last long in mine since I just walked 20 blocks and bussed about the same, and I never wound up eating the congealed cheese at lunch, so by this time I was starving. She'd laugh at how I shoveled the food in, telling me to take a breath. She had an iced tea maker that she never used until I moved in. She poured me a glass and it was the best iced tea I'd ever had; another thing I still try to make but have yet to succeed. I'd thank her and help with dishes. She'd wash, I'd dry. She could use scalding hot water, even with steam coming out of the spigot! That always amazed me because her hands were so frail and soft. She kept a little Tupperware dish of hot water and soap she'd use to wash and rinse with the lava water she insisted never bothered her. To the right of the sink was all her medication. I never knew what she needed it for, but eventually I'd need to. We didn't use the dishwasher; that was used to store the pots and pans. And I'd never ask why out of all the plates and dishware she had; we didn't use any others except the white Corning Ware ones with the green flower border. I'd eventually inherit these very plates and use them every single chance I got. Once things were cleaned up, Gram would turn off the big light, that seemed to stay on only for me until I got home and finished eating. Then she'd shuffle across the frayed green shag carpet and sit on the old tattered black and gold flowered love seat that she once shared with the love of her life. I'd go get changed while peeling off the remnants of my day that stuck to my uniform like glue. I'd toss it to the side in a ball but only to find it on a hanger pressed the next morning. Once I cleaned up, I'd go find Gram either watching Jeopardy or Wheel of Fortune. It didn't matter the show, she would call everyone stupid that didn't know an answer that she did, although she didn't know many. "You stupid!" she'd yell at the TV, then look at me and laugh. Once they got an answer right, she'd say to me "see I told you!" as if I was somehow connected to the competition. She'd eventually doze off and I'd go upstairs to do whatever homework I had and pass out to do it all again the next day. Gram never slept in her room, but always on the little love seat. She was small enough, but I imagined it was not very comfortable. She had a pillow with a golden silk case, and she'd use the Afghan that draped the back of the couch during the day. I never pressed her, as I was adjusting to her as much as she was to me. As a kid, she seemed larger than life. But this would only be the beginning of watching my superhero start to lose her powers that I so very much loved and very much needed.

Chapter Thirteen

What year it was, how old I was, even what was happening in the world is all a blur during this time of my life. I knew I felt very alone and the only friends I had still lived in Jersey. If I called them, it was a "toll call" which meant if it wasn't local, it cost money. And I had racked up quite the phone bill thus far and unless they called me, I was forbidden to call them. So, I immersed myself in my schoolwork, even earning two awards acknowledging my academics: one in Biology and one in the Who's Who in American Students. I had no idea what the requirements were for either of these, but I was given certificates that Gram proudly framed and put on display next to the bin of glasses on the marble table no one was still allowed to touch. The weather started to change, and I didn't have a winter coat. Why was I left *without* a winter coat? Aunt Gio offered to buy me one and I took the bus to Center City after school which was well past my normal bus stop. She told me where to get off and she'd be waiting for me. And there she was. Hair whipping in the chilly wind, perfect makeup, and her long denim skirt. She wore the same Mickey Mouse pocket watch on a black string around her neck and black lace-up boots. I only had on a sweatshirt over my uniform and couldn't wait to find something warm to wear. She escorted me into some department store filled with racks of coats and jackets and told me to look around. Everything she showed me seemed so bulky and hot and I declined everything. I eventually settled on some cream-colored patchwork coat that I was able to put right on instead of them bagging it up. Aunt Gio needed to get back to her store, so time was limited. She ran a rare memorabilia store nearby, sort of like an atypical toy store. Her store was the real-life eBay before there was an eBay. People would come in looking for a rare Barbie or a 45 record they had as a kid or a gift for someone and sure enough Aunt Gio had it, in mint condition. Lewis ran the store with her but had another job as well. Lewis was very quiet, kind, Jewish, and tall. He now had white, coarse, long hair he tied in a small hair band at the base of his neck. Even though I watched him during my life go from dark hair, salt and pepper to totally white hair, he never aged. He was very nice to my Gram, always fixing something, helping with a TV antenna, and he loved her food. They'd come on Sundays from time to time and eat dinner and hang around watching TV while Aunt Gio questioned my Gram about why this and why that. She always responded with "will you leave it alone, Giovanna?!" No one called her that except Gram. Then she'd shortly after tell Lewis they were going to miss the bus home, so they'd gather their things, and we'd say our goodbyes, and he'd always seemed disappointed as if that was the first time he got to sit down, and he was now being rushed out the door. This went on every weekend like clockwork. Lewis worked at the same deli as my dad had, called Applejacks, like the cereal. Bill no longer worked there, but Lewis stayed around. They didn't want to drive their old green and white VW bus because otherwise they'd lose the parking spot. Parking in the city isn't easy. People hold spots by putting a folding beach chair or an orange cone in the spot to prevent anyone from parking there. It never prevented it; they'd just get out and move whatever the holding item was, park, and go about their life, no matter who was yelling that it was *their spot*. I kissed Aunt Gio on the cheek and thanked her for my new coat as the bus pulled up. I waited for the people to pile in as I thought, well, at least the top half of me is warm while my feet numbed in my now beat-up saddle shoes. The lights came on inside the bus as it was getting dark. I was the last stop, and as I stepped out, the cold wind hit my face, and I was so grateful for my patchwork coat. As usual, Gram was waiting at the door and commented that she liked my new coat. I took it off and hung it on the banister. My feet were now burning and cold. Due to the now daylight savings time, I went to school in the dark and now started coming home in the dark. I missed my friends and wondered what they were up to and if they thought of me. I don't know how I figured it out, but if I took the same bus to City Hall, walked to Market Street, then a few blocks to the Speedline station, I could take that to Jersey, and someone could pick me up! At least for a weekend. Same Speedline my mom was stalked on, but I didn't have a deranged ex-husband looking to kill me...but who would pick me up? Where would I stay? I planned this initiative as if I had money to spend and time to kill. I did wind up doing this a few times, and it not only worried me, but worried Gram. I don't know how long she'd stood at the door waiting for my return but grilled me like a sandwich when I arrived. Gram must have told everyone because all of those people, and by people I mean those who share a bloodline, like her kids and grandkids.

But they never cared if she or I were OK but had opinions on my doings and told me I'd be on drugs and pregnant in a year if I kept it up. I'd lock myself in the brown bedroom and cry at how my mom just up and left me there not even so much as making sure I had a winter coat, let alone having to be an adult well before my time. Gram started asking me to go to the grocery store to pick up a few things. This was something she normally did, but I didn't think too much of it and happily obliged to help. Why weren't her daughters able to help, I wondered? Aunt Gio and Lewis could easily go when they were here, and Aunt Fran and the boys only lived a few blocks away. My uncle Mario and his wife had moved to Virginia to get away from city life, so I had no reason to blame him. He called often; being her only son, Gram laughed and was so happy to hear from him. She'd hand me a list and I'd walk to the market and ask for paper bags inside the plastic ones, so I could carry them without breaking. I'd get home and put away the items that she requested, and a few days later she'd ask me to go again. I'd repeat the process, and I'd also stop at the pharmacy next door for her medicines. They'd ask me how she was, and I just said she was good, just helping as it was too cold for her to come on her own. They said it was good I was there to help her. I didn't know what they meant…she didn't need my help; she was invincible. I'd just smile, say thank you and shrug it off as being polite, but the thought still stuck with me. As I got to the front walk, the door wasn't open with Gram waiting for me as she usually was. I fumbled around for my key and opened the door, locked it behind me, and found her in the kitchen cooking dinner. She smiled and asked me how school was. I said I was already home from school, and she asked me to go to the store. She would laugh and say she had lost track of the time and brushed it off. I got a job as a server on the weekends so I could make some money as Gram was on a fixed income and I wanted to be able to help at least pay for groceries. I was another mouth to feed, using water and electricity, so I had to contribute somehow. I'd work late and by the time I'd get home she'd already be asleep on the love seat. She said the rosary most nights and they'd always be next to her or wrapped in her hands. I'd gently take them and place them on the arm of the small couch. I went to the kitchen to get some water to find dishes in the sink. That's never something she did. Even her teacup from the morning was still unwashed. So, I cleaned up what was in the sink, put them in the drying rack, and dried my hands. Something was off and I couldn't put my finger on it, but I was so tired. I chalked it up to my own exhaustion and went to sleep.

Days passed, months dragged on, and now I have a red ribbon affixed to my uniform acknowledging I am finally a senior. Along with puffy red sheer shoelaces in the same beat-up saddle shoes. Fan-frickin-tastic. I hadn't made any real friends in this school yet, just a few acquaintances; but I still had my Jersey friends who, by this time, could drive and it wasn't so difficult to see them now. Occasionally I'd get picked up by the guy I was dating, who was a train wreck, but he'd drop me off at one of my girlfriend's houses for the day and drive me back that night. I think he had friends in the city somewhere (who were entirely questionable company), so I wasn't too out of the way. But no matter who I was around, or who I was an acquaintance with, everyone was preparing to go to college. From applications, acceptances, student loans, to how much fun it would be to finally be away from their parents. While the only thing I could think of was that I'd give anything to be around parents who loved me, and you can't wait to get away from them. I'd just nod and be as excited when good news arrived from a letter in the mail or a conversation about planning a graduation party to celebrate in advance. I didn't come from this world of higher education or even the thought of it, although I very much wanted to. For me, college was never a discussion I had with anyone in my family. No one had thought to consider what I'd do after high school. The conversation was never even so much as uttered to me; what my plans were, or what I wanted to do. I had no parents to push me along in the right direction, help me financially, or so much as ask me what I wanted to be when "I grew up". I had planned on going to Juilliard and living in the Big Apple, and that would've really been a contributor to any college conversations. But even that dream was taken from me, along with so many others. While everyone is opening college acceptance letters, I just got a card in the mail. It was in a pink envelope with no return address. Gram sat perched as I opened it. My birthday was approaching, and I was going to be 18, but no one knew where I was except for a few friends and a dumb boy who was nothing but trouble, so I didn't know who it could be from. I opened it slowly, swallowing the air I had stored up in my throat. A check fell out for $15.00. I flipped open the card and it read something about a daughter on her birthday, and then I saw the signature, "Wow! 18! I can't believe you're 18! Love Dad". I tossed the card to the side as if it was on fire. I looked directly at Gram and as much as I tried to hold back my tears, they flooded my face, as I said, "I hate him, I hate him, how does he even know I'm here?!" I sat next to her saying who knows what in the state of anger I was in and just she handed me a tissue while holding my hands in hers. She said in her curt but kind voice, "Honey, you listen to me. He is a jerk, he always has been, and should've never sent that. He probably knows because your mommy had to tell him before she moved. You're safe; *he won't dare come here.* You don't need his penitence". I asked what that word meant; she said pity or remorse. To this day I've never forgotten it nor ever used it in another sentence except the one she used that day. She told me to send it back. I had assumed he still lived in the little yellow house, so that's what I did: mailed it back to him. I had no idea if he ever received it, but I didn't care if he did. I'm not scared of him. I willed myself so hard to believe that; but I was so terrified of him.

I had no grand celebration when I graduated high school; quite frankly, I don't even remember it. I have no evidence of a cap or gown as a keepsake, heck even a diploma. Some would later question that very evidence, and I chalked it up to being lost in many subsequent moves. I dissociated so much that it wasn't until much later in life that I would realize how important these memories would be to recall. I did find my senior photos tucked away in some box many years later, showing me with a white robe and red cap affixed my head, airbrushed red lipstick, all while never knowing the hell of three lifetimes I had endured behind that very fake smile. I hadn't spoken to my mom, nor did anyone ask me what I planned to do after graduation. So, I did what I knew, survive. This is how I wound up getting two extra jobs and eventually was able to save for a car. I hadn't needed a license up to this point as public transportation was all I knew, but I was now out of high school and needed to get around, especially at night, safely. I took my driving test in a tiny friend's hatchback with no power steering and had to parallel park. The large man who was my driving proctor kept the driving very short because I think he was 1- cramped in the little car and 2- the car didn't just have no power steering, but also had no A/C. I passed, and he was relieved, because the back of his shirt was sweating when exiting the car. Then the same friend took me to some random used car dealer, told me it looked legit, and since she had a car and I knew nothing about buying one, I trusted her expertise because, well, she was the one driving. She stayed there with me until I eventually got in the driver's seat of a used blue Chevy Corsica. I drove out of the lot feeling happy and accomplished that I had worked for this all on my own. My new "used" car signified some sort of freedom and being able to come and go as I pleased, or so I thought. But driving from Philly to Jersey was no easy feat. But I was somehow convinced that the friends I thought were waiting for me somehow would be relishing the new car experience and happy to see me. But I was about two years behind everyone not just on getting a car, but a license to drive; so, no one was impressed. More like an "it's about time". I ventured to see the knucklehead guy I was seeing at the time, and I pulled up to see a garage full of people, some outside and some in; and many of them were my 'friends'. So, much to his surprise and mine, I wasn't the girl that could live in ignorance of a life I wasn't a part of, but one that he, or they, didn't want me in either. That seemed to be the running theme in my life; no one wanted me around or in their lives at all. Perhaps I reminded them of a part of their own shame they tirelessly tried to run away from, or perhaps I was being kept away from people who would otherwise single-handedly ruin the life I was attempting to build some semblance of. Either way, I said my hellos and my goodbyes, and he walked me to my car and said he'd come by Grams over the weekend. I just nodded and smiled, got in my new used car as he shut the door for me. I drove off in the big piece of metal that should've made me finally fit in but did the complete opposite. It made me feel further alone than I already was. Thankfully, my new used car was able to help get Gram to her doctor appointments and made going to the grocery store that much easier. I felt safer not taking the bus to and from work, but now I was just working to pay for this hunk of junk. I had a friend I knew from my brief stint in the Jersey high school; at least that's where I think I knew her from. It all runs together, especially when I get a *friend* request on social media now; where on earth do I know this person from, because they surely knew me. I try to piece together if there are any mutual friends as I'd prefer to leave my past where I left it...far away from my present. Anyhow, she had family in the same area I lived in, and I saw her occasionally. She heard of the many jobs I was working and recommended I try a temp agency she recently found a job through. She said they were really looking for people for some company she was currently at. She said the name, but I didn't retain it. I took the number and put it away for a later time when I wasn't so far away. What I didn't know at that time was that the very company I'd get a job at many months later would change the trajectory of the next two decades of my life.

Gram was much slower at getting around now. She shuffled when she walked and held on to the furniture or chairs as she moved about to wherever she was heading in the house.

I watched her go from a vibrant, indestructible woman, to a woman who was rapidly aging in mind and body right in front of me. The caregiver becomes the one now being cared for. She always refused help, but most times she wouldn't even realize the help she was given because she forgot it that quickly. I still hadn't heard from my mom…I assumed that whenever Gram talked to her, she'd convince her all was fine with me AND with her. But that couldn't be further from the truth. She was good at making others not worry about her, which is probably why no one visited or helped in any way. Or maybe it was me. Maybe I was a reminder of what they should have been for her, so it was easier to keep their distance. Whatever the reason was, I was determined to show the naysayers and the cynics that I would become something, and I would do great and amazing things even if they thought I'd be pregnant and on drugs at 16. Well, I'm just about 19 at this point and so far, no drugs and no pregnancy. Just wait, they'll see.

Chapter Fourteen

I called the temp agency. They had an immediate opening with a company that was growing, just as I was told a few months prior. But the company was in Jersey. But it was a full-time day position, which meant if I took it, I no longer would have to work my other three jobs that kept me out till all hours and exhausted me beyond measure. They asked me to come in and take a standard typing and comprehension test to determine if I was a good fit. They had no idea how I'd not pass but exceed their "testing". They explained it was a mortgage company (I thought, what *is* a mortgage exactly?) but it was administrative work, so it was unnecessary to know all the specifics. I started the job the following Monday. A strip of office space, a sea of cubicles, a few small kitchens with coffee makers, refrigerators, and vending machines. The woman I reported to was very welcoming, showed me around, as the feeling grew in every way that there was no way I belonged here. I wait tables, I work in questionable establishments, and I have never taken a college class in my life. And even though I was in the "business casual" dress code, no part of me fit this corporate world environment; or so I thought. My initial role was to deliver faxes to the various people throughout the office. It was a room that had about 15 fax machines in it that were relentlessly in motion receiving documents. There were shelves of paper beneath as it was necessary to constantly refill the machines, or they'd beep loudly until you did. Twice a day, people who sorted the mail would come into the room to bucket the mail for delivery, the same as they did with the faxes. A girl named Claire, who had a sweet British accent, was also put in the fax room with me, also a temp. We became work friends and would have tea and share a strawberry pop tart once the initial morning deliveries had finished. Everyone had their names on the sides of their desks, so it was a lot of figuring out who sat in each area so we could be more strategic and efficient in delivering the faxes to those waiting. Once I had that down, there was no stopping me. I was able to not just know where people sat to deliver their paperwork, but I was friendly and started to know everyone, and they me. I shared pleasantries each day with people, and some with influence, but this wasn't foreign to me. Connecting with people was a breeze for me, and being helpful came easy. This wouldn't be made known to me until much later in a larger capacity. I was getting a real paycheck, I was getting home at a decent hour, and it was only one job, no longer three. So, I continued as I had been, friendly and efficient and helping where I could; the random ask to file things in my downtime, the can you organize this or that. It was only a temp job, so I figured this was what came with the territory. I continued my fax duties and the random other things I was doing for some time until it started becoming noticed by the woman to whom I reported. She asked me to come to her cube when I had a moment. Great, I'm done here, no more paycheck, back to waiting tables and questionable establishments, I thought.

But I smiled and said I'd be by after this delivery; to seal my fate, my job's temporary time had reached its end, and they would show me to the door. This is how I catastrophize things; I do it even to this day...I think of all the worst-case scenarios I can think of, so I'm not blindsided. Maybe it's from having to survive, maybe it's from trauma, maybe it's because I think I'll somehow shield myself from pain if I'm prepared. I took a breath and walked over to her giant cubicle. She didn't have a regular one where you could see the person in front of you; she had the same partition walls all the way up about 5 feet and another foot of glass above that. She was very happy to see me and told me to have a seat. She asked me how things were going and if I was liking it there. I gave my obligatory yes, of course it's great, and I'm happy here. This was so she at least thought that I was content and maybe somehow that would guilt her and ease up the blow of letting me go. She said she was glad I was happy and that many people had been giving her compliments about me on how quickly things were getting done and that other areas had asked her if they could use me for help; they needed (ah, ok, that's where the filing and random organizing tasks came from). I was flattered and said I was just doing what I thought was right and the people had been great. I was just waiting for it, thanks but your time is over, even though I hadn't finished my three-month contract of temping, but there's the door, don't let it hit you on the way out. But none of that happened. Instead, she asked me if I wanted to accept a full-time permanent position in the closing department, her direct team. I told her I wasn't done with the temp job, and she said she had already worked that out and if I wanted to accept, she'd get me all set up with the HR people, get me a desk and a computer, and let the team know. I immediately blurted out, "yes, thank you so much!" She said, "great! I'm glad to have you as a permanent part of the company and the team; you're going to do great things here". She had no idea what that statement would entail in my life for the next 17 years.

I learned in no time and became adjusted to the various things this team did, and everyone was, for the most part, gracious and helpful in my learning; they already knew me from my "fax days," which gave me a leg up. I adapted and became a supportive person on the team, even if I was the glorified assistant. I drove back and forth daily but at home Gram seemed to be a little less like herself each day. It worried me, but she was so happy I got a full-time job that I didn't want to ruin it with the book on those worst-case scenarios I was writing in the projection room in my head. The underwriting team, who basically said yes or no to people trying to buy houses, was adjacent to us. Most were okay and had to know a lot about a lot of things, but some were cocky and loud as if they wanted everyone to know the slight power they were given to say yes or no. One girl who was apparently fed up with working on a team full of arrogant men quit there on the spot! The manager tried to stop her, but she was yelling and cursing that she was now being disruptive. One guy led her outside who I'm guessing talked her off the ledge and came in afterwards alone. He went to the manager and told her something as I just watched from a distance to see what drama was next to unfold. He looked up and saw me staring, and I instantly looked away, hoping he never wondered who I was or why I was so concerned with what was going on. I heard people talking a few cubes behind me… he was talking to one of my co-workers with whom I was guessing he was friendly, telling her what I assumed had happened. I no longer heard anyone talking but heard footsteps coming behind me. I sat at the last desk and my back faced everything and everyone. Usually, people would come down the aisle past me for supplies, to go to the printer, or to grab the random bagels brought in for breakfast. I heard a tap on the edge of my desk as this same guy passed my desk looking at me as he walked by and said "hey". I looked up and I nodded once to acknowledge whatever his tap was. He kept walking and as he met the end of the aisle, he looped back over to his area talking about how they now had all guys on the team, all while seeming too pompous and egotistical for his own good. I shook my head in disgust and went about my day. I did meet some friends and in no time found my place, at least with the females in my age demographic. I had been sought after by a few random guys, to which I wasn't interested, but that did not stop their pursuit, as this was a business-critical area that a lot of people funneled through daily. It was amusing to me that no matter how much I appeared not interested, they'd stop at my desk and try to have a conversation about whatever mindless nonsense was spewing out of their brains at that moment. I'd nod and smile, not hearing a word they were saying, all while I could feel the eyes of others burning through the back of my neck, thinking the "who does she think she is" thoughts; I was the youngest on the team, and it was full of peri-or post- menopausal women. Hormones were not forgiving in this space. My boss visited me again, asking if I had a moment to chat. Here we go again, let me pull out the chapter on "let's get rid of this girl she's disrupting the ecosystem of the hot flashes and moodiness and so see yourself to the door." I, of course, obliged and she asked if

I wouldn't mind helping another team as they were falling behind, and I was good at getting ahead of things; only caveat is they are on the other side of the building. *The other side of the building*?? YES! Without a doubt, *sign me up*! Tell me where to go and let me pack up my desk while you're at it. She asked me if I knew the team lead of the area and I did; she was always so kind to me over my deliveries in that area. She was of Indian descent, but very Americanized, and had long, inky black, beautiful, thick, shiny hair. The next day I walked over with my things, and she smiled and said she was so glad and relieved I was there to help. She gave me a checklist and a mail bucket full of 2-inch files filled with paperwork to look through and make sure all was compliant and done accurately. Wait...I'm checking the potential mistakes of the team I left? Oh, how beautifully ironic. As I was settling into this new gig, I got word from my Gram that Sam would eventually be coming home to the States from Brazil once she graduated. She too will live at Gram's with me. It will be like when we were kids and my mom was hiding us from Bill, except this time there was no one to hide from, or at least that I knew of. She's about three years younger than me, which meant she'd be graduating in about a year's time. Maybe I'll give her the number to the temp agency when she gets settled in. I thought about changing the path of her life, but as soon as the thought came in the "don't plan her life," that's been done to her far too much already, the thought went out as fast as it came in.

Chapter Fifteen

There are times in our lives when we know we are doing hard things, but there are also times when we know full well that those hard things aren't making us better; as a matter of fact, they are making us worse. When you find yourself at the end of your rope or at your rock bottom, they say, there is nowhere else to go but up. Who are "they" and what bottom did they come up from? My life always felt like I was at that rock bottom just barely seeing over the edge of the things I was faced with. I'd climb out and before I knew it, I was not in Wonderland, but down Alice's rabbit hole not knowing what awaited me at the end but somehow came out alive. I didn't meet any white rabbits, nor have any magic potions to drink along the way; but the only thing I did have was many Queens of Hearts trying to take me out or as she'd say herself, "off with her head!" At least that's what it felt like, as if I was in a constant state of trying to survive until the next blow. I was the boxer who went every round and could never be knocked out, hanging on the ropes, beaten and tired, but never a knockout. I pushed through everything and didn't let anything get the best of me. Until now.

Gram's ability to care for her daily living had started to decline, and her mind could no longer identify even me on some days. She needed full-time care, and as much as I tried, I couldn't give her what she needed. I wasn't medically trained, and I was scared I'd come home and find that she'd tried to do something she'd otherwise normally do that she no longer could. Like leave the stove on, she'd taken a fall, or something worse. My uncle Mario, who lived in Virginia, the one whose little brown room I was occupying, had a few conversations with me about how she was. He was the only one who seemed to care if I couldn't care for her. Everyone else assumed because I lived there that they could wash their hands of her care. She did too much for me, and there was no way I wasn't going to allow her to keep her dignity even if she didn't know who I was at times. The plan was my uncle would move her to Virginia and she'd move in with him and my aunt. Their kids were teenagers now and it wouldn't disrupt their lives too much as they'd have a room just for her, and they were looking into a daytime nurse that could be with her while they were at work. They'd eventually get all this settled; additionally, the logistics of starting to prepare to sell her house once she was settled in her new home. This was all a lot for me to take in. Although I was glad the focus was on Gram's care, this was my home too. Where was I going to go when she left? Where was I going to go when they packed up her things in the only place, I ever felt safe? There was no for sale sign, just a menagerie of a life lived that was gone in an instant. What will happen to this house? Is no one concerned that I won't have anywhere to live, to feel safe? Did *she* understand she'd never return to the place she raised a family, kept her daughter and her kids safe from an invader only looking to destroy them? Did she know she wouldn't return to the place where she raised her granddaughter? The granddaughter whom she cared for and loved unconditionally? Would she know she would never return to the place where she cooked endless meals and served with love? Would she know she'd never return to the place where her granddaughter watched her in awe and knew she was protected and loved? Would she know she'd never return to the place where her granddaughter knew why she'd turn the big light on...

While preparations were being made, I knew I had to act quickly to find a place to live. I had a car, a job, but barely any money saved since I was taking care of Gram and things at home. I had a few friends who offered up their space until I could find a place of my own, and I wound up taking them up on these offers. I'd sleep on floors, couches, even my car, in the freezing cold winter nights. No one could know the agony I was living every day. I eventually secured a one-bedroom upper-level apartment for $500 a month. I had no idea what living on my own entailed, and I had no furniture or even a bed. Friends found items on consignment, and I was able to buy a secondhand bed and couch. I even got a small kitchen table at a thrift store. It wasn't close to work, about 25 minutes away, but at least I didn't have to pay tolls each day driving from Philly to Jersey. It was an OK place, not in the greatest neighborhood and a very active tavern next door to the apartment complex with very questionable patrons who walked, or rather stumbled, through the streets late at night back to their very own one-bedroom apartments.

Gram was leaving. And my heart was broken into a million pieces that were scattered throughout her house like two giant handfuls of glitter. The thing about glitter is, it gets everywhere, and you can never clean it up enough that it will fully disappear. The broken pieces of my heart and soul will forever be strewn about in that house like the remnants of the glitter embedded there forever. She thought she was just going to visit. I kissed her goodbye and said I'd see her soon. They locked the door and didn't ask me if I was moved out, or needed anything else, or to just make sure to lock up when I left; it was a cruel way of making me walk away from all I knew, all the security I had. I see it now as a blessing because I never was in that house without her, and it would've killed me then to be alone in it. As I walked away and waved, holding it together, it was like my whole sense of safety cracked and I was exposed to everything that big green steel door kept me from. My body felt like it was dripping with sadness as I walked to my car. I left parts of me outside of her house, everywhere and sat in my car just staring; I was in shock. I couldn't cry, I couldn't move, I couldn't breathe. This was my first sense of what real anxiety felt like. It was like for the first time my body just erupted emotions I had been keeping locked up for years. I knew there was a God, but if he was so good, why did I feel so bad? I screamed, "Why!!! Why did you not keep her well?! Why am I alone, *again*?! Why are you doing this to me? I hate you for this!" I was convinced that if there was a God, he was not anywhere near me and sure as hell didn't care about what happened to me. I put my key in the ignition. I took one more look at the house and tried to see it through the rose-colored glasses I had worn of Grams so many years before. I didn't see anything but a house that would eventually be someone else's. And I hoped they felt as much love as I did and that they left the big light on for someone they loved, too.

I now live in this tiny apartment alone but fill my days with work and my nights out with friends at whatever club has the best scene of the week. I had a fake ID that worked quite well, and I never had an issue getting in anywhere. Or maybe it's because I'd barely wear any clothes and had on either stiletto heels or thigh high boots. Some places even wanted to pay me to dance on giant boxes, behind shadow screens, or be a shot girl-a shot girl? I can't say I didn't take them up on some of the offers to make some extra cash, but even this scene grew tired, and I was filling my time just to avoid feeling the inevitable crushing that my soul was enduring. But I had three very good girlfriends by this point, and we hung out quite frequently. They came to my place to get ready most times we'd go out because it wasn't normal for someone my age to have their own apartment, as they all still lived with their families and seemed to annoy them when they wanted privacy or just to be themselves. They had no idea what I'd do to switch places with them. I was living a lie and only trying to numb the excruciating grief I felt of being abandoned by the very people that were supposed to care for me. The guy I dated, the knucklehead, showed his face a few times here and there and tried to coax me into thinking he was more mature somehow, and for whatever reason I thought to believe him. I'd later find out he was physically abusive and would break my hand with one squeeze of his hand, quite literally. But this is not useless information now; but it becomes very useful for me later in life. As time ticked slowly by, I dreaded each day more than the last. Night after night, I'd jolt awake with nightmares and my own screams echoing in my ears, my body drenched in sweat, convinced some nameless horror was about to swallow me whole. This continued for weeks, and I tried to ignore it, but eventually I'd be scared to sleep.

110

So, I'd stay out all night at whatever club or bar was open, then go to an after-hours place, come home, shower, and go to work. I felt like the tavern crawlers I watched many nights from my window, probably not able to sleep or face their lives either. But I had to go see a doctor as I couldn't keep going at this pace. I had health insurance now, and I was facing so much in my life it was probably manifesting into some fatal disease, or at least my worst-case scenario chapter told me. He told me, in fact, I was not dying; I was having night terrors. I didn't know what that even meant or how I could rid myself of these. He asked me questions about what stressful things might be going on, and I froze in place. I didn't know how to answer that; I mean, what stressful things *weren't* going on? He asked if I feared someone or if someone was trying to hurt me. Oh no. My thoughts froze. Will Bill find me now? My refuge was now gone, and I was alone. I needed to make myself disappear, and this time there was no big green steel door in sight to hide behind.

I sat there at the top of the stairs against the wall, feeling the warmth of the blood flowing from my arm. I watched as it dripped onto my pants and then the floor. I don't remember planning anything, feeling scared, or even pain. I don't remember what blade I used, just that I wasn't afraid when I sliced into my wrist from the top down to make sure I was not going to survive. I felt like the disastrous life I was living was slowly draining from my soul, and I felt a calmness come over me that I craved for so long because I was so tired.

I didn't want to die, but I didn't want to live either-not like this. I was in and out of consciousness but lucid enough that I heard the door unlock. My friend Alaine had my spare key as she always came by unannounced, but this time it was because no one could get a hold of me on the phone, so she decided to check in on me. It wasn't like me to not be ready for a good time. She called my name, saying something about how I can't disappear and not answer my phone, all while she climbed the stairs. She dropped her bag and keys in shock. She saw me there covered in blood slumped against the wall, and I heard her faint whisper… "Oh my God." She grabbed a towel from the closet and wrapped my arm in it and put pressure on the wound. I winced and for the first time I felt pain. What did I do? Am I going to die? She called 911 and an ambulance came quickly. They too climbed up the stairs, but they had a gurney in tow. They were both male and big, but kind, and said they were going to take care of me. They removed the towel as blood continued to pour from me like a faucet. They wrapped a tourniquet tightly around my arm as they carried me to the waiting ambulance to take me to the hospital to seal my fate. As I felt the cold air hit my face, I suddenly took a deep breath in knowing I didn't want to die. I just didn't want to hurt anymore. I turned my head for a familiar face and saw that Alaine was close behind me. I heard her say through her brave, fearful tears that she was going to follow the ambulance and she'd be there waiting for me when they "fixed me right up." The emergency room gurney with the bright blue surgical draping was waiting for me upon arrival. The nurse put an IV in my right arm while the doctor worked on stitching up my other. "The tendon is severed, and there could be potential nerve damage; you will need surgery." I just replied," Okay." Someone had opened the door, and I was able to see into the small waiting room. Alaine was there, perched on her seat, waiting for word on whether her friend was dead or alive. I had 15 stitches placed in my wrist and was put in a giant splint with as much cotton and ace bandage wrapping as I think the hospital had in its full stock. I was groggy from the medication they gave me for the pain, but once stable, they eventually brought me out to the waiting area as Alaine was handed the number for the surgeon and asked if she could make sure I called them and a script for painkillers. I left with her, and we drove in silence. We pulled up to my apartment, and she walked me up, both of us stopping briefly to step around the blood soaked carpet, all while making sure I was able to get into bed. I told her I was sorry. I was sorry I frightened her, but in that moment, I didn't want to live because everything hurt. She grabbed the fingers I had peeking through the top of the cast and said, "God was with you tonight. You can't die. He's not done with you yet."

The next morning, I woke to sunlight peering into the slits in the blinds. I wasn't dead; I was very much alive and very much in pain. I'd go over the next few weeks to have surgery to repair the detached tendon along with the nerves I had severed. I wore a cast for a while to ensure the wound healed. I played it off to everyone just as I did to the ER nurse when she asked me if I had done this to myself, only lying to her to keep me out of a psychiatric hold. I made up stories so no one would know what I had done to myself when they asked what had happened. I'd eventually get the stitches out but have the visual reminder of what happened with a giant scar on my wrist that I very much live with each day. A token of the grace of God and that He was with me even when I very much thought He wasn't.

Chapter Sixteen

As I adjusted to this life of wondering what I was being saved for, things started to seem different. I'd go to work, come home, and play off any questions that arose about how I felt from my 'accident'. And by accident, I told everyone I was carrying laundry down the stairs and slipped and broke my fall with my arm and needed surgery to repair the break. That was a load of crap just as much as the story I told the nurse in the ER...that I was trying to lift an old window up and the pane broke. As if I was on the outside of me looking in; wow, what a mess. I decided in that moment, no one got to come into my world of chaos and trauma. It was far too much for me to take, let alone try to explain it to someone else. I trusted no one. Hell, I didn't even trust myself. I built a web of lies to protect myself from others seeing who I really was. Where I came from. What I've endured. What I've done. I was full of shame and abandonment, but I held the reins now, and I promised myself that I would gain control over every part of me that felt exposed, tarnished, broken, and bruised, and I'd build a giant wall around it. And that's exactly what I did. The big green steel door at Grams had nothing on the fortress I'd built to keep everyone out. I was so deeply in pain that pretending it didn't exist was so much easier than dealing with it. Even today, as a grown woman, I'm still chipping away at that wall, and it's hurt me more than it's helped me. I can cut anyone off in a New York minute and not even think about it from that moment on. People have tried to love me, despite the stuff behind the wall, but I built such a stronghold that it's taken decades for me to let the right people see behind the curtain, mostly for fear they would see a very damaged and fragmented woman, and they too would leave. What I didn't know at the time is all those pieces I tried so hard to keep locked away could be made into something of value. A piece of mosaic art must start from various broken pieces from different places and things to create something beautiful. I am a work in progress, and God is not only the master artist putting me back together, but He's allowing me to see that I am a culmination of all my broken parts in hopes of encouraging you to keep going and not to give up. Because your broken bits and pieces are too, being made into something wonderful.

I kept myself busy and wasn't ever in one place too long. I didn't like being in my apartment alone, and my friends slowly distanced themselves knowing that what I faced just scared them; it's not that I wasn't a good friend, just not the right one for them. I was used to enduring suffering and pain, but they only read about it or heard it on the news. I was a real-life mess that they were not equipped to handle, understandably so. It also didn't help that every time I reached the top of my stairs, there was a huge stain of blood where I had hoped to escape the life I was living. No matter how much I scrubbed, it never came out. Indicative of life, isn't it? Sometimes you just need to cover it, or hide it rather, with a doormat instead, which is exactly what I did.

I never did get to thank the people who cared for me in my darkest moments; but the thing is, I'd have many more where those came from, so they all mesh like the people who send me social media friend requests, what school do I know you from again? Thankfully I still had a job that I poured myself into and moved up the salary chain quite nicely for someone who didn't hold a college degree. What I had was work ethic, determination, and tenacity as needed. I had no idea how those very characteristics would come into play throughout my life, and many more I'd discover.

Remember the girl Dani whom I met on the bus? My very first school bus experience way back in freshman year of high school? Well, out of a glimpse from the corner of my eye, I saw someone being shown around the building, and sure enough, it was her. She must have gotten a temp job…don't look, she might recognize you or even worse, start asking questions if I was OK from the "accident" I was in. I knew she had third degree of separation friends so I'm sure I was the talk of everyone's "oh my God did you hear what happened?" And of course, who do they bring her over to? You guessed it, yours truly. COME.ON. She recognized me and said some surprising statements that I don't even remember but said she hadn't seen me in so long and how happy she was to see me, and how coincidental it was that we'd work together all these years later! I had no issue containing my enthusiasm, as I had none. Just dread of 'where have you been and what have you been doing' conversation. But I chose to adult and tell her it was great to see her and if she needed anything to let me know. My team lead took over, so my fake pleasantries were in fact short-lived. I could see her looking up from time to time smiling and she'd wave, and I'd just smile briefly and go back to the piles of files that stretched across my desk. No one knows me here and no one is messing this up for me, especially a blast from the past ghost who wants to make herself known. I was making a whole worst-case scenario chapter yet again based on conversations with her that hadn't even happened...yet. She asked me if there was a place she could grab some lunch. There was a cafeteria in the building across the street, I told her, pretty good made-to-order sandwiches, and the like. She asked if I could walk with her there as she didn't have a badge to get back in the building. Great. Here we go. "Sure, let's go," was about all I could muster. She chatted away about this and that, and I just mm hmm'ed and said the occasional oh wow or whatever cliché saying came out of my mouth in that moment. She was still living at home, same house, same friends, same life. Well, good for you. Oh, what about me? Oh, well, my mom moved to another country, I took care of my grandmother who has dementia, I was physically abused by the guy we went to high school with, and I had a mental breakdown where I attempted to kill myself in my apartment. So, no, not too much. I just told her not too much to talk about, same old same old, just working and keeping out of trouble. It appeased her but she said we should hang out sometime, go to a bar or a club, and she knows some people that work there, so we'd be hooked up. This is NOT a part of my rehabilitation plan. But I gave her my number and let her back in the building hoping she'd never call. She called alright, and I fell again into a spiral of good times and late nights. I can still name the clubs we'd become regulars on a first name basis and the bars in which it seemed everyone gravitated and wanted to 'be your friend'. One night when out, I was sitting at the top tier of the club we frequented, and never saw anyone there I knew, and it was dark; both a draw for me. She was chatting to my left with some guy, and I was sipping on a very cold martini staring at the lit up mirrored shelves holding the various bottles mesmerized in random questions of who drinks all this, and does it ever expire thoughts. Then the bartender put a drink in front of me and tapped me gently on the arm. I looked up and he said it was from the guy at the end of the bar and pointed him out as if I was to gesture a thank you or even worse a conversation. I looked to my right and dammit, this guy...this same knucklehead who would physically pick me up and slam me against walls, and yes, the same one who broke my hand in one squeeze of his. He waved...I stared at him pensively and pushed the drink towards him. He started to rise out of the stool he was on, as if to come speak to me. Then my friend Mike who was a male, but strictly a friend, who too frequented this same club sat down next to me, as if he knew there was trouble brewing. He always kept an eye on me, and this time was no different. He was now the barrier, a *very big barrier*. He motioned to the bartender to get us another round and gave him the drink I pushed what seemed like a world away. Knucklehead walked behind me, and I could see him in the same mirrored shelves I was lost in moments ago as the hairs rose on my neck. He whispered as he walked by in my ear, "see you around. And I WILL see you around." I did not engage, and he walked past me down the stairs. Mike *and* the bartender asked me what the hell that was about and if I was okay or needed the police. I told them it wasn't necessary, just the past trying to haunt me. That's what got me into this... just another ghost from the past and their clanging chains. I think it goes without saying but there were no more good times and late nights with Dani. I stopped all communication with her, and she wound up getting let go well before her "temp" role was up. And as far as the ghost at the bar, the news said his house was raided, and his dad was put away in jail on major gambling ring charges. And I never heard from him again.

That's the thing about the past; it tries to make you hold on to the baggage you left behind, and it will get heavy if you let it. But the thing is, it's only filled with the demons you haven't faced. As for me, well, I am a professional demon slayer at this point, and my prayer for you is that you armor up and go to battle every time a ghost comes knocking.

Chapter Seventeen

During the chaos of life, my sister arrived back in the States as anticipated. Among all my own confusion, I forgot she was coming back, but I was glad she was here. She had planned to stay with a good girlfriend of hers that she kept in touch with, and I was able to land her, you guessed it, a temp job. I picked her up and took her back home each day, as she was trying to save for a car of her own. Although I did enjoy the time I got to spend with her now and cherished it. The closeness we had all those years had been tarnished by the decisions of others, but I was determined to make sure we found that bond again. Eventually, she did save up enough money and bought herself a car...a bright blue Dodge Neon. You couldn't miss her if you tried! I was proud of her, and we kept in touch at work and hung out as much as we could. But we never spoke of the past, my time with Gram, her time overseas, or the collateral damage it all caused.

My department grew and space was cramped. Mail buckets of files were everywhere, and people were barely getting through the aisles. So, they moved us into the building directly across the street, where the cafeteria was. It was much more open, more space, and there was a whole seating area we could eat our lunch in now, instead of at our overflowing desks. Everyone still made the trek over to the cafeteria from the other building, so unfortunately, I could not escape the loud, ego-driven guys that I had been so graciously removed from sharing space with a few years earlier. I hear a tap tap on my desk, and I look up at the same guy who had tapped on my desk when I was one aisle over from him when he'd pompously pranced down the aisle in a sea of arrogance, when he did something good, or gossiped to whoever he knew behind me. He stood there carrying a Styrofoam container filled with something that didn't smell all that inviting, and he said, "Hey, I see they moved you all over here now. I don't see you anymore." Out of all the people he *did know* over here, he stopped to talk to *me*. This can't be for real. But I remember I am trying to adult, so I just responded with a quick look around and said, "Um, yeah, seems that way." As if his small talk was going to invite some profound response from me. He said, "Might be a long shot, but I was having some people over and thought you might want to stop over for a bit." I thanked him for the invite, but I'd have to pass as I had plans. I didn't have any plans. I just didn't want to be around a group of people who barely knew I existed; let alone around Mr. Pretentious himself and his self-absorbed friends for any length of time. He just replied with an "Okay, maybe some other time then," and walked back to wherever he came from. The company migrated other teams over to the building, and now the once-quiet space was filled with muffled chatter and the occasional laughter or singing of a happy birthday. Thankfully I was in the back of the aisle away from anyone in eye shot who entered this now-active office space. Time just kept ticking, and all I was trying to do was endure another day.

121

The weather was getting cold, so people stopped coming into the building for lunch as often, except for a few. Including Mr. Arrogant, (he graduated from Mr. Pretentious) continued to tap on my desk when he was leaving; of course, this is when he'd done his rounds of socializing. What does he want from me? Come to think of it, he might be gay. He was meticulously groomed, dressed awfully well for some regular guy, and walked with a flounce, not a strut. He was about fashion, money, and obviously women as that's all he talked to, and even drove a Mitsubishi Eclipse. Maybe he just likes those things; hell, I'm not to judge anyone, but either way he was clearly giving off some strong America Psycho Patrick Bateman vibes. It had snowed during the workday, and I knew I had to find a way to clean off my car before my long drive home. So far, I've been able to survive everything up to this point in my life but prepare myself for northeast winters by having a snow scraper in my car; but nope, didn't think of that. I looked for manila folders or even the top of a box of copier paper I could use. I MacGyvered my way into some makeshift snow removal tool, bundled up, and headed outside. I could see people peppered in the parking lot removing the snow from on and around their cars, and some were just hiding *in* their cars until they warmed up before they faced the foot of snow they were hoping would melt off their windshields first. I arrived at my car at the end of the lot, seeing it cleared off. I looked around and didn't see anyone, although I was thankful for whoever the good Samaritan was. Nonetheless, as puzzled as I was, I was freezing and went to open my door to start my car. I heard scraping, but it was coming from behind me. I turned slowly to see if perhaps someone needed help clearing off their car.

Well, if it isn't Mr. American Psycho himself. I reluctantly called over, asking if he needed help. He walked toward me as the snow crunched underneath his shoes. Why is he coming over here if his car is over there? My feet are numb now, and I don't think this is the appropriate time for small talk. Most of the cars had left the lot and there was no more humming of engines heating up to be on their way home. If you know anything about fresh snow, it has a weird way of making everything feel very still and quiet. He was wearing a dark grey peacoat, a black beanie, and black gloves. He shook the snow off them and again, I asked if he needed help. He thanked me but said he was okay and didn't live too far away. I told him he was lucky I had about a 40-minute drive and probably much more with the snow and traffic, but that someone was kind and cleaned off my car and saved me some time. He stared at me not saying anything and I immediately said, "Wait, it was you! You cleaned off my car, in the freezing cold and snow?" He smiled and nodded and stared at me with sort of kind but weirdly dark eyes. In true Patrick Bateman fashion, he must turn into different people and personalities upon entering the building and exiting. I thanked him and, without thinking (probably because my brain and feet were frozen at this point), I hugged him flimsily out of obligation mostly. I said I'd see him tomorrow, and I smiled and turned to walk away. He walked me to my car and grabbed my arm gently to face him. I don't know him, and he sure as hell doesn't know me, and anyone who grabs me, I immediately see red. "OK, thanks! I gotta go!" I opened my door and got in and quickly locked the doors. The warm air immediately started to thaw my frozen hands and feet as he held up a hand in a wave as I started to pull away. What just happened? Well,

I'll save you the time and shorten this ghost story as there were no sparkly vampires or young girls that needed saving, just a big bad wolf in sheep's clothing.

We had our first daughter, Cecelia. She was and is still amazing, now a college graduate.

Then, we had a courthouse wedding. Little did I know then that this wouldn't be the first time or the last time we would visit this very place, all for very different reasons.

Then, I bought a house. Again, *I* bought a house.

Then, a few years later, we had our second daughter, Ava who was and is still amazing. and is about to graduate college with honors.

Both of them are the kindest, most selfless, and toughest people I know.

Between those years, I saw glimpses of the very American Psycho Patrick Bateman I knew was there all along. But those camouflaged glimpses became a prominent part of my daily life and escalated into a person I did not know anymore.

Chapter Eighteen

I went through the motions of life, working, figuring out how to be a mom, trying to get some normalcy, but as much as I wanted that life, it didn't work that way for me. I had gone to work as usual, started my day mostly living in a fog of regret and shame, and my desk phone rang. I didn't recognize the number, so I had to answer in my corporate voice. On the other end of the phone was my brother. I thought he was calling from Brazil, but it turned out he was now living in the States, but none of that mattered in that moment. He wasn't calling me to check in or see how I was; all he said was "Hey, I wanted to let you know Dad passed away today." I froze. The room plunged into darkness, silencing my voice. He continued, "He died of a massive heart attack. He was working for a food vendor and died on a delivery." He rambled on about where his funeral would be, and by this point, I had stopped listening. All I could reply with was "OK". I hung up the phone and could feel the blood leave my face, and I was in shock. A guy who sat in the cubicle next to me asked me if I was okay. I replied, "My father died." He gave his condolences and suggested I take a few minutes or even go home. I thanked him but said I was fine and went about my day. I can only recall certain key moments over the next few days. I was in a fog and not sure how I should feel. Bill was dead.

The man who beat my mom, physically abused me to the point of bruises and blood, and quite literally used me as his personal punching bag was now, dead. I wrestled with even attending his funeral, but a morbid part of me almost wanted to make sure he was, in fact, dead. There was a viewing, a funeral mass, and then a military burial. I went to all of it. I was the last to arrive at the funeral parlor. I saw his wife, Judy, puffing on her Vantage cigarette. She saw me coming up the walk and tried to embrace me, saying she was glad I came. I did not reciprocate; I nodded my head in retort. I entered the tiny room with blue carpeting and tacky décor, where his casket lay in the corner by a window and walked slowly over to it. I scanned him from top to bottom, locking my eyes on his hands placed so peacefully on him. All I saw were hands that had been used so many times as weapons that inflicted so much pain. I saw that people had put pictures on the casket lid. Among them was a wallet-sized photo of my daughter, Cecelia. I whipped only my head around as if I were transfixed into a protective mama bear in that moment out for blood protecting her cub. I said, sternly, *"Who put this here?"* His wife, off to the side, replied meekly, "Your brother got that for us. It is his granddaughter, though he's never met her." I looked pensively at my brother who was standing off to the side. He could only hang his head in shame at what he did without my permission, or even knowledge. I leaned over the corpse of my dead father, took the photo of my daughter out of his casket, and walked out. Leaving everyone speechless. I went to the mass and sat in the back, and I went to his burial, which was full military honors when he was laid into the ground. People were crying and sad, most of whom I didn't know. It was as if everyone knew what he was and did but pretended he was some hero. I understood his true identity, which was far from heroic. It was evident they didn't know the real him. But I felt nothing. I felt nothing for his passing. I was completely numb. Inside, I was glad he was gone, and still am.

God's word tells us no weapon formed will prosper. It doesn't say the weapon won't be formed. His word also says you only need to be still, and He will fight for you. A weapon was formed, many at that. But no matter how many times I tried to escape, mentally and physically, God was behind the scenes fighting my Goliath. No more hiding, and no more fearing for my life, for that giant is now dead.

Chapter Nineteen

I lost track of time in a whirlwind of days, even years. But I was home each night with a toddler and soon-to-be kindergartner. The man I was married to, Mr. American Psycho himself, a monster hiding behind a suit and smile, deserves no name but the fictional killer from that horror novel: Patrick Bateman. Well, Bateman started going out several nights a week. This was normal, as his work often required him to meet clients. But it wasn't until he started coming home very late, and when I'd question this new behavior, he would become enraged. So enraged that one night he threw me against the wall, (seems like I've been here before) and then threw me to the ground and got on top of me, wrapping his hands around my neck, choking me... "I hate you! I hate you so much! You ruined my life!" as he slammed my head to the ground over and over and squeezed my neck harder in hopes to what I think to this day, kill me. I fought for my life that night. I kicked and punched and whapped him in the side of the head and startled his actions; he squeezed my neck one more hard time and came to his senses of what he was doing and let go. I screamed through the coughing of trying to catch my breath, holding my head in pain and told him to get out that I was calling the police. He grabbed his stuff and left before they arrived. I was in a cycle of repeating what I'd seen Bill do to my mom so many times before. A cycle of high school boyfriends who treated me as a rag doll to throw around. Here I am, an adult who has fought her whole life on multiple occasions, just to survive having the police on their way to my house, while I have a 2-year-old and a 5-year-old sleeping upstairs because their mother was almost killed. This isn't just about my survival; now, this is about theirs. We still worked for the same company but in different buildings for now. I was very much a single parent even before his shift to Bateman, and the pressure immense. Add the stress of being a good mom, with no blueprint for it, compounded everything. This was not a good environment for the three of us, and I needed to work to get us out. I took up running to lose the baby weight I had put on, but it became so much more than that. It became an outlet, a therapy. I was running on my lunch breaks every day, and not only did the weight fall off, but I felt stronger and more alive than I had felt in a long time. I went a step further and investigated the local YMCA for any type of classes I could take surrounding defending myself. No defense classes, but a boxing class. I'd never put on a pair of boxing gloves in my life but sign me up; I need to know how to duck and move so I'm not thrown to the ground again. I feared for my life, for my kids, but until I could save money and leave, I had to at least prepare for which personality I'd encounter on any given day. I showed up to class, clearly with fear in my eyes, but also a sort of fire that the coach knew right away was personal. He taught us to tape our hands to protect our knuckles under the gloves. In many classes, we learned the basics of the six standard boxing moves in every major fight you see. It's about learning your enemy and what their next move is and how to either get out of the way or hit back when they don't see it coming. I caught on so quickly, and he knew the intensity I brought even in our warm-ups. One morning he slid my black gloves over the yellow tape he put on me that day and looked me square in the eye not knowing anything about my situation, tapped my gloves with his and said, "I'm him. Now fight!" This was the time to spar. Hair in two french braids like I was Maggie from Million Dollar baby and I felt it too. I squared up and, holding back every ounce of emotion that wanted to come out of my face, and I punched hard. And good thing he was wearing protective gear because I wasn't holding back. He punched, I weaved. I saw every punch coming and attempted to land and counter each one with one harder. Jabs, uppercuts, rib shots, you name it I threw it. I was fighting in that five-minute sparring match with a professional boxing coach and all the years of pain I felt inside were coming out. I heard him say again, *"Fight!"* I moved around this gym with the whole class watching in awe while sweat was pouring down my face, and now tears. I was so, so tired. Tired of the match but so tired of fighting in my own life for so long. Boxing is about having a strategy for your fighting and not getting knocked out by your opponent. That day I won because I knew I still had more in me to fight for. I collapsed on the floor to my knees trying to catch my breath, and the coach knelt and lifted my chin and said, "now, *that's* how it's done!" He pulled my gloves off and unwrapped my tape. My hands were maroon-red and bruised from top to bottom. I kept showing up, perfecting my craft, and this coach worked with me to condition me to top shape. I'd kept up running, even doing half marathons and any long-distance race I could find, 23 in total as of today.

But because I knew I lived with an enemy, and I needed to have the endurance and strength for the next time he thought of killing me, I'd be ready.

Chapter Twenty

I drove back and forth to Virginia to see Gram every other weekend. Bateman knew she raised me, her condition, and that she was my world and never dared to argue this. I'd take the girls with me, and sometimes Sam. But this was mostly a time for me to be with her and hope that she knew who I was when I arrived. My Uncle Mario and his wife, Aunt Kat, have always welcomed me with love, grace, and hospitality as they knew the bond and love Gram and I had for each other. This stemmed as far back as being a little girl digging through her purse and putting on her rose-colored glasses that filled my entire face; even before I knew she was an angel dressed as a grandmother here to protect me, sent by the God of the Universe Himself. Each time I'd visit, we would talk about funny moments and reminisce about the silliest of things. She loved my girls, and they her. The unfortunate thing about dementia is you can seem fine one moment and there is a trigger that can get you stuck in a place of memory that is not conscious, but it is very real to the person encountering it. Being around my kids helped, but I think it overstimulated her at times. She'd go in and out, staring into space saying things like "you keep that up, Giovanna, and you're going to find out what will happen!" In her mind, she was in a memory of her and her oldest daughter, my Aunt Gio. Aunt Kat told me to ignore her; it would pass. I was in shock as I'd never seen her transition elsewhere like that. She'd eventually come to the present moment, but my heart was breaking again into another thousand pieces. I continued to go see her, hoping one of the times she'd be her old self for just a few hours. The dining room was essentially transitioned into her room so she could be near everyone if she needed them, but also so she could be watched easily. All her furniture, her bed, the very one where I cried until I had no more tears left years earlier, was affixed in this room among all her photos of her kids, grandkids, and anything to keep her remembering who we all were. Except this time there was an oxygen tank, and she was wearing a nasal cannula that pumped 24/7 of oxygen because of newly diagnosed COPD. Dementia wreaks havoc on not just the brain, but your body deteriorates too. I knew this, but still I was surprised as if it were the first time, I came to terms with it. My Aunt Kat, who will forever be a saint in my eyes, took care of Gram, even when she could no longer go to the bathroom herself. They got a nurse to come in during the day, Bridgette, to keep Gram company but who was also medically trained to help with the bouts of incontinence, outbursts of dementia, and to make sure she was eating, and her oxygen levels were at their peak. I watched the very person who was and is still my hero disintegrating right in front of me. It was like I was watching a movie and someone else was experiencing this, but it was me and I had no idea what the next scene would be. She called me into her room and told me to sit on the bed. She said she had something for me. She was lucid, so I went with it. She dug into one of her drawers and seemed to have found something wrapped up in a cloth, but very purposefully done. Her hands trembled as she handed the object to me, motioning me to open it. As I opened it, I saw the anticipation on her face waiting for my reaction. It was a soft figurine of the Pillsbury Doughboy. I looked up and smiled, my heart crushing now into two thousand pieces. This very object sat next to her kitchen sink for as far back as I can remember. She'd let me play with it as a kid, but I didn't know it was a logo for many various dessert ingredients; I just liked that he was soft and rubber-like and I couldn't break him. He'd always wind up back by the kitchen sink when playtime was over. But she was handing me something she remembered about *me*. She said, "I want you to have him, but don't tell anyone else; they are all asking me where it is; he's yours! Now go hide it!" I promised her the secret was safe with me, and I thanked her. I hugged her and inhaled her smell any chance I got, as it was complete nostalgia for a time when I was loved unconditionally. She always smelled like safety. Part anise-anise perfume, and just, well, Gram, and it was the best. I came back again two weeks later as I always did, but this time she didn't know who I was most of the time I was there. Aunt Kat would keep assuring her who I was and that I was her granddaughter—she said she didn't think she had any. Something inside me shattered beyond repair. Dementia is a fast-progressive disease, but her not knowing who I was had put me on a whole other kind of level of worry and sadness. I told her I loved her as she stared blankly into space. I had to leave because this was not the person I knew, and I was not equipped mentally to handle the ramifications of what I'd inevitably have to face.

Two weeks later, I got home from a long workday, picked up the kids from daycare, and got a phone call as soon as I got in the house. My mom was on the other line…she said Gram was rushed to the hospital. She said she and Aunt Fran were there, Uncle Mario and Aunt Kat. I asked, I begged to be there but was told a firm NO, that this was not how I wanted to remember her. I was crying, I was angry, I yelled and said, "I took care of her, I should be there! I can drive there, it's just a few hours!" But there was nothing I could do even if I was there. Gram's disease took over her small, frail body and she couldn't fight any longer. My mom said she was awake, and I asked to talk to her… I took in a hitched breath to prepare myself. Gram got on the phone with her classic "Yeah…" I replied trying to fight the break in my soul, "Hi Gram, I miss you so much, I hope you're being treated well there" as I sniffed through the tears and tried so hard to hold back my emotion for the love and honor, I had for her. I didn't do a good job; not only did she know that, but she knew *who* I was *and* my name. She replied in a drawl I knew too well, "Nicole honey, why are you crying?" I said voice trembling, "I'm not crying, Gram, I'm just happy to hear your voice. And I'm sorry I'm not there," she replied, "Oh honey, it's ok, everything is going to be fine. Tomorrow is another day so don't you worry, ok?" Those are the same words of encouragement she'd tell me when I was 16 years old sulking next to her on the little love seat after my ever so many bad days. Same words as she tapped on my hands and held them there until I was assured, tomorrow is in fact another day. I replied while fighting through tears, "Ok I will try, I love you so much, Gram, so, so very much. Thank you for loving me when no one else did." She said so clearly, "I love you too, honey, always. Now go on, I'm going to be just fine". That was the very last time I ever spoke to her. She died the next day, and I was completely shattered. And I still am to this very day.

The funeral was in South Philly, and I waited as long as I could to enter the funeral parlor where her viewing was being held. So many people in there were the "I'd be 16 and on drugs and pregnant" people, and I felt like I had combated that, but I was in an abusive marriage and faking my way through everything that crossed my path. As I entered the room, a hush came over the space, and everyone's eyes were on me. No matter how anyone viewed me as a person, no one could deny that I took care of my Gram, and the bond we shared was so much more than anyone could ever dream of having. I could see my mom and her siblings, less one Aunt Gio, who sat in the lobby, and in that moment, and I wished I was there too. I took a deep breath and walked over to her casket. My Aunt Fran, who many years ago said she had 'no room for me' when my mom moved said, "It's okay; you can talk to her." I stared at her with such tension in my eyes that she immediately backed away. I reached in the casket and felt Gram's hands, which had held mine so many endless nights, and held rosaries praying for everyone. They were so cold. I collapsed on my knees and cried silently. I told her I missed her, but I'd continue her legacy and I promised I would make her proud. I then stood up and gazed at her…I knew the entire room was waiting for a show, but I was poised and in control, even though I wanted to break down and go into the ground with her. She didn't look like herself, maybe 25 years younger, or maybe that's God's way of saying this is what she looked like when I created her home to be a refuge so you would feel my presence and protection. God was certainly in my Gram…I was so busy watching her decline I forgot the fun, vibrant woman who showed me my worth, my value, and loved me more than life itself. And the one who always left the big light on, only just for me.

Chapter Twenty-One

My mom had moved back from Brazil the year before my Gram passed. She didn't tell me she was in the States; she was staying with her longtime friend, who I endearingly call my Aunt Sues. She's known me since I was an infant and knew the entire series of unfortunate events not only my mom endured, but also me. She despised Bill, and she equally despised my mom's now soon-to-be ex-husband. The infamous Tiago. The third husband didn't abuse her, but he was unfaithful. She left her family, her daughter, and all she knew for a man. She lived there for 17 or so odd years, only to move back to a life where she had nothing but shame. My Gram was gone, so there was no house to run to keep hidden behind the big green steel door until the terror passed. This was a decision that came full circle that she'd have to now face. She eventually fessed up and told us what happened; I can't say I was surprised, but I was in no position to offer her anything except grandkids she barely knew. Call it ironic, call it ridiculous, but Sam married Bateman's best friend a few years earlier too. I shake my head as I type those very words. I'll spare the details, but he and I do not speak, even to this day, and that's fine by me. He didn't like the influence I had on her or rather just being the person that I was. One who would fight for my life, so he did his best to keep her at a distance. They lived in Delaware, and that's where my mom wound up staying for a while, in their spare room helping with their now two kids. She got alimony until I'm guessing she saved up enough, and she got her own apartment close by and did exactly what I was forced to do so many times: start over from nothing. How I was feeling at that time could only be summed up by a song we all know well, by a very underrated band, The Verve...called, Bittersweet Symphony. "I'll take you down the only road I've ever been down," were never truer lyrics that rang over and over in my head in a loop. What I had experienced up to till now was nothing short of a bad horror movie you can't help but watch through the view of your peeking fingers. An accident where the car is upside down and the authorities scratch their heads trying to put the pieces of how the wreck happened, but you managed to climb out and survive without a scratch. That's the thing about survival; on the surface, I physically appeared okay, but internally-I was bleeding. I had endured so much torment because of decisions one person made and didn't care how it affected anyone else.

But I was supposed to have empathy for the crash of the single-handedly largest decision she made? I allowed the men in my life to abuse and degrade me because that's the only path I was shown? The path she laid out like a map for me, like a 21-step program, except this one almost costs you your life. I watched from afar, while her life was in the process of starting over, and I truly did want her to succeed, and I felt sorry for her. But simultaneously held this anger and bitterness inside of me towards her. My whole existence was shaped because of the very person who was supposed to protect and care for me, didn't. She never knew how many times I had to "start over" and figure out how to take care of myself. She didn't know the moments in life when I would rather die than live another day in the living nightmare I was facing. And here I was confronting another ending that I would have to pick myself up, dust off, and keep going; but this time with two little girls. I sacrificed my whole being for them, and every decision and choice was made with them in mind first. She was used to playing checkers with her life, whereas I was playing chess. I had to be strategic about every decision I made because I saw firsthand the destruction one bad move could cause. Hurt and tired of cleaning up the collateral damage, I got news from my mom that my cousin Nick purchased my Gram's house. He was planning on gutting the whole thing, top to bottom, which would take years; but he planned on living with his wife and kids there eventually. Although a part of me was glad it didn't go to a stranger, he might as well have been just that. And just like that, someone who didn't come around, take care of Gram like I did, or anyone, takes her house and destroys it. You might as well have burned it to the ground. When I thought about this news, my fingers curled around an imaginary chess piece, the queen perhaps; ready to sweep every painful memory off the checkered battlefield of my past.

I actively started looking for someone else to live; a safe environment for me and my kids. Bateman never hurt them physically...but they were witnesses to his verbal abuse towards me, and at times the threat of physical harm. In my hunt for another new place to call home, I was met with nothing but rejection by various apartment complexes and townhome communities. I never felt so stuck in all my life, but I was determined to be prepared just like I had been physically months before. Until one day, I was browsing the work intranet's sale section. Imagine it like today's Facebook Marketplace, with everything from used cars to kids' toys. "Condo For Rent" immediately caught my attention. 2 bedrooms, 2 baths, first floor end unit condo, and a photo. It was PERFECT. Close to work, a great school system, AND far enough away from the abuse I was living in. I'd been rejected so much that I ran through the worst-case scenario chapter in my brain again. So, I mentally had to prepare myself and finally emailed the girl who posted it. She responded and I let out an audible sigh. She said it was her dad's condo and gave me his phone number. I thanked her and went about my day. He's probably looking for the perfect tenant and not some woman with two kids trying to escape an abusive spouse. I decided to give him a call later that week as I couldn't take another denial, not when the wound was so fresh. I'd replay each day picking up the girls from school, heading back to the house praying to a God I had no idea if heard me, to please let Bateman not be home. And most times he wasn't, thankfully. It was peaceful when it was just us, without the walking-on-eggshells feeling we all had when he was there. Once I'd settled the girls, most nights I found myself with my face in a book and a glass of wine, listening for anything that would alert me to leave the vicinity. It wasn't long before many hunches I had over time about the whereabouts of Bateman were confirmed. He was having an entire relationship, not just an affair, but living an entirely separate life with a co-worker, under my nose the whole time. I can't say I was surprised, but it still stung and was a huge blow to know I was stuck and sharing a house with not only a maniac, but a cheating maniac. It all made sense now. Get me out of the way and he can live the life he thinks will change the terrible life *I* caused him.

"Hello? Hi, my name is Nicole, your daughter gave me your phone number about the condo you have for rent. I hope it's okay I'm calling. Is it still available?" "Yes, hello! My name is Bob, nice to meet you. Yes, it's still available; would you like to come and see it this weekend?" This weekend I thought, wow, can I take another blow after the one I just had? "Yes, that would be great, thank you." "Great, does 11 a.m. work for you?" Bob replied. Trying to sound excited, I said "11am Saturday is perfect!" "I'll text you the address. See you then!" It has snowed, and I refused to call Bob and tell him to reschedule. I arrived on time, walked through slushy snow in the parking lot, and saw a very tall man standing near the doorway. "Bob?" "Hey, you made it!" and he shook my hand and said it was too cold out and let's head inside. He's in his 50s, at least 6'4", and looking down at my 5'2" self- and I felt so small in that moment. A tenant was preparing to move out, so he told me ahead of time not to mind the boxes and such scattered about. He walked me through the place, and it was perfect. It was so much space just for the three of us, but there is no way this guy is going to rent to me. I thanked the tenant for allowing me to invade her space and headed back out into the cold. "So, what do you think?" Bob said with a smile. I replied with real excitement, "I think it's perfect!" He asked me a few questions like where I grew up-South Philly. "No kidding, I have family there! "How long have you been at the mortgage company?" For over a decade. Then he asked, "Is it just you?" I sighed audibly. "No, to be honest Bob, it's for me and my two young daughters; they are 5 and 7. I'm in an abusive marriage and I'm trying to get us to a healthy environment," I replied shamelessly. He said, "Well, I bought this condo for my daughter, and she didn't want it, so if you want it, it's yours!" I was so taken aback. I said, "You don't want to see my income or credit or have a reference?" He replied, almost chuckling, "No, that's not necessary. You have a good stable job, you grew up in the same place I did, and you want to get you and your girls safe. I have 7 kids. If any needed my help, I would. This includes someone who hurt them or broke their heart. So, you're no different. Rent is reasonable and lawn care/snow removal are included. When do you want to move in?" I was in shock. Was the God I was praying to and not knowing if my words just evaporated into the air, heard me? But something broke for me besides my heart. "Are you sure?" "Yes, absolutely! I want to paint and clean it for you once the tenant leaves, so how's January for your lease? It's a $1200 deposit, so if you pay that ahead of time and don't worry about the rent till you move in. Once everything is painted and cleaned, you can bring anything over you want to keep it here even though you don't officially move in." I can't grasp how someone can be so gracious when all I've faced was rejection, and January is over 45 days away. But I blurt out an immediate "Yes!" Absolutely, thank you so much," as tears welled in my eyes I couldn't keep back if I tried. Bob, the father of 7, put his arm around me and said, "It's going to be okay; I promise you that." No truer words were spoken as my entire life's course was about to change into something I had never seen coming. I felt a huge weight lifted, and I felt confident in my new decision. How was this going to fare with Bateman and telling the kids? I had to strategize. The next day, I got up and got dress and wore a black-and-white wrap dress, tights, and big black 5-inch stiletto boots. This was nothing out of the norm, but today, I felt much taller in them. I dropped the kids at school, while keeping the news of a new life to myself. On the way home, the girls chattered on about their day, as I pulled up and saw his car already in the driveway. Damn. Well, no time like the present. We weren't even on speaking terms. So, when I said I had something to tell him, you could see him tense up and his jaw tick. I got the kids fed and in bed to ensure they were not around for any of the carnage that was about to ensue. I stood in the kitchen, watching him ponder about what bomb I was about to drop while cooking something for himself. I started out by telling him I know he's sleeping with someone else, and that I was leaving *with* the girls. He immediately lost his faculties, glared at me, and threw the plate he'd taken out for his food. It was like a frisbee aimed at my head. I ducked, and it shattered against the wall. He grabbed me by my neck and attempted to throw me again against the wall. Not this time. I jabbed the heel of boot into the front of his foot, and he let go, reaching back for me, but I ducked. This is where my training came into play. He charged at me, and I weaved, and he hit the wall. He wasn't giving up... I punched him in his ribs as hard as I could, and he hunched to the floor as he gasped for air. I pushed him on his back and laid my boot square on his chest. I looked down at him and said, in a deadly tone I had never heard come out of me before, "If you *ever* touch me again, or even *think* about it, you will go to jail for a *very long time. Do you understand me?*" This time I had the power. I didn't need anything from him; he got exactly what he wanted.

Me to stop ruining his life. I told him, "I want a divorce." He just nodded as I removed my foot from his chest. This was yet another Goliath I had to face, but this time I did it in God's strength. I went upstairs and took off my boots, my tights, and my dress. They were so tainted now that I never wore them again. I signed the very informal lease I was sent via email and met Bob the next day, which was during my lunch break, with a check and picked up the keys. He said he had to run, and the place was mine. I opened the door and locked it behind me. I walked around and even though the silence was deafening, it was peaceful. And it was mine. I stood in the corner of the room and just slid down onto the floor; I had nothing, but I had everything. I filed for divorce, and it happened quickly, no contest, child support, but joint custody. Great...nothing like a narcissist. But I couldn't lose focus—I spent so much money and time putting together Ikea furniture and doing my best to make a home for my girls. I got them new bunk beds, dressers, bright pink curtains, and all the accompaniments that little girls love. I got couches on consignment and tried so hard to make this place feel like a home. All while going to work and pushing through each day like I always did. This feeling was all too familiar. It took me back a few years, to when I was doing the same thing, starting over. I took the day off work when I knew Bateman wouldn't be home. I'd spent the past month packing mine and the girls' things and stashing them under the beds. I piled my car and trunk with as much of our things as I could fit. I pulled out of the driveway, took a deep breath, pulled away, and never looked back. I sat in the parking space staring at the place that I had to start my life over again. All because of someone else's actions and decisions, yet again. I felt frozen in my body, like I was standing outside of myself looking into what seemed like a kaleidoscope of moments in my life I had no say in; but I was left cleaning up every mess I suffered. Why not let me go in any moment of Bill's abusive rages, or on the top of the apartment stairs, why not let me go when I was on the floor being choked out by Bateman? Why keep me alive to just start over *again*? I sat there and cried. I pleaded with the God who I didn't know if heard me, "Why is this happening? I can't take any more, please." I cried and cried until my eyes were swollen and blotchy red. What I didn't know is my girls were one of the reasons why I was not taken out all those times before. I didn't know what was ahead of me and how much of a pivotal part I'd play in their lives, or they'd play in mine. I stepped out of the packed car and took a deep breath. I braced myself and opened the door to not only a new home but also to a new beginning.

Chapter Twenty-Two

The girls really loved this new home, playing Barbies or Polly Pockets in their new space. I think it was just the peace that they now felt. They were halfway to finishing out the school year, so I let them stay in the school they were in. It worked as it was just temporary, and I knew they'd need time to adjust to not just a new environment but also a new life. They are resilient, flexible, and trusted me more than anyone that this was all going to work out. I had no idea how much love I had in my heart, or in my soul until God gave me these little humans. Their hugs could heal a bad day, their caring hearts and empathy for others were palpable, and their smiles would light up a room. But what they didn't know and probably don't to this day is that they saved my life more than once as I lived for them, as they were all that mattered in my world. They'd go with Bateman half the week and every other weekend. This was joint custody...and it sucked. He'd pick them up after dinner, and I'd walk them out, as he was *not* allowed in my home. I'd watch them pull away and, without recourse, start crying. Although I had been theoretically alone for so long, I now felt more alone than ever. That silence I heard the first time I entered this home wasn't just deafening; it was now screaming. I'd work extra hours, go to the gym, and run more on the days they were not with me just to limit the time I was home alone. I was still running at work during my lunch hour, and they had showers off the bathroom that I would use to wash off and clean up before heading back to work. I'd seen this same girl a few times a week, and I'd exchanged pleasantries with her when I saw her until one day, she introduced herself as Anne. We became fast friends, and I now see her around the building and go out of my way to say hello and have a quick conversation. But she always was accompanied by this tall, handsome guy with meticulous pulled back dreadlocks, kind brown eyes flecked with hazel, and a smile that could melt you. I assumed they were together and didn't think too much of it. Until she said "her friend, Cliff" saw me and inquired what my story was. The first Cliff I introduced you to covered up for me when I forgot the lyrics in an eighth-grade talent show and did help in a pinch, but this one...this Cliff would alter my existence as I knew it. My life was so messy that whatever she told him was probably not that inviting. Yet, a day or so later, I got an email from him just with the salutation "Hello". We engaged in conversation, and he asked if I wanted to get lunch sometime. It's just lunch; what could happen? He picked me up in front of the building, and we went to a local sandwich shop. Standing next to him, I felt so small. He was much larger than me, 6'2", defined muscles, big hands, but so kind and gentle. To the regular person, he was extremely intimidating, still is to this day, but is a big softie inside. We had good conversation, and he told me about his life and his past adventures in the entertainment industry, dropping many names that made my mouth gape. I had to get back, so he said he'd explain more later, as he could visibly see I was feeling a bit unsure if he was lying or if this really happened. I thanked him, but I didn't think anything of it after as I was just trying to get my life together and didn't need another relationship to unload my cargo of baggage on. I had to take some vacation time, or I was going to lose it entirely, so I just took casual days off around the holidays and one day found myself randomly walking through Target. I was not paying any attention and my cart accidentally hit someone else's while I came around the corner. I looked up and said, *"I'm so sorry!"* realizing at that moment it was Cliff. Same guy who was name-dropping celebrities just a few weeks back. He said he was on his lunch hour looking for fillers for his artificial Christmas tree. I laughed and said I'm not sure they make those, but good luck finding them. He was so much bigger from this vantage point that when I talked, I had to look up at him. And his smile was so inviting that it was hard to look away. I said I was off for a few days, so I was just walking around the store, and I hoped he would find what he was looking for. I'd like to think that day Serendipity herself was working overtime to make sure we "bumped into" one another, at Target of all places, because when I left, I could not get him off my mind. I'd given him my number the first time we had lunch, but it wasn't until after this encounter that he used it. I got a text from him saying it was nice to see me today; I obliged and said, "likewise." He asked if I wanted to come to his apartment to hang out one night and watch a movie, have a few drinks. He seemed harmless but also very protective at the same time. We made plans but unfortunately Ava had an asthma attack, which made me cancel. Ava suffered a long time being sick as a baby only to find out she had asthma and struggled even with play and exercise at times; she was on breathing treatments several times a day, but I was used to the height of it being bad and getting her calm so the meds would work. Bateman never had a clue how to take care of her, so I'd sleep on her floor in her room just to listen to the sounds of her breathing in case of so much as a wheeze. Cliff knew I had two kids but didn't realize the magnitude of them or the situation I was in until a bit later. I rescheduled till she was better and headed to his apartment in black leather 4-inch booties (cause, well, short people insecurities), jeans, and a white long-sleeved shirt. He greeted me with his giant smile, and it immediately smelled of vanilla upon entering. Why *vanilla*? It smelled like the vanilla air freshener trees people put in cars, and I am a not a fan, but I mustered through. I had been carrying a bag of drinks and mixers that I awkwardly handed over to him in a now torn brown paper bag. Basketball was on the TV, and he handed me a red Solo cup to make myself a drink. A red solo cup. Cause I'm 16 at a house party apparently. We chatted for a few while we made our chosen poison of choice, in said solo cup, and I felt awkward, apprehensive even. But he was hospitable and told me to have a seat. I took a seat next to him on the oversized couch, which seemed fit for him, but as for me, it swallowed me up whole and my feet just dangled off the front. As we chatted, it was rather warm, so I said I was going to step outside; this was all just too much to add to the chaos that was my life, to which he was oblivious. He walked me toward the hallway, and before I could open the door, he gently wrapped his arm around my waist and pushed me against the wall. Oh no, did I make the same mistake again? He seemed *so nice*. Then he had one arm on the wall and one on my face and gently kissed me. I was *not* expecting that, but I went with it; he knew I was stunned. I'm rarely speechless, but he told me to go ahead outside, he'd see me when I came back in. Now I really needed air. Cold air. I closed the door behind me while the temperature outside was a mere 20 degrees; my insides were on fire. What was happening and why was I suddenly feeling no scary tension with a man? I asked myself what felt like a million questions, and I headed back in. It wasn't long before we wound up watching a movie, and he quickly fell asleep. I woke him and said I had to go, and I'd see him soon. I left feeling like I needed to see him again.

His birthday was a few weeks from there, and he said he had plans to go to Atlantic City with friends for the night. I had no right to have an opinion, but I found myself up late that night eating Oreos at 3am while he was there "celebrating". I sent him a text and asked him, "How many Oreos at 3am are too many?" Not expecting a response, he replied to me a moment later, "Well, depends how many are left?" I laughed and I asked him how his celebration was, and he seemed very uninterested and said it was "Okay" and he was up while everyone else was asleep. Again, Serendipity has a way of pushing things right when you don't see it coming. I went about my life, continuing to box, run, be a mom, and all the stuff in between. When I told him I boxed, he said he felt it was unfeminine, but he didn't know the history behind it. So, I boxed more. He'd learn eventually that I am very stubborn and extremely determined. My birthday is the following month from his and he took me out for sushi…he doesn't like sushi but heard me mention I did. So, he endured the raw fish and various rolls just to make *me* happy, and *this* type of treatment I was certainty not used to. We engaged in such intense conversation as if we were the only two in the restaurant. When it was time to leave, he asked if I wanted to go get ice cream. Ice cream? How about a drink, I thought to myself, but I decided to indulge his unexpected suggestion. We left and before I knew it, we were pulling into a 24-hour diner at about midnight. We sat down and a very tired older Indian woman came over to take our order. Two ice cream sundaes. "We only have vanilla and caramel," she said tiredly. He ordered two and we sat there again engaged in conversation, bringing in a new day together eating ice cream.

He knew I had my girls on certain days, so I only made plans with him when they were with Bateman. I missed them when they left so much but reveled in them when they were home. He invited me to a get-together in Philly one weekend at the same friend who connected us; it was her cousin's house. It was in South Philly...of course it was. He picked me up, and I asked where it was as I knew the area well so I could probably get us there with no GPS. He handed me a printout of a map with a red star on it. Puzzled, I asked what I was looking at. He said, "That's her house, right there, where the star is." I said, "What is the address?" We both laughed knowing his method of navigation was not getting us to this place any time soon. He texted and got the address, and I put it in my phone's GPS, and I knew exactly where it was. We parked on the tiny little street and headed to the tucked away rowhome, walking in the cold. He'd always hold my hand, and he was always so warm. My hand got lost in his and he'd hold it close to him as to offer protection and comfort that he was not about to hurt me like so many had in the past. We entered the house foyer, steps to the right, kitchen to the back. I'd never been here before, but it felt like a blast from the past because I know these rowhomes like the back of my hand…I knew the home's entire layout and where everything was already just upon entering. It was rather eerie stepping into a place I felt a knew where every room already was, but we wound up having a great time. He drank a bit too much, so I was now the designated driver. Driving in the city in someone else's car was not something I was accustomed to, so this was new. I pulled out of the spot and headed through the backstreets I knew to get us to the bridge. He was passed out next to me, so I was on my own. Now in a panic as it was late, dark, and I had only taken a bus or driving one way back and forth to Grams. Where I was now driving in the city for real. We arrived safely at my house, and I woke him up and said to come in so he could get some sleep. He came in and sat up on the couch. I went in my room and changed and cleaned up, thinking he'd be passed out upon my return. He was still sitting there with his coat on. I helped him take off his coat and guided him to lie down on the couch and put a blanket on him, and he fell fast asleep. When I woke up, he was gone. I texted him, but I didn't get any answers all day long. Let's flip through the worst-case scenario chapter again and see what this could mean. I ran, I filled my day with nonsense, and eventually he called me around 6pm. He said he left as he felt sick and slept all day but felt better and asked if I had plans. What do I say, am I available based on his not even telling me he was leaving? "Sure, I'm here" is all that came out of my mouth. He arrived about an hour later with a canvas painting he purchased of Marilyn Monroe. He said he saw it and thought of me because she was beautiful and unique, and I needed some artwork instead of just stark white walls. I smiled, watching as he measured the wall with his eyes, tapped a nail into the drywall, and carefully positioned Marilyn's face so she gazed down at us with that famous half-smile. We stayed up in the dimly lit room sharing stories and philosophies on life. He had no idea my philosophies came from the life baggage that could be stacked up in my closet floor to ceiling. But he didn't seem phased, and the more I let him in, the more he wanted to know. Is there nothing I can say to push him away? Nothing about me scares him. And I realized in that moment that every new beginning comes from some other beginning's end.

Chapter Twenty-Three

At first glance, Cliff was a 6-foot-2-inch-tall handsome as they come caramel colored man with perfectly groomed locs gathered at the nape of his neck by a hair tie and a precisely trimmed goatee framing his jawline, which only added to the commanding presence he carried with him everywhere. Some even mistook him for a pro ball player on many occasions. However, he's not a pro ball player but he was and is still the gentlest giant I've ever known. Except at this time, he had a fan club of sorts from what I found out; a fan club of women; not that he entertained that notion, but he was friendly and engaging, so I coined him "the mayor" of his work area. I didn't like these women "friends" who would ask him to lunch and the like. Even though I tried to make light of it, I disliked those women, and I couldn't be hurt again. I built a huge wall to protect myself from this very thing. I started pulling away, answering his texts with one-word replies and finding excuses to cancel plans. But he wasn't fooled. I told him I didn't like the "we're just friends" women who hung on his every word. Those women had to go if he was serious about us. He said he understood and in no way was intentionally trying to make me uncomfortable. After that, several days went by and I had no communication with him. Well, nice knowing you. And like clockwork, my brain was scanning the chapters of my worst-case scenario book in my brain, or so I thought. Before my brain had time to figure out what chapter to land on, a few days later I got a flower delivery. Twelve long-stem purple roses (there isn't even such a color) were sent to me at work. They were in a beautiful arrangement and the card read, "It must be nice to know the Mayor." Well played, sir… well played. He approached me in passing, saying what beautiful flowers they were, and someone must think I am very special. I closed my eyes for a beat and quietly mouthed "thank you." It was a sweet kind gesture, and they were in fact stunning flowers, not to mention the clever card. He smiled and nodded, and he went about his way. I watched him walk away until he was out of eyeshot while damning my brain for always thinking negatively first. But hey, can you blame me? Not much positivity I can draw from; the scales are completely tipped. At least that is how I justified what I really felt: unworthy. My desk was at the end of the aisle right by the community break room. When I tell you if looks could kill, I'd have fallen out. "Oh, they are so pretty; who are they from?" "A friend," I'd reply. But they knew. This was a general message to the female fan club, who were asking. I was his his. So, back off. I kept them there for a few days even until they started to wilt, and until the eye rolls and whispers ended. He was proud of his work without even saying a word and let me know I was the only one for him. All I've known are men who are abusive, physically, mentally, and emotionally, and complete abandonment. I realized he wanted nothing from me. He only wanted to help me heal from the torment that had plagued me for so long. I've had a hard rule that my kids are first, but he knew each time they'd leave I'd hate to be alone in my house. The silence had become sounds of screaming and I'd hear phantom calls of "mommy" if left with myself too long. One Saturday he told me to get dressed, wear something I would be comfortable in but still presentable, and that he would be over at 3pm and we'd head out. He didn't tell me where, not even a hint, no matter how many times I asked. I heard a knock at the door... right on time. I opened the door and could only muster "Hi," probably way too breathy for a greeting. He stood there, basically the size of the doorframe, wearing light blue faded jeans, an untucked white casual long-sleeved dress shirt with the sleeves folded up slightly, and tan beat-up vintage shoes. He stared at me as I was mesmerized in a trance staring at his gorgeous, well, everything. He spoke, and I was taken out of my daze, and he said, "Hi to you too. You look beautiful." I widened the door for him to come in. He asked me, "Are you ready to go?" I ask him hesitantly, "Yes, I am ready to go, but where are we going exactly?" He replied, "New York City, well Manhattan really." "Oh cool, sounds fun!" I said acting as cool as I could knowing full well, I was *internally freaking out*. "But what's in New York City?" I knew full well *what* was in New York City; this was my dream for so long and he's taking me TO my dream! He replied, "Well, YOU are New York City, so I thought you'd like to get acquainted". He kissed me on the cheek and grabbed my hand to leave. Safe is the only word I could use to describe how I felt with him, and still do. Manhattan, New York, became part of not just that day, but of many days and nights for a long time after. I never got to be on Broadway as I always hoped, but I did get to experience it in a way I never thought possible. He once surprised me with a weekend away there and even better we were seeing a matinee of West Side Story. As we entered the theater, I took a big breath in while trying to keep every bit of composure I had. He grabbed my hand and led me to the theater doors. I have been in many a theater, but this was different. This day I felt like a kid in Wonka's factory. Chandeliers everywhere, red carpets, and woodwork only an old building in a city would have. And he turned as I must have been trailing behind, he smiled, and said, "Are you ready now?" I shook my head a little, trying to come into reality. He handed me a playbill with the bold West Side Story logo on it as I rubbed my hand over the glossy cover. Admiring it fondly, to when I was brought to my first theater performance by someone else who thought the world of me, and here I am with another. We found our seats eventually, but we were a bit early. As I flipped through the playbill, an usher came by and approached us. And here I am, now not flipping through a Playbill, but flipping through the worst- case scenario chapter again. Great, we probably have the wrong seats, maybe even worse, the wrong day! But they kindly said that we could move further down as the seats were open closer to the stage. This meant it wasn't a sold-out show and we could move down as far as we'd like. I heard nothing after moving closer to the stage! I grabbed my things and moved as far down as we could. The lights eventually went down, and the orchestra started to play. It's showtime. I felt a flutter in my belly as the overture started. The show was mesmerizing. He watched me in awe as I leaned up in my seat, filled with joy. I was transported, as if I were Natalie Wood herself dancing on that stage. I could see myself in the pastel crinoline dresses and the DeLuca soft sole palette character shoes that seemed to lift them gracefully off the stage with every move. This was my dream, to sing and dance on Broadway, but I was just watching from a seat, wondering why someone else's decisions allowed them the right to be an official dream crusher. I had sunk back into my seat in defeat. He sees me, grabs my hand, and smiles. To which I believe to this day he knew exactly what I was feeling in that moment. Afterward, he took me to what would become our favorite restaurant, Vice Versa. A tiny restaurant hidden away where you went down a set of outside stairs leading to a door of romance and intimacy. This was the day I fell irrevocably and undeniably in love with him. We'd have months of day trips walking the city, dozens of Magnolia cupcakes later, picnics in Central Park, and overnight trips to hit the nightlife. And many times, I tried to sneak in various stage doors along the way that never seemed to be open. What I did know for certain is that he saw me and made it his mission to make sure I felt every corner of that city to which I, to this day, know I fully love and fully belong.

Chapter Twenty-Four

It was time Cliff met my girls. A year had passed of us together having the best time, but I was enduring so much with the girls leaving and returning and having to reprogram them every three days from Bateman's narcissistic ways. It was time they saw the person who could not only love me but could be a door of love for them should they choose to accept it. There is a chain water-ice place called Rita's. Depending on the area of the country you're in, you may call this "Italian ice"; yes, it is, but it's just water ice to those Italian Americans and those of the Northeast. School was out for summer, and since this was a place we frequented to cool off in Jersey hot summers, I suggested we go and do just that, "some cooling off." What they didn't know is Cliff would already be there as if it was a "oh what a coincidence seeing you here" moment. The girls knew I had a "friend" and asked when they'd meet him. We got to the counter and ordered our favorites when I saw Cliff approach us. He was dressed in a yellow polo shirt and jeans and eating his favorite water ice, mango. I pretended to be surprised to see him and introduced him to the girls as my friend, Cliff. They didn't care, as I don't think they initially comprehended this was who they had been asking to meet; they just wanted to know if mango was good to get for next time. We laughed as we sat on the bench enjoying our now sloshy ice, but I said it was time to go. They asked if he could come back to our house with us to hang out and that he was "so fun." We both looked at one another, and I said sure if he was able. He said he had plans with his nephews later but could come for a little while. The girls were on fire showing him this and that, and we finally settled on a game of Connect Four: Ava against Cliff. And he did not hold back-he destroyed her. Afterwards, her comment to him was, "I don't trust you. My mom doesn't have a lot of friends, and my dad is mean to her. How do I know you won't hurt her?" He only beat her in a game, but it was a fair honest question, nonetheless. She was so in tune with me laughing and what she had never known for me to have, joy. So that she questioned the very person that contributed to that to make sure it wasn't a sham. She waited for an answer. I recall this as if it happened yesterday, and he responded, "Girls, I care very much for your mom, and I promise not to do anything to hurt her. She means so much to me, and I also promise not to hurt either of you, so long as you allow me to show you that." They were slightly speechless, as they had only seen their dad be abusive to their mom, and this man clearly was more than a friend, but a man who truly loved her, fully. He explained that he had many nieces and nephews around their ages that they were more than welcome to meet. The idea of a real extended family is what I believe went through their minds. It was time for him to go, and we all said goodbye, and they asked again and again when he could come back over. I don't recall the flow of how that worked, but he was never not present when they were there now; it was organic, and nothing was expected from them but being themselves.

They looked forward to watching shows like iCarly, Good Luck Charlie, and Victorious with him any chance they got. He was a big kid with them, and they appreciated it, and so did I.

I was hesitant to meet his parents, mainly because, well, I am white. Will they accept me? Will they accept my children? But as God has prepared this for me already; my kids are biracial. Bateman was the whitest black man in the country, but still, in fact, African American. As awful as Bateman was, I was thankful for those two beautiful humans that looked like God's Photoshop. Cliff decided that it was a good opportunity for the girls to meet his family and his nieces and nephews, but we had to do one thing first. Meet his mom, dad, and his sister. Denise is five years older than he is, but they grew up very close, so I'm sure she had an opinion of who the new girl her brother was dating was. So, we all drove over, me *with* my kids as we are a package deal, and instantly felt, upon walking into this house, the warmth and love it exuded. I met his mom Bernice first. She was so gentle and kind and so happy he brought a "nice" girl home. And from what I gathered based on the past females she had encountered; she didn't care too much for them. She instantly embraced my girls with a hug and asked them if they were hungry, as all mothers and grandmothers do. In grandma fashion, I let her do her thing as I walked to the living room with Cliff and met the other man who would eventually love me like his own daughter. I entered the room, and his dad Mr. Clifton George, stood up in perfect chivalric fashion; Cliff introduced me, and he hugged me just like his son had done many times before. Hugs of genuine protection and love. We chatted and laughed but I felt I needed to be honest about my situation; he assured me we were safe, and he was happy I was there. His sister had stopped in and she met me and the girls. She was kind and friendly, but you could tell she wasn't fully sold on this new white girl that was in her house. But, once she saw the way the girls interacted with her brother, I'd like to think she was instantly sold that I was here to stay. The girls came in next holding Sunny D's and Entenmann's little brownie bites, and Cliff's dad greeted them with smiles as they shared laughter and silly stories just as a grandpa's do. I didn't want to overstay our welcome, but I did ask for his mom's attention separately. She seemed concerned but obliging. I thanked her for her hospitality, but something in me said "tell her." I know now that was the Holy Spirit as it was a pulling at me, almost pulling me towards her…I took a breath as she looked at me sweetly and patiently. I told her I cared deeply for her son, and I was fully in love with him. She looked down at her hands; oh no, worst-case scenario chapter full speed ahead, great, she's not even looking at me, she hates me…but I continued. I told her I'd do everything I could to protect her son and us together and ensure his happiness and joy. She looked up, smiled, and lit up like a Christmas tree and embraced me and said how happy that made her. What I didn't know is that she was battling cancer. For her son to be settled with a woman who loved him was what I believed to be an answer to prayer, or perhaps just the start. A month later, in August 2010, Cliff moved in with me. With us. The girls eventually met their amazing now what are cousins, and three of them were the same, including Ava-all six years old-which meant one word: trouble! The other two were older, twin boys about 12; no matter the age, they all loved their uncle. Their Uncle Todd. Wait, who? Todd? His whole family referred to him as Todd, and he immediately knew the confusion I felt. Todd is his middle name, and since he and his dad share the same first name, he has been called by his middle name to just decipher who was who. He's still called Todd to this day by his family, and it's very endearing to know how much they still very much love their 'Uncle Todd'. The girls inherited an instant family that they never saw coming. Sleepovers upon sleepovers, 'kids got talent' shows, riding bikes round and round the condo parking lot, plenty of video games, and being told I was the best "cooker" ever were just some of the perks of being a future aunt to these amazing kids. We would visit his parents often, and his mom always greeted us with hugs and love and wanted to know all about the kids, ensuring they knew they felt safe. Plus, Sunny D and brownies were a staple they grabbed as soon as they walked in. His dad and I became close, like I was always just another daughter to him. He was interested in anything I had to say. I could talk about the weather, any of the kids, about the next race I was planning for, and even the drama I was still enduring with Bateman, and he hung on every word I said. I loved listening to him tell me stories of the life he's lived, his extensive Air Force career, and the travel and amazing places it took him to. Being with him, a father like this, was something I only imagined, something I dreamed of, and never thought I'd experience. But the best part about all this was the unconditional love you felt as you became a part of this new family. Time passed, and with every other week it seemed to put the girls in a funk to leave to see their dad. The saving grace is their newfound best friends, their cousins, also had to do the same. But absence truly makes the heart grow fonder. Cliff and I stayed local in

Philly to see what kind of places we could explore and make memories from. We were always looked at as what I'd imagine a power couple when we entered places; full of confidence and like we belonged there. We acted as if we belonged there even if it was our first time. We frequented places until they got old, and we couldn't fill the place we longed to be which was either in Manhattan or with the girls. Until one chilly day in April did my whole life get turned on its head. A hard part of divorce is splitting holidays. It truly was the worst part for me by far. Saying goodbye to my babies, praying their dad did something unique and important for them no matter what the celebration. It never happened like that, so we decided to share the holidays. I felt something was off with Bateman, but I couldn't quite put my finger on it just yet; giving up time with his kids seemed, well, typical for his narcissistic self, but not for this. I took any time I got to spend with them and ate it up with no questions asked. But he specifically took holidays to spite me. This holiday was Easter; it wasn't a big holiday, but do not put me in an Easter basket challenge because I *will* win! That's the key to a happy morning is watching them dig through what they thought a giant bunny left for them. We had them Saturday, and Easter was Sunday, so we made the best of the day, so when they had to go with Bateman, they missed absolutely nothing, and their hearts were full. We even did an inside egg hunt because it was a rainy day and I wanted to make sure they had the full treatment....I still do. I love Dunkin' Donuts. I don't just love the chain; I truly love coffee, even the richest Italian espresso you can find, but the munchkins you can only get either in Lollipop Land or Dunkin'. So, since I wasn't planning a trip to Oz anytime soon, the chain of donuts will do. Cliff knew how much I put into this, and everything for my girls, so he graciously went out to grab me coffee. When he arrived back, the girls were still digging through the mounds of candy and eggs they found, with more candy and even a few dollar bills hidden amongst them. Upon his return with coffee and said box of munchkins, I inhaled as many as I could. I heard him say, while I held a chipmunk-cheek-sized donut holes in my mouth, "I think there is one more egg no one found, a blue one. I think I see it behind the box." I thought we got all the eggs. I sipped my coffee unphased, and I looked in the directed area, and this was in fact a bright blue plastic egg unopened. The girls came over, but he said, "that one is for your mom." I froze. He grabbed the cup from my hand placed it down on the table, then led me to the couch. He knelt in front of me and handed me the bright blue egg and he told me to open it. I was trembling, and the girls were in shock, standing there in awe of the love that was pouring into this room. I opened it…it was a shiny, beautiful princess cut diamond engagement ring. He said so many wonderful things about spending my life with him, how beautiful I was, and what an amazing mother I was…and he's never felt this way. All I could think was I was dressed in a green pair of beat-up sweatpants, an old, oversized t-shirt, and an old lady cardigan sweater from Good Will. And he still sees me this way, beautiful. I don't know half of what he said as I was transported to a place where I only saw his eyes and kissed him and said yes, a thousand times. He placed the ring on my finger so steadily, kissed my hand, and told the girls how much he loved me and loved them. They were in shock but smiling because all along I believe they were secretly hoping this family they loved so much would eventually become theirs, fully and officially. No time to waste; we were married a month later, Friday, May 13th. Fun fact: I was born on Friday the 13th, so what a perfect way to start redemption. We had a reverend we had found that was more than willing to marry us, and even in her own home outside overlooking beautiful greenery and surrounded by the people who loved us, well most of them. All the kids were our "groomsmen and bridesmaids," and we wrote our own vows and to this day we have kept them even more than when we said them that very day. Cliff's mom and dad were elated, and in every photo, you can see pure joy permeating from them. God was at the center that day and made sure we found each other despite our previous mistakes and missteps, and He's been ever since. That day I didn't just marry my soul mate; I married my very best friend.

Chapter Twenty-Five

I was constantly, and probably still am, always waiting for the other preverbal shoe to drop. There had been no constant in my life up to this point, so it's going to take a lot of undoing to change that preset mindset. But I had a husband who loved me, or so he told me; and as much as I wanted to trust him, a small part of me kept a tiny part of that internal wall up, just in case. Love is funny like that; the moment I give my all, they bail. And I don't just mean the male species. Even Gram left, and she was, to me, immortal. But I had to see this through as I had way too much skin in the game now. Cliff didn't have any children of his own, and truth be told, that was one thing that kept me moving along in this relationship. I could not deal with any baby mama drama because I had plenty of my own. I came in with a moving-size truck full of baggage, plenty stored up for decades, and this man didn't flinch or say it was too much, or he couldn't deal; he embraced it all. He loved my girls, and he wanted to add to this family we were so joyfully living. We talked about us having children, but I was so damaged from the last time I was terrified at the though; the thought of going through all that and being left, again. What my body would have to go through and a pregnancy or that a baby didn't fit into my current plans. It's funny how hard we try to avoid what God wants to do in our lives because He's very good at changing our "want to's", because suddenly I found myself aching to hold a baby in my arms again. And sure enough, Cliff and I were pregnant on the first try and we were both over the moon with joy. But that happiness was short-lived. Just days later, I noticed bright red blood soaking through my underwear, and I was bleeding profusely. I called the doctor asking to come in, and they called me back a few hours later. When they called me back, they said I did not need to be seen, as I was having an early miscarriage. The doctor kept talking and explaining what was happening and going to happen and I heard nothing but the sound of tears screaming in my body. I was devastated. Every thought of blame ran through my mind and how could I fail Cliff at the one thing he wanted that I couldn't give him. But instead, he comforted me, and reassured me it was ok, it wasn't God's best, and we'd try again another time. His calming presence was and still is an anchor but is also my net that I know will catch me before I fall and give me a sense of grounding, only he can provide. Life as I knew it continued but felt like I was in a funk I could not shake. I started having nightmares and even waking up again from night terrors, not only in tears but in a complete fear to sleep, again. The last time this happened stress was the cause, and I was under so much of it at this point that no number of miles ran or trips to the gym could end this feeling of heaviness I dragged around daily; and believe me I tried. I'd get this overwhelming sense at times where I felt like I couldn't breathe, like an elephant was sitting on my chest. I'd cry uncontrollably and my body would tremble, all while scared I was physically dying. I knew my body, and something clearly wasn't right. I went to the doctor, told him everything and he assured me we'd find out what was going on. My bloodwork was ok, my weight was fine, and my physical check led to nothing remarkable, except a diagnosis I was sure they mixed up with someone else. 'You have anxiety, panic disorder, major depressive disorder, and CPTSD'. What? No, that cannot be me; the life I've lived, I'm as tough as they come, there's no way. I've endured abuse, and trauma my whole life, heck I've even slept in cars in the winter and managed to keep myself out of the psyche ward with a very thorough attempt to un-alive myself, and a whole bunch of other stuff that's too many to list. Ok, well maybe I have all that that. Ok, I do. Hearing this and coming to terms with this terrified me. None of this was my doing, but I have this as another collateral damage souvenir to add to the list that's forever growing, and not in my favor.

In Manhattan, the city empties out on holiday weekends during the summer. Memorial Day, Fourth of July, Labor Day and so on. The people who can afford to *live* in the city can also afford beach houses in places like the Hamptons and Martha's Vineyard. What that meant for us was, the perfect time to go and enjoy ourselves. It meant lesser crowds and tourists, no waits at restaurants, and no one packing out bars or any form of entertainment. By no coincidence, Fourth of July was that weekend, and the girls were with Bateman so Cliff being the masterful Super date planner, and all things considered I was dealing with, planned not just an overnight trip to Manhattan, but leaving early and spending the whole day there doing what I always wanted to do, be a typical New Yorker. We stopped on the way at Juniors in Brooklyn and got cheesecake to go and that did not stand a remote chance to our destination. We'd been there many times and it's nostalgic as Cliff spent time in Brooklyn as a kid with his mom and grandma. We crossed the bridge, and I knew and soon as we came out of the tunnel, a calmness would come over me. I cannot explain it, but in the busiest city in America the city's chaos wrapped around me like a blanket, offering a stillness within my soul that no other place has ever managed to replicate. We found our hotel, parked the car, and spent the day walking just experiencing all the things this magical place has to offer. We spent time in Bryant Park, in little tables drinking iced coffee, walked the outside food festival and shared random ethnic foods from around our globe, and to top off what was the best cannoli I'd ever had, and that's saying something being of Italian heritage. We eventually made our way back to the hotel as we had dinner reservations across town. I felt no anxiety and no panic, just butterflies of anticipation of where the night would take us. We hailed a cab that took us to what looked like an office building or a highrise apartment complex. I didn't question Cliff's choice of dates as they go far beyond my expectations, so I stopped asking a long time ago. We get into the elevator, and he hits the very top floor. Then I feel a bit nervous and ask where we are going. He grabs my hand as the doors open to a beautiful restaurant that as far as I could see were floor to ceiling windows overlooking the city. Top of the Tower. He was greeted by the hostess who led us to the table by the windows overlooking West Side Highway- this is the Hudson River that separates Manhattan from Brooklyn. But this was also the place where they would put on the fireworks display. Cliff knew exactly what I needed-not just an escape from my surroundings, but a glimpse of the woman he believed I was. We enjoyed an amazing dinner, and at dusk an ambiance of candle lit tables that was completely transcended by the lights from the city alone and I looked to my right and, fireworks in all their independence splendor burst like my heart was. I watched them, and he watched me. As the show came to an end we paid and left but the night wasn't over. We went to a place we liked to visit called Tonic. A terrible name for a bar that pumps loud music and serves tables of food to families and the like. But again, this weekend it was relatively empty. We arrived and I'm feeling pretty good and friendly- he initially didn't like this about me but it's a necessary character trait he will later come to appreciate. I noticed a group of people were timid to come up to the bar to order drinks and I kindly as best I could over the music to please come up here with us. We found out they were from Canada on their first trip to the states, and they run into the two of US?! What lucky ducks! We spent the night laughing and me more than a dozen times me saying, "I just got married 6 weeks ago" to random strangers and bartenders who would give us free shots that did the job of 'fun'. We left Tonic and went to a rooftop bar Cliff knew of (super dates have all kinds of surprises), so we hung out there for a bit, but it was late, and I was not in a state where I could be fun any longer. We took a cab to the hotel, slept, and woke with a wicked hang over. But I was no longer thinking of panic and anxiety, just how many ibuprofen is too many for my pounding super date hangover. We arrived home and I slept off the New York state of mind for most of the day. Fast forward to a few weeks later. I was a bit tired and feeling worn down a bit. I was late for my period but only by a few days, so I chalked it up to stress like everything else. But for the heck of it let's check. Wait. 2 pink lines? Pregnant. Ah,

Manhattan as always, you always come through in clutch.

Chapter Twenty-Six

As many would understand, being in this moment of excitement also comes with a state of fear based on the culmination of just the experiences you have had up to this point. I knew a doctor's visit was imminent after my last experience, and thankfully they understood. I entered the dark ultrasound room, lay on the cold protective paper-strewn table, watching monitors facing away from me, well, just in case. The warm jelly-like substance was put on my belly, as the wand moved to and fro, and the tech marked measurements and typed random things; then she turned the monitor around and turned on the sound. *Thump thump thump thump.* A live little baby with a strong heartbeat, 7 weeks old. Tears of joy fell to the sides of my face while I tried to keep my composure. Cliff squeezed my hand and in that squeeze was not pure gratitude. They printed some souvenir pictures to take home, almost to prove the miracle that was living inside me. As amazing as this news was, it was followed up with a visit with a doctor of all the things to do and not to do, especially as I was now 35 years old and in the OBGYN world you might as well consider yourself "geriatric." March 22nd was our due date and the first person we needed to tell was Cliff's mom. Her fight had become harder. We hoped this would bring her joy and a push for the new baby she had yet to meet. And telling her any other way but in person was unacceptable. Upon arriving at their house, I said, "Mom, we have something to tell you." She responded, "You're pregnant!" I just smiled and was a little perplexed about how she *knew* that. She said, "Oh, I just known it!" and she jumped up out of the recliner she rarely left, as if all the sickness had left her body. She hugged me and her son and was genuinely happy. We told the girls and Cecelia was happy, but it took some convincing to get Ava to see it was a good thing. I still worked out, ran (much slower), but I was much more tired this time. I had to go for non-stress tests weekly starting at 32 weeks, and being 35 years old, they give you tests and scans to make sure you and your baby are okay, which I complied with, reluctantly, but I complied. Including a test for Down syndrome and the gender at 10 weeks old. No Downs, but another girl. Cliff, a girl dad. Seems fitting. So far, the non-stress tests were all okay, but as usual, I had a morning appointment at 34 weeks now that I planned to go to work afterwards as I always did, alone, but this morning Cliff wanted to go with me. He even got me a Dunkin' bagel with cream cheese to take with me to eat on the ride after.. You can't eat or drink anything before the test, and I was planning to head to work after the appointment; he knows me too well. I was there longer than normal this time, and the tech left the room several times. I still had 6 weeks to go, so perhaps it was routine since I was rather big by now. Cliff and I shared worried, telepathic glances. In a demanding tone, I said, "What's going on?" the tech said to get dressed and meet the doc in the next room. He was super calm, told us he wanted us to go to the hospital to get a better look as they had more high-tech testing there but "not to worry", his colleague would meet us there. We complied, unaware of what was happening. We went to the hospital, but no scan was waiting for us. I was shown a room and given a hospital gown to put on. I was then hooked up immediately to a contraction monitor while the nurse fiddled with the settings to capture the activity. The doc came in no more than ten minutes later and said calmly that the baby's heart rate was decelerating, and she needed to be delivered today. TODAY? This wasn't the plan; we were supposed to go 6 more weeks and have a full-term baby! The doctor promised she'd keep me stable because Cliff had to pick up the girls from school as they prepped me for induction. He took a pit stop in the bathroom and puked even though he swears to this day he didn't. They moved me to a labor and delivery room, started me on Pitocin, then not long after, Cliff and the girls arrived. They had no idea this was scary, just that the little person they had been waiting for was arriving today; if she didn't come soon, a C-section was imminent to save her life. He called his family and mine, and they stopped everything they were doing and stayed in the waiting room of the hospital, anxiously awaiting the new member of the family. I was terrified, defeated, and I still had to go through labor. All NICU staff surrounded me in this cold delivery room. Nothing stopped me before, and it won't now. Our daughter, Olivia Grace, was born on none other than February 14th, Valentine's Day, a day meant for love. Ironically, my birthday was the day prior, and she was and will always be the best gift I've ever received. They whisked her away to analyze her as I was cleaned up, showing me a full knot in her umbilical cord, which was the cause of all this. Most babies don't make it through that, but

I was shown a miracle on a screen months prior that showed me differently. The nurses let me kiss her quickly and took her away in an incubator. Cliff went with them, but they made sure to pass all the family in the waiting room who were awaiting her arrival, and they all cheered and snapped quick photos. But I was now cleaned up, fresh sheets, and...completely alone. Everyone was somehow gone, and I had no baby, no husband, and no one to assure me my daughter, whom I didn't even get to hold, was okay. The nurse eventually came in and saw me with tears streaming down my face. She hugged me, and I collapsed. I had endured so much that day, and I asked her if I had caused this. She assured me I did not; it was a freak thing that happened, but my baby was obviously meant to be here. She asked if I could get into a wheelchair because she wanted to take me to see her. I used every ounce of energy I did not have and forced myself into that chair. She covered me with warm blankets as I was shaking from the shock of the delivery. She wheeled me to the NICU, and I was terrified...my breathing got heavier; was she okay? And of course, here comes the worst-case scenario chapter starting to fill up my brain again. I was wheeled in and brought over to a baby warmer with a beautiful pink 4lb 12 oz little human who was moving with force, showing everyone not only the fighter that she was, but that she wasn't staying here much longer. Cliff squeezed my hand just as he did at that first visit looking at our miracle on that screen 8 months earlier. I was told she was doing well, but they needed to get her body temperature and weight up, and if she was stable by morning, I could spend as many hours with her as I wanted. The doctors and nurses knew how traumatic this birth was and knew I needed rest and an extra mental watch on me. She was so tiny but so beautiful...and she was made from love, so there was no way I was giving up without a fight for her. I sat back down in the wheelchair doing my best to hold back my tears as the hormones raged throughout my body, making it all that much more exacerbating. I was settled in a post-labor room, and the nurses made sure I was comfortable and warm. My head was replaying all that had happened, but I was again alone with no baby and no husband. I couldn't sleep because all I heard were the cries of the babies the mothers got to keep in their rooms and weren't fighting for their lives. I remember putting a pillow over my head in hopes of drowning out the sound. Techs would come in to check my vitals quite often, and it seemed all standard procedures. Until the night nurse, who I hadn't met yet, came in to see me. She was a little rough around the edges but friendly and concerned. She helped me get comfortable and got me ice to reduce my pain from pushing a human out of me. She took her stethoscope and listened to my heart. Was something concerning her? Did the tech notice something odd in my body's postpartum ability to acclimate? She listened, then asked me, "Are you a runner?" I would have proudly answered an emphatic yes, but all I thought was that my ability to run and keep working out did this to my daughter. So, I calmly said, "Yes, I am, why do you ask?" She responded, "Your heart rate is very low, in the 50's, and after all that's happened, we need to make sure you are also taken care of as well." She left and came back with a litany of juices and ginger ale and all kinds of crackers and said by the time she came back it should all be gone. Again, rough around the edges. But I wasn't hungry—I just felt a empty ache in my belly a heaviness in my chest. But I sat up and drank and ate everything she left. I felt sick; what was wrong with me? My baby was in the intensive care unit; was I next? No! I fought like hell with everything I had to know that I'd wake up and be able to hold my daughter and revel in the smell of her newborn head and let her know who I was, her mommy. Anxiety had a funny way of creeping up when you least expect it no matter how much you fight it or will it away. The nurse came back and seemed impressed, but I wound up vomiting it all up within minutes. She sat on the bed next to me, and I just cried. I told her the sounds of the babies crying were so hard to hear, and she just held me and didn't try to talk me out of anything I was feeling in that moment. She started to talk about how her husband is a fisherman and he goes out for months at a time but brings back fish for a year's worth and they can store it up and how they do it. I knew where she was going with this; it was to distract me and to get me out of my own head as this was not how the birth of my daughter was supposed to go. She gave me pill, sat down and just stroked my head, like a mother would do, and told me it would help me sleep. It did just that. Until I saw the sun peek through the blinds. Today was the day I was going to meet my daughter.

I was even sorer than I was the day before, but I got up and somehow showered, washed my hair, and put on actual clothes, not this hospital gown madness, put on makeup and made myself presentable. Cliff walked into the room and brought coffee and handed me the menu to order food. He said my mom took the girls home with her and they were having fun and doing what kids do. It was early, so we ordered a light breakfast that was delivered rather quickly. I scarfed down whatever soggy breakfast was on the plate and said I wanted to go to the NICU *now*. Again, I felt like I was in Alice's rabbit hole, except this time very small and there was no potion that would help me feel bigger. Before you enter the area, there are bins of packaged soaps and scrub brushes at a sink that you must use each time upon entering. Just like surgeons on TV, I was doing the same thing. Fully cleaned and sanitized, I rang the bell and said who I was, and I was buzzed in. The nurse met me and led me to a curtained-off area that, in my mind, was prepared to see the worst. Instead, I saw a big blue rocking recliner, and to the left, monitors beeping and cords leading to a small crib that held my very tiny daughter. We were told she was doing great and even took bottles overnight. I bent down to see her, covered in several blankets and two hats trying to keep her body temperature up; hearing that was the biggest challenge so far. She was hooked up to monitors to watch her heart, pulse, oxygen, and who knows what else. I asked if I could hold her. The nurse picked her up and placed her in my arms as I sat in the big blue chair holding the very human that very well may not have made it. I held her and took in her scent, and she turned towards me as if to already know who I was. I took turns with Cliff as he was always an approximate 108 degrees, so if anyone could warm her up, it was him. We fed her; she gained weight continuously, and I was in that NICU each day from morning until they kicked me out each night to make sure I was resting and recovering. Each day started the same: breakfast, scrub in, and make sure this little girl knew how much she was loved. The girls were finally able to visit, a bit hesitant, but immediately knew they had a bond with this tiny little human. They made notes and cards to tape into her crib letting her know how many people in this amazing family loved her. Eventually, Cliff's parents were able to visit as well. And his mom did the same thing; sat in the big blue chair and hugged this little human as I knew simultaneously, she was thanking God for allowing her to be here for this. It was a sight to see that I still have etched in my mind. We were eventually told that she gained enough weight, but I could no longer stay in the room I had been occupying. So, they put us in a "nesting room". Which was basically saying she's good enough to leave the NICU floor and she can room with you now, to bond, and to make sure in case anything happens, we're a call away. We stayed in this room for a few days and figured out how to be new parents together to a small human Cliff could hold merely in his forearm. We were told we needed to get our pediatrician to give the approval on whether we could take her home or not. Eventually, she showed up and was very confused about why we were still there. Olivia was eating, gaining weight, and she knew this wasn't my first rodeo. She signed our discharge papers, and off we went. We said goodbye to the nurses as they said they knew she was a fighter and were so happy we were going home as a family. We took a very slow ride home, as I sat in the backseat admiring this sleeping beauty. It was cold; February is always one of the coldest months in the Northeast, and today was no different. As Cliff helped me out of the car, he carefully lifted the car seat out and into the chilly air. Olivia took some quick breaths, not used to this outside air, and we chuckled at her ability to recognize the difference in her surroundings. I still had to keep her bundled up to ensure her temperature stayed steady. We were home with a new little person who was entering into a family that already loved her. Unfortunately, no one could visit or be around her for at least 10 days while she built up strength and saw her docs for vaccinations. Eventually, family trickled over, and they too were in awe of this tiny person they had waited so long to see. Cliff's parents continuously showed up with boxes of diapers, clothes, food, and everything in between every single time. We'd eventually make our way over to their house as Mom was not feeling herself too much lately and was resting more than not. She'd light up when we'd show up and be able to hold her granddaughter and talk to her, and immediately the oxytocin was ignited in her. We came as often as we could, but eventually Mom wasn't well enough to even visit with us. Dad would still bring over diapers and ask what we needed, trying to keep himself busy along with the pickups and drop-offs of his other grandkids. His wife was dying, and there was nothing he could do to fix this.

Seasons changed, and I was given the go-ahead to start running again. I pushed Olivia in a jogging stroller every day for miles. It would put her to sleep, and it gave me a much-needed break from the worry of her and what life was handing us. A birth and an impending death. We reached the end of summer and Olivia was growing so fast, and she was a light in every room, and she still is. I went back to work and thankfully at home. Because she was still small enough and hadn't built up the immunity needed yet for a daycare setting, I was granted remote work until she was bigger. Cliff's mom had an appointment that day to see how her cancer was and if it was any better or worse, as she had stopped all intervention at that point. While en route to the oncologist, Mom said she wasn't feeling well. Dad was taking her to the doc, so he said he'd be sure to mention it when they arrived. But she asked to be taken to the emergency room instead as she could not wait. When they arrived, even before they could assess her, she took a turn for the worse. I saw Cliff calling me, thinking he was checking in on his girls as he often did, ignorant of all that was happening. This time his voice was full of fear. "Babe, Mom had a cardiac arrest. I'm at the hospital now; my dad called me". I replied as anyone in that situation would, "Oh my God, is she ok? Is she stable?" He replied quietly, "No, she's gone," I questioned, "What do you mean she's gone?" He cut me off and said "She didn't make it. We have to say our goodbyes now." As I tried to hold back the tears all I could say was, "I'm so so sorry" He replied, "I'm okay; I'll talk to you later. I have to go; I love you." And he hung up. I wept on the floor while holding this little girl who I knew had a grandmother that held on with everything she had left in her body and soul to experience. She was a wonderful woman, mother, grandmother, wife, matriarch. If I can be half of what she was I consider myself not just lucky, but extremely blessed. Olivia was the light that we didn't know we all needed in a very dark time. And she needed to meet the angel that she'd be standing in for. Once that exchange happened, then God turned Olivia's light on, and it hasn't faded yet. She is still the biggest light in every room she enters and is pure love and sunshine even on the cloudiest of days. Mom's birthday is the day after Olivia's… she's never left; she's always right next to her watching her shine…But God made sure we'd see *both of their lights every single year.*

Chapter Twenty-Seven

Grief is not something you can truly prepare for. It is like a train you hear in the distance, and seeing the blinking railroad crossing signs knowing you must slow down and come to a complete stop. Except this isn't a middle of the town freight train that moves at a sluggish pace, but a bullet train that arrives with such intensity that you have no chance to fathom the speed at which grief can strike you at any given moment. You sit there stunned and awestruck thinking, "I prepared, and I slowed down to accept what was coming". No matter how much preparation went into the inevitable loss, grief is something that is out of our control, and if you're anything like me, I like to be in control.

I was a divorced woman with two girls, who lost not only her mother, but her grandmother who took care of her all her life. And I'm now recently remarried, with a new baby, while my husband faced one of the hardest moments he has ever endured. Let's say I knew something about grief. He needed to process this, and he spent days at his parent's house to watch over his dad, who had lost not only a wife but also a best friend. But my grief was coming from a place of anger, and not from the person I loved dearly with whom we all lost. I was working full time with an infant and had to care for the older girls and felt like a single mom all over again. But I didn't push, as I knew grief looked different for everyone. But I too was grieving, and that was slightly discounted. I have dealt with so much grief and loss that I was a pro at this point in identifying the waves of when they come in, and when they go out. He eventually came home, and when I tell you he immersed himself in this baby, it was like built-in therapy for him he didn't know he needed. He slept with her, he'd hold her, and he'd make sure my girls knew they were just as important, as they too were feeling the loss of someone, they knew loved them but was now gone. Grief is another ghost that comes knocking when you least expect it, but you don't have to answer, at least not right away. And that's what we decided to do. We went back to New York, back to the things we knew made us "ok" until life dealt us a hand we didn't see coming, again. And quite a few this time. I was let go from a job I'd been at for almost two decades but thankfully was offered another one the same week, AND Bateman was moving out of state and could no longer keep the girls for joint custody. Talk about having to adapt. Ok, that's fine; I knew he'd eventually find a way out of his responsibilities, and the more time with them the better. But the small condo we were in was not ample to house two growing girls, a toddler, and a married couple. Also having to acclimate to a new job was a lot of plates to spin, to say the least. So, I started looking for a bigger place to live. Once again, someone else's decisions affected my life with no say in the matter; notice a trend here? These are my kids, and if he was giving up time, well, I'm going to make it official. I filed for sole and residential custody with Cliff's full support in doing so. We found a twin home on the other side of town. It's a cute place with plenty of room for the girls. They would each have their own room, and Olivia would have hers. It was more money, but I also filed for child support to be withdrawn from Bateman's checks along with that motion. He was giving up on his kids; well, I will make sure they are protected in all aspects. Court date received. I took off work,, and well, Bateman was a no-show, shocker. He never showed for custody, visitation, or support for his kids. So, the judge, by the sheer virtue of seeing my kids meant everything to me, gave me exactly what I motioned for.

The girls were living with us full time and now it was official. It was October, and we had to wait until April to move into the new house, so it was a bit tight, but we managed. I had started my new job, and it seemed to be going well. But I started to not feel well a few weeks in; super tired and lethargic and pains in my abdomen. I went to countless doctor visits who treated me for everything from Lyme disease to an infection they weren't sure of by pumping me full of antibiotics and various pain medications which only made it worse. One night in so much pain and the feeling of dying (again) I drove myself to the ER. They ran a bunch of tests and found out I'm fighting a virus called mononucleosis, aka, mono. My spleen was enlarged from it which was causing the pain. Mono? Again? How? The last time I had this I slept through Christmas and New Year's. They told me since I had it before it was dormant inside of me but ultimately is caused by none other than my good old friend, stress. And I needed to change everything as I knew it. I went home the next day and recovered for a few weeks. I had a gracious new boss allowing me to work at home temporarily and a husband who refused to let me do anything. But I bounced back quickly knowing we had a move coming and had to get ready for it and get myself to a place of health and return to work. We signed the documents for our new place in March and everyone seemed excited and anticipatory for a new change and environment. We have a few weeks to go and with the swirl of life I started to feel, well... off. Had I pushed myself too hard? I hadn't been running and I had taken good care of myself so what could this be? We must move in 2 weeks, and I cannot be down again. Maybe I didn't take enough time to heal or rest, but I was *so* tired. I opened under the bathroom cabinet to pack my hygiene and ancillary things up. I saw there was an unopened pregnancy test, leftover from Olivia. There was no way, I joked to myself after all I've just been through, as I tried to will myself to throw it out. But instead, I shut the bathroom door as I could hear my heart pounding with an audible sound from my chest. In 0.10 seconds flat, two bright blue lines showed up like the night sky itself. *Pregnant.* God is big on giving you miracles when you least expect it. But when you try to reason the how or the why, it becomes more about the questions instead of embracing the miracle fully. This time I wasn't scared; I was excited. Another light to add to the family that needed it the most. I called Cliff into the bathroom to show him what I had discovered. He too was just as shocked, but as happy, if not happier than I was. He embraced me and held me there, burying his face in my neck. Just holding me as if to take all his grief and let it go for a while. He held my face and kissed me and said, "Thank you for being you. For staying through all this." All I could think of was wait, *me* that stayed; *he's* the true hero here lugging that 18-wheeler of baggage I have around me like it's a part of my body. But none of that mattered. We were now becoming a real family. We moved into our new home, and even Cliff's dad and nephews came along to help move and to see our new place. His dad mostly sat and supervised, which was fine. He was there, smiling and present, surrounded by people who loved him. We pulled up in the giant U-Haul, and it was all of three miles from where I started over (again) and had spent my life for the past five years. Time to start over again. Except this time, I wasn't alone, and I had a new life growing inside of me and a whole family behind me. We eventually moved in and got settled. There was no disruption to school for the girls as we were now closer, even within walking distance. Well, maybe on a nice day. We'd now been to the doctors to confirm the pregnancy, and everything looked as close to perfect as you can get. Given my age, I was offered genetic testing again, to which I opted for again. I waited 10 days for these results, and when I saw an incoming call from the OB's office, my anxiety kicked in. I answered it bravely, my mind racing with the worst-case scenarios. But she said everything is great! Phew, thank you God. "Do you want to know what you're having?" I paused because all I seem to produce are females. "Yes, of course." "It's a boy, you're having a little boy!" I cried on the phone with her, laughing tears of joy as she too laughed and congratulated me. I thanked her, and she told me she'd see me soon. We knew the news of a new baby was something that could help heal so many people, but first we told the kids. We gave them baby announcement cards, each with a little saying of how they would all be big sisters in December. What none of them knew was what we were having, including Cliff. I gave him a special card knowing how much a son would mean to him. He embraced the card but was confused. I asked him to look and read it again. It was a card announcing a little boy. He said, "You're having a boy?!" He jumped out of the chair and cheered like I'd never seen him do, a moment I've never seen matched since. Everyone was crying and so happy for this anticipatory human that we all needed. Including Olivia, who was so excited to finally be a "big sister." We went to see Dad and we were hoping for this new life that was to come, would in fact give *him* life…and sure enough it did. He was over the moon excited and even more so when I told him he was having a "grandson." He jumped up just like his son did and for the first time in a long time, I saw actual joy in him. This was already going to be his little buddy and he wasn't even here yet! I continued to run slowly, but this time I felt different. I was more tired than the last pregnancy with Olivia. I'm working full time, raising a toddler, and now have the girl's full time. I'd come home, cook dinner, clean up, and put Olivia to bed, reading "If You Give a Pig a Pancake" about 200 times that I even know it by heart. Life is so much different now that I rarely have downtime. Or when I do, I am so tired. Considering I was building a human, it's understandable. I'd rather lie in bed watching TV, drinking tea, and eating cookies. This little boy was surely different and so much more active than his sisters, especially at night. I went for my anatomy ultrasound around week 20, and all looked fine, except the doctor said he had a small hole in his heart from what they saw. I was sent over to maternal-fetal medicine immediately. No. I will not go through this again; it's too early! *What is wrong with me?* I did as they said and went through a 3D ultrasound to see the defect the other docs questioned. I met with the doctor afterwards. She explained my son had a small hole in his heart called a patent foramen ovale; which means it is a hole in the upper two chambers of the heart. She assured me that this was common and should close almost instantaneously at his delivery. "Should? And if it doesn't?" I asked her. "Well, he would need open heart surgery right after birth to repair the hole. But I am 99% sure this is not the case. But, to ensure the care for you and your son, you must come here now for the duration of your pregnancy. You and the baby will be monitored weekly, and you will also see a neonatal cardiologist for an ultrasound of your son's heart monthly. We will induce you early to ensure we are prepared for any intervention needed. But, in the meantime, no caffeine, chocolate, or tea. Nothing that would make your heart or his heart work harder. Do you understand?" she said curtly. *What. Is. Happening.* You just said he would be okay, this was common, and now you're planning another NICU *with* cardiology standby in my delivery room? I left the conversation mentally but could still hear her talking; I was no longer listening. Eventually I was being led to the door and told to set up as many appointments as I could in advance. No matter what, I'd make sure this kid had a fighting chance. I went to the cardiologist appointment, and he assured me it was "no big deal" and he'd be fine. "Fine?" I questioned with every bitter tone I did not intend to come out. The doctor could sense my unease, "He is growing well. He has a way to go but when he is delivered, his first breath should act like a suction and close even the tiniest of holes." There's that word again, "should." And I *should* not be dealing with this, but here we are. I went about my life, resting, working, and taking care of myself as best as I could.

But, between my weekly doctor visits and a pending heart problem of my unborn baby, I was at capacity for worst-case scenarios. Since I was being induced, I had to be on standby and was told they could call at a moment's notice when a high-risk bed became available. Standby is something you do for a flight, not the birth of your child. But sure enough, the hospital called me in a week before Christmas to come in the same day for induction to mitigate any issues. Great. Here we go again. It was about 5pm, and I was placed in a labor room, and within minutes, a nurse came in to stick me with an IV; ya know, just in case they needed to cut me open in some emergency so I couldn't have any food, just this stupid tube of saline. This seemed routine for the staff. They placed the NICU warmer, heart monitors, and wires in their places. Then more staff came in to check things and bring supplies. But for me, I was freaking out inside. I had made it to 39 weeks, and I did everything I was supposed to. I seemed as confident as one could expect-minimal. I put on a brave face as I always have, and no one knows I'm screaming inside with buckets of tears and a terrorizing fear that will not leave me alone. Cliff didn't leave my side as he knew the traumatic birth with Olivia and how hard that was, and now I'm here to deliver his son in what feels very eerily similar. The nurse came in and started the Pitocin to start contractions. And this time everyone was monitoring deliberately, no matter the level of pain they caused me. It was suggested I get an epidural as soon as they were giving me higher doses of this baby-come-out medicine. I obliged, even though I didn't want to do it. The pain was manageable, but I understood the reasoning of not wanting to risk having to put me under should I need a C-section. I'm in active labor now, and the contractions are so intense that no amount of epidural can take away the pressure I'm feeling. Until the baby's heart monitor slowed to an almost complete stop. The many nurses in the room acted swiftly and flipped me on all fours to take the pressure off the baby. One nurse yelled for the doctor by his first name; oh no, this is bad. I'm in view of only feet that are entering the room, and I could see the sneakers walking towards me. The person knelt next to me, and it was the same amazing doctor that told me to go to the hospital with Olivia, who saved her life. I said, "I'm so glad to see you." as I fought through anxious tears. He put his hand on mine and said, "Do I look worried? Because if I'm not worried, you shouldn't be worried either. Your baby was struggling to get through his final descent and sometimes they work hard to do that. So…are you ready to have a baby because he must *really* want to meet you." The calmness he provided to me amid the chaos that was in that room with so many people in a panicked state not only helped me, but them too. I pushed a few times and our son, Xavier, was born. The doc held him up as if he were Simba from the Lion King and said, "X-man! It's nice to meet you!" and he passed him off to the team that was waiting to tell me his fate. While the doc was fixing me up, the nurse looked over and smiled. She said, "He sounds and looks amazing; I see no issues and a strong heartbeat." They weighed him, and Cliff took pictures as I gazed over again without being able to hold my baby. The nurse brought over a wrinkly pink little boy with a blue hat and placed him on my chest. They call this skin to skin, and it's supposed to help with bonding and warmth. As she placed him on me, he felt like a pile of warm laundry you first take out of the dryer. He was crying, and that was a great sign for his heart, but in that moment, *my* heart was overflowing with gratitude. I spoke to him in a soft voice, and he calmed down right away. They let me lie there for a while with him, not wanting to disrupt the connection. I told them it was okay, and they could take him to clean up, intending to clean me up in the process. I was able to move to a recovery room *with* my baby this time. Cliff held him and sat with an almost awestruck state of happiness. I imagined he sat and looked into his eyes at who this little boy would be and how many people were waiting for him. Cliff went home to be with the other girls and said he'd be back in the morning with all of them. I held this beautiful little boy all night and expressed my gratitude to God for allowing him to be safely here. Nurses came and went. They took my vitals and stocked the bassinet with formula and diapers. It's all up to me now; this little human is mine to care for while I am still caring for myself. Morning came and I don't think I slept much, but I got up again and, as what felt like a very real repeat. I forced myself to shower, put on clean clothes, and makeup. I tried to make myself as presentable as possible considering I had given birth less than 12 hours ago. Cliff entered the room, holding a giant cup of coffee. I think I heard angels singing, because I had to be sworn to no caffeine for what felt like a year. The taste and the smell were intoxicating. The girls followed, then Cliff's dad. Olivia was looking a little apprehensive, but I hugged her and asked her to cuddle with me on the bed. I introduced her to her little brother, the one she had eagerly anticipated. She was in disbelief that he was now a real live person but held him and talked to him, and he squirmed as if to know her voice. The girls passed him around one by one, and when Cliff handed his son to his father, I knew that moment would be imprinted in my memory forever. The light that this little boy carried was illuminating between them. Dad started calling him "my little buddy buddy." He chatted with him as you watched the sadness, he had been carrying melt away, at least for a little while. Not only was my coffee magnificent, but the view I had of everyone full of love and joy in that moment was too. Both Olivia and Xavier came at times when darkness tried to make its place in our lives. They were light, in its purest form. And that's the thing about light...when it enters an atmosphere, the darkness has no choice but to disappear. God made sure they had an illumination that to this day, still shines and fills every room they're in.

Chapter Twenty-Eight

My light had been in a constant state of trying to be extinguished. From Bill to my mom, and everyone in between, they kept me in darkness. Or so I thought. When I saw any semblance of light, I tried to grasp on, but it was snuffed out before I could identify what it was or how I could keep it. Perhaps for fear of those in direct opposition being exposed. I brought a light they knew wasn't a good one for them to shine in, so it was easier to make me feel that I wasn't worthy of being a light for anyone, especially myself. So, if history repeats itself, why would this time be any different? Cliff got a new job about a month before I had Xavier. Double the salary, but an hour-plus commute each way and we considered it good. Even though he'd be gone before the sun came up and home well past dinner time, it would help us financially and he was getting more experience, or so we thought. Xavier became a fast addition to our lives, and quickly invaded everyone's hearts. The other thing he invaded was my sleep. Of course, an infant wakes every few hours for one reason or another, and this wasn't my first rodeo. But this time was different. The feeling of bonding with your child while sleep deprived, and a slew of hormones I hadn't recalled being so intense, was not something even my best efforts were allowing me to do. And I cried, a lot. But, I'd blame it on hormones. When I'd have time to sleep, I'd lay there awake while intrusive thoughts, one after the other, played like a movie in my mind. And again, I'd blame hormones. I was home alone all day, except for school drop-offs and pick-ups, and in the winter doing that each time with an infant and a car seat was exhausting. I didn't look like myself, I didn't feel like myself, and I sure didn't like myself. I was so lonely, even with this tiny human I waited so anxiously for that was healing so many hearts, except for mine. I missed my husband who was working countless hours and away twelve or more a day. I realized I had lost myself and I had fallen into a deep hole of depression. Like a functioning alcoholic, I was a functioning depressed human. I went through the motions each day, loved my baby and my girls, and they'd all never know that the smile I showed on the outside really felt like I was dying on the inside. My light was being smothered, and here I was in the dark, again. I spent my days numb and waited for some relief that I had hoped would come as time passed but it only worsened. And I was now fearing something was wrong with me. This wasn't me. I'd had three other kids, I bounced back, I pushed through.

I survive...that's what I do best. God didn't let me just "survive" this time. I lay in bed and told Cliff how I'd been feeling, and the tears I'd been pushing down flowed like a river out of my eyes. I was tired, worn out, depleted, and nothing I was doing was helping. He told me he thought I should see a doctor, that maybe I had postpartum depression. There is no way that's the case, I thought, and that made me even more upset. But he knew this was something he, nor I, could fix, whatever the issue might be. I called my

OB and told them I needed to make an appointment, and as all medical offices do, they had no immediate openings. I told them I thought something might be wrong with me and since I'd already been to my post-natal visit, they got me in for the next day. I got myself together as best as I could and buckled my now two-month-old son into the car and drove with my heart pounding the entire way. I pulled into the parking lot, took a breath, and got out, carried my son in with me, as if he were some kind of support animal for what I was possibly facing. I checked in and sat anxiously waiting and hoping Xavier stayed asleep. I heard my name called, and I gently picked up the car seat and smiled and greeted the nurse as best I could. She asked why I was there, and I said I just was having trouble regulating my emotions and not feeling like myself. She handed me a paper with several questions to rate. This is called the EPDS (Edinburgh Postnatal Depression Scale), which I'd learn later. She asked me to fill it out and give it to the doctor, then, we would review it together. I smiled and skimmed the questions while she jotted her notes in her laptop. My eyes focused in on one specific question: "The thought of harming myself has occurred to me": A: Yes, quite often B: Sometimes Hardly ever, C: Never", welp, I'm guessing they are asking about *right now*…so I answered "never." My doctor came in and asked me how I was and said how beautiful Xavier was. But appeared like she was way more concerned for me instead of" how are you?" She said the assessment I took, that the lower the score the better, and out of 10 questions I answered I scored an 8. An eight. And everything I was experiencing was a very real signature of postpartum depression. I just sunk in my chair and could feel the darkness continuing to snuff out the light. She placed her hand on mine and said "it's ok, we are going to get you well and it will pass. You need to be ok for you before you can take care of anyone else." She might as well have been talking another language as her words were just waves in my head. I heard her say something about calling in a medication that would take a few weeks to work but considering my already other mental health issues I was being treated for, this was one I should surely start to feel better soon. She wanted me to come back in 2 weeks and see how I was. I asked if I could skip the medication and just run or walk. I couldn't stand the feeling of taking any more pills every day to feel somewhat normal. She said sure I can do all those things too, but medically I scored high on this survey and my hormones are still trying to find balance. And then she told me to take this seriously as I can go into a state of postpartum psychosis. Which is basically when you lose touch with reality, have delusions and/or hallucinations; great. I just sighed and said, "ok I understand". As any semblance of light that was left in me was now completely gone. She hugged me and assured me it would be ok and picked up the car seat for me and walked me to the bright red exit sign. In that moment I wanted to walk through an exit sign that wouldn't take me to a reception desk but take me anywhere but where I was.

When I arrived at my car, I put Xavier in, still sleeping, as I sat there clutching the steering wheel and not sure of what to do next. I was riddled with anxiety about something that felt as though it was taking over my body, and now my mind. I sat there for what felt like an hour to see it was only a few minutes by way of my phone buzzing with a text message that my medication was ready for pick up. Can I wrap my head around what just happened? What is happening *to* me? Can I at least get out of the parking lot? I found myself in the drive-through of the pharmacy—a woman at the window said, "Name and date of birth?" I wasn't sure who I was in that moment but somehow answered, and she asked me if I had any questions. I just shook my head no, "Make sure to take this at the same time each day," she replied. Again, I just nodded, and half smiled. She handed me the long brown bag with what seemed like an instruction manual stapled to it. I looked at it and in what felt like an inanimate object screaming at me, "Zoloft 50 milligrams daily. Wow, you're even more messed up now huh? One more to add to that already long list of stuff you take..." I hurled the pharmacy bag onto the passenger seat like it was radioactive and pulled out of the parking lot. As I pulled into the driveway, a wave of emotions that had been building up completely flooded out of my face. And I cried. And then I cried some more. Then Xavier started crying too. I felt so alone just like so many moments before that one, I *was* alone again to muster through the darkness I felt. I went inside, cleaned myself and Xavier up, and fed him a bottle. I sat there in a silence that was so deafening I couldn't hear anything else. I looked at this amazing little human who didn't ask to be here or be given to a mom who was barely holding on. How can something so wonderful, pure, and full of love and light be paired with a darkness that was almost blinding? That's the thing about darkness; it's just the absence of light. And I had to learn how to allow that light in. It's what I imagine a person who is color-blind is like. They go for so long not seeing colors the way everyone else does, and then get a special pair of glasses. They are overcome with emotion and gratitude as they are now seeing the beautiful color of the sky, the grass, and people. But it's all just an illumination of light they couldn't see before. I could see all the colors, the green grass, the blue sky, the pink on my son's cheeks, but I had no glasses to help me see through this. What I had was a several pills and now a blue one that was supposed to help me see the light again; I felt it would keep me in the Matrix all that much longer. A nurse called me the next day to check in on me; her name was Hillary. She had the kindest demeanor and a genuine voice of concern for how I was. Asking me if I had started the medication and if I had any questions. I hadn't started taking it yet but lied and told her what she wanted to hear so she could check me off her to-do list for the day. I guess I was on her list each day because she called me at the same time for the next six weeks. During that time, I decided to keep the idea of another medication to myself and wouldn't dare tell a soul for the shame that was attached to taking any anti-depressant outside of those I was already taking for all the other things. Especially a mom who now has four children who need her. We should not be ashamed of mental health. It's just like any other part of our body that needs help. A broken bone, a headache, even a scraped knee and no one bats an eyelash. But I never needed to rely on anything for my brain's health. As a society, mental health is taboo; as if you are getting help, you must be crazy, or worse. I felt that stigma 100-fold as I secretly started taking the medication. After a few weeks, I noticed I wasn't crying all the time. I felt less anxious despite my endless sleep deprivation. I was due back to work in about four weeks, and I'd be in a new role as my job was being eliminated, so they found me another spot in IT and knew nothing about it. But what I did know is I couldn't go back to work in my state, let alone learn a new job. I was hoping something would break in me before that happened and I'd suddenly be "fixed." Then I would feel the sense of life I had, the one I remembered was still inside of me somewhere. But I just found myself like Neo living in a simulated illusionary reality and believing whatever I chose to think real. After about 12 weeks of this little blue pill, I decided I'd had enough of this numbing effect. It was time for everyone, including myself, to stop allowing me to walk in this path of perpetual darkness. And that's the thing about darkness; you can choose to flip the switch at any time; it's how hard you are willing to fight for it. My life has been full of battles, some I've won and some lost, but *this* giant was not going to defeat me.

Chapter Twenty-Nine

I went back to work into a new role entirely, and I felt the weight of every ounce of it sitting on my chest daily. I had no idea what I was doing, nor why anyone thought I would. I am in a spiral of not just postpartum hormones and mom guilt of having my three-month-old in daycare, but a spiral of self-doubt and insecurity. I went from a job I was confident in my abilities for almost two decades to a role now as a Project Manager in IT. This was like stepping into a completely different universe. I didn't know anything about IT, let alone how to be a manager of the projects it held. I was totally ill- equipped, especially just coming back from maternity leave, as I made no conscious effort to research what this new job's expectations were. I consider myself to be relatively intelligent and a quick learner, but this was not easy, and I'm the *only* female. I'm by nature an extrovert, but if you looked up these guys in the dictionary, their photos would be next to the definition of "introvert". Some call them nerds, some call them geeks, but one thing I found out quickly is yes, they may be those things, but they are extremely smart and creative. They didn't know how to communicate with a female either, which I also quickly discovered. I reported to Jay who was the VP of IT and faked my way through seeming that I knew what I was doing. When you don't have the levels of protection between you and the Vice President, it hits different in making sure you don't mess things up. I felt a level of anxiety I'd not experienced before in a job, and I found out that he was in the military, so my "orders," per se, were explained, and my expectations were made clear. Great, I am now the human shield to this world, and I get to communicate and defend what is being built or not, for that matter. Ok, well if that's the job, I am going to do it the way I see fit. There was no other "me" there, so what did I have to lose? I reveled in the challenge of getting these guys not just out of the dimly lit dungeon of a room they worked in, but to show them I was not a threat, but an advocate for them. There was an entirely separate IT area of admin guys; these are the guys who fix your computer, get you a new keyboard, fix your hard drive, etc. Smart for sure, but very different from the dungeon dwellers I was used to dealing with. They were on the other side of the building and surprisingly didn't work in the dark, nor were they introverts at all! I guess helping fix things all day, you get some people skills to go along with that. One guy liked to cook, and he was always bringing in food and desserts for the team to try. The dungeon dwellers never took part, but they made sure to call me and include me in all the taste testing. My job required me to meet and communicate with people with whom I didn't know existed before, but I would eventually find my footing and start to excel in this new world. We were launching a whole new platform for the company to use; it was being built long before I arrived, but I gained trust and confidence from the very people who would use it, so I was responsible for that transition. People don't like change, but I had a way of letting people know how it could help them rather than hinder them, a skill that remains one of my most valuable assets. The developers saw their work come to life and saw I could make it fun all the while; hell, they even let me put a standing $7 halogen light in their dungeon, but of course compromising to leave it on the lowest setting. But change in executives caused chaos on the ground level, and it was disrupting the ecosystem I built for myself. Adapting to situations that are less than ideal seems to be a running premise for me, and I had seen enough. My boss Jay, who became a shield for me and always went to bat to protect me, was leaving the company. What would happen to my job? Was it safe? He told me there was a director job opening for the very people I helped, but the favoritism was palpable. I needed a job, so I immediately applied. Then I had my interview and waited. What I didn't know was the person I interviewed with was the very person who got me the job initially at the company and she's still a good friend to me even till today. Favor or not, I got that job and did well. I was able to turn the whole operation on its head and they were thriving in both productivity and exceeding metrics. Just when you think things are looking okay, life has a way of ensuring you don't get comfortable in that space for too long.

Cliff's dad had been having heart troubles over the past year and eventually had a pacemaker put in and seemed to be doing well, or so we thought. The man who had been holding every bit of himself together since he lost the love of his life was slowly dying of what I still believe to this day was a broken heart. He was in and out of hospitals and cardiologists who eventually placed a mini defibrillator along with his existing pacemaker to ensure he'd get a jolt to keep his heart pumping.

We were there often, making sure he wasn't alone, along with the many grandchildren who scurried about the house. He'd made Olivia his little sugar puddin' and would even sing a song to her about it. Xavier, just a little over a year old by now, would just sit calmly next to my now "Dad" and watch TV with him as if he were an old soul who'd known him in another life. I can see Dad slowly losing weight, deteriorating before our eyes, but he had a smile for anyone who met his gaze. He'd sit on the porch with me, telling me about how he was going to pay off some things and help Cliff and me buy a big home. He seemed excited and determined. He was a man of his word, so I always believed every one that was uttered from his mouth. But a few months later, he was in the hospital in heart failure. He was placed in the ICU and unfortunately, he had many complications now from the preexisting diabetes he had, that his organs were no longer functioning the way they needed to. His extremities were now black, and we knew there was no recovering from this. Our entire family, adults, and kids surrounded him in that small ICU room. There had to be over a dozen of us, and no one dared tell us to leave. The plan was to move him to hospice to be more comfortable, but we were going to spend every moment in that room, savoring every breath in his presence while he was conscious and alert. We laughed and told funny stories you could see he felt brightened by. We all individually told him our I love you's and see you later's. They had his face covered in a BiPAP machine in hopes of helping his oxygen levels sustain a little longer until he reached his hospice room. We asked to have it removed temporarily, and the nurse obliged. She was kind, with short blonde hair, wearing dark purple scrubs, and a softness in her eyes that she knew this might be the last time many of those that stood in this room would ever see him alive again. She smiled at us, but mostly at all the kids, so many grandchildren who were watching their grandpa, their very earthly guardian angel slip away. A son stood guard at his bedside while watching his hero become weaker but knowing all the strength he held inside was from him. And a daughter sitting holding his hand as he had so many times for her. I felt almost frozen as I pleaded inside with God to not to take the only father that ever believed in me away. A path was made as I walked to his bedside holding Xavier in my arms, his youngest grandson. I looked in his now glassy eyes and I smiled as I fought the lump in my throat and the tears that were welling up like an ocean behind my eyes. I thanked him for loving me, and I thanked him for being the dad I never had. I had always told him that, but this time I held his hand and told him I promised to take care of his son, just as I had promised his mom just a few short years before. He was barely able to speak but touched Xavier's foot as he giggled happily to see his buddy, even if for the last time and closed his eyes briefly to take in the impact of what I had said. Olivia, in all her little five-year-old self, stood there overwhelmed by the beeping of machines, tubes, and wires, but bravely took my hand and walked past all of it to get to her grandpa. He immediately tried to sing his sugar puddin' song, merely just slightly closing his eyes and moving his head, but we knew. She hugged him by laying her head where she wouldn't disrupt the extensions of machines keeping him alive, and he placed his hand on her head. She squeezed my hand and in her little voice told him she loved him, and he waved to her like he always did when we headed home. I think this was the moment everyone knew the wave wasn't just to her, but to all of us. Everyone started to leave knowing they needed to prepare him for hospice. Eventually, they took Dad away on the stretcher to settle him there, and Cliff and his sister Denise were signing papers outside the door when the same nurse came into the room asking if I was okay. I was the only one left and had the kids with me and I thanked her for all she had done for Dad. She fought tears that eventually fell in cascades on her face. She said she had never seen so many people stay and surround anyone with as much love as we did for him. She said we were a special family and she had never experienced that in her whole time as a nurse. I hugged her and thanked her again for letting us be with him. Cliff came in with a pause and a hitch in his breath. We locked eyes and he said quietly to me, "Dad made it to hospice but passed just as soon as he arrived." I was stunned and couldn't move, and the oceans of tears finally broke as I could no longer contain them. He placed my head on his chest while we stood there holding our kids, somehow knowing God let him live long enough until he could say goodbye to everyone he loved. But now Dad's heart was no longer broken and was with the love of his life. I miss him so very much, but he left me the very best part of him, his son.

Chapter Thirty

About 6 months into my new job, I got a call from my old boss, Jay. He asked if I wanted to join him at his new company and work for him again. It was the same role, but it was a 45-minute commute each way with no traffic. I said the best I can do is agree to interview, but I'd need compensation for the new wrench that was now thrown in the plan. I had a baby, a toddler, and two older girls prepping for middle and high school. I was trying to be a mother and a wife while overcoming a depression that I never knew when it would arise. It was all very consuming, and I was in over my head in my regular life, and I'm about to take on something else? Plus, as if life hadn't handed us enough, Cliff was laid off from the job that kept him out for twelve hours a day, so I had no choice. I would be the only one working, so I had to go to the interview. I met with a panel of interviewers who peppered me with questions while I sat rigid in an uncomfortable conference room chair. When they finally finished, Jay came back to rescue me from what felt like an interrogation... I said, "How'd I do?" He replied, "Considering you're the only candidate, the job is yours if you want it". The salary number he named made my eyebrows shoot up and my breath catch, far beyond what I'd dared hope for with my childcare juggling act and that brutal commute. So, I gave a verbal yes. Reuniting with Jay felt like slipping into a familiar pair of shoes-comfortable, predictable, no surprises waiting to trip me up when I was already juggling so much. Plus, I felt good starting a new job with someone who had my back. I gave notice at my current job, to which my boss, who was and still is my friend, cried. All. Day. Long. But I had already crossed the point of no return in my mind. The new executive leadership was causing more upset than I was paid to deal with. I handed her my office key and said it was my last day. No two-week notice: With everything hanging in the balance at home, I couldn't afford to stay in a place that drained what little emotional energy I had left. I walked out that door with my head high, refusing to let that chapter of my life follow me home. I started working at the new place and was doing well considering I knew nothing about what the company did, and the commute was brutal. I had a great boss, met some nice and not-so-nice people, but I played the game and kept to myself. But here we are at the six-month mark. (What's with six-month marks?) The HR lady came into my office. I thought it was just a pleasant good morning, as the coffee room was right next to where I was. She did in fact say good morning normally, but that was not why she came to see me. She came in and quietly closed the door behind her holding a stack of papers in her hand. I immediately thought I did something wrong and said, "Is everything ok?" She half smiled and hung her head slightly, then looked up. She said I was not in any sort of trouble and pulled a chair that was sitting against the wall closer to my desk. I immediately felt unease. She sat for a moment organizing her papers while I stared at her pensively. She looked at me, took a breath, and said this was my last day. Unfortunately, my position was being absorbed by others. I was being laid off, again. Wait, but I just got here. In a calm but rigid tone, I immediately asked if Jay knew this information. I could simultaneously hear my phone vibrating over and over and tried to ignore it, but it persisted. She handed me the papers she was holding and went over them in quick detail. Something about a small severance, and my release to basically not sue them and hold them harmless in my sudden departure. I don't know what I signed; I was overwhelmed that Cliff and I would both now be without jobs. I felt myself coming into a full panic attack and needed to get out of there as quickly as possible. I slid the papers back across the desk. She tapped them into a neat stack, then looked up with that HR smile that never reaches the eyes. "You'll be a tremendous asset to any company fortunate enough to hire you," she said. The words caught in my throat, but I forced them out anyway: "Except this one". She waited as I packed my things, which thankfully weren't much, and escorted me out the back entrance as if I were some kind of criminal. I walked down the stairs to the street and opened the steel door to be met with blazing sunlight and a chill in the October air. The daylight and fresh air felt foreign after weeks spent under fluorescent lights in climate-controlled office. In sort of a tunnel vision, I walked to my car, not sure how to process what had just happened. My phone started to vibrate again; I looked, and I had 8 missed calls from Jay. I arrived at my car and answered, saying I was sorry, but I was predisposed by being laid off. He had been calling insistently earlier, trying to warn me as they too let him go. Guilt by association had cost me my livelihood. He apologized profusely, asked if I was okay, but I was numb and didn't have much to say other than I had to go and get home. I felt badly for him but not as badly as I felt having to tell my husband I lost my job, and we were now incomeless. Driving home at 10am ensured there was no traffic, but I took the long way. I was trying to process the shame of feeling the punch in the gut I had just endured. When I walked in my house, putting my small paper Starbucks bag down that held my belongings, Cliff looked at me puzzled. He walked over to me, thinking perhaps I had left sick. I'm sick all right, but not how he thinks. I sat down and told him they laid me off, hanging my head. He was silent and still. I looked up, wondering his thoughts and searched his face, and without saying the words, we were both thinking "now what?" I immediately applied for unemployment, one thing I had never done in my life up to this point. I wasn't feeling the shame I thought it would bring, considering I'd been paying into the state fund for decades. I had a few paychecks as "severance" to hold us over. We managed to keep things afloat until weekly benefits started. I must have applied for a hundred jobs and made countless resume submissions. Only to be met with rejection after rejection. We knew we only had a few months of unemployment to count on, so jobs were critical for us. We were not going to be able to sustain ourselves in these current circumstances. But if my experience had taught me anything, it was to always be prepared to move quickly should you need to. Both figuratively and quite literally. We searched for recycled boxes from behind grocery stores and strip malls. We collected any we could find. The plan was to purge and pack. Even if we got jobs in the interim, getting rid of things that were weighing us down was a smart thing to do. We got a storage unit, and as we packed, we would take trips

211

discreetly during the day while the older girls were in school. I had to pull Xavier out of daycare, and Olivia only went for a half day to preschool. They were thrilled that both mommy and daddy were home with them. Inside, I was seething at the thought of not being able to provide a life for them of stability that they so very much deserved. Christmas came and went, draining us financially with the little we were living on. Time ticked as if every second was louder and louder, letting me know that it was not on my side. I was falling into a dark place, and unfortunately, I knew this place well. Panic attacks resumed as if they were just paused, just waiting for the moment they could consume me. Springtime is upon us, and we continue to pack and hope for employment, which is like looking at a dead-end street. We are not going to be able to make rent except for a month or two more. I let our landlords know what we were facing and empathetically let us use our security deposit to buy us some more time.

I'd give my life for my kids, but what I wasn't giving them *was* a life. The white rabbit was in my head daily, taunting me with a clock just making the case that time was slipping away from me, from us. I lived in a haze of functional depression. I searched for something to stop me from wanting to find the highest bridge to jump from. I scoured the internet to look for some form of affirmation, some sign, anything that would keep me sane for that day. I found a clip someone shared on social media of some pastor talking about struggles being the same for everyone. But no one realizes it because of the shame attached to it, so we hide it; and I was surely hiding. I don't know why, but it stuck with me, and I needed to know more about who this man was. I did some searching and discovered he was the head pastor of a church a few states south. I grew up Catholic and only knew church to be "mass" with rules and regulations, never an experience. But this church was different. It had an online platform, which meant they streamed live and there was a band that sang. Then the pastor would preach his sermon just as if you were in the room with him. I started watching each Sunday as my part of hoping a God I barely knew would not let me suffer any more. That was such a lofty hope, because each day my hope was chipped away and fell to the ground mostly in tears, and all I heard was parts of me shattering inside. Each week after the service concluded, there was an invitation at the end. The pastor asked viewers to surrender control, to let faith guide them instead of fear. And they offered a button on the screen to do this. Wait, it's a computer; what could my clicking it possibly do? Was it some magical portal to peace and a job we desperately needed? One Sunday, I was going through the motions of packing up the kitchen and having no idea if we'd have somewhere to go. Or if homelessness was imminent. I stopped to watch the service online and heard a message called Barriers and Blessings. This impacts me to this day as if God were talking directly to me through this mega global ministry. I saw the bright button at the end of the sermon starting at me on the screen, reading "surrendering your heart to Christ, let us know!" I debated, knowing I'd tried everything I knew how and lived in survival mode my whole life. If something I could not see, feel, touch, smell, or taste could get us out of this, well so be it. I proceeded and clicked the button, thinking in my mind "well, what do I have to lose? I'm out of ideas." I waited for some angel to come from the sky to enlighten me. I looked around, hoping some booming thunder would crash acknowledging that what I did was the right thing. But I got no angel, and I got no thunder. I got a box and continued to pack up my life again. I contemplated for the next few days that I was done with this state of just surviving and constantly chasing the next spot of safety to land. It was a never-ending loop replaying all the instances where I tried and failed and carried other people's collateral damage from decisions I did not make. But I was left to clear out the destruction left, and I had had enough of cleaning up other people's messes.

Everyone has a junk drawer somewhere in their house usually found in the kitchen. These junk drawers hold various nonsense that you think you may use at a later point and wind up in this drawer. Things like batteries, screws probably left over from Ikea furniture, maybe a half- put-together sewing kit where the one thread you need is just tangled up everywhere. Old rubber bands, receipts from years prior, old phone or tablet chargers, and a slurry of you insert yours here, are all part of one's individual junk drawer. I stared into our junk drawer, sifting through to clean it out, but I couldn't help but just stare at it. This is what my life felt like, just a mishmash of stuff thrown into a drawer with no reason for it but held on to for dear life. I hate this representation of what I'd become and never amounted to. I was prompted to open the notes app on my phone, and I started to write out my wishes for when I die. I made a clear, concise list. My final wishes would be crystal clear, and no one would have to wonder if I was thinking straight or debate what I would have wanted. I wrote this as I planned not to wake up the next morning. I planned to take my life because any life without me in it would be better off for my kids and my husband. Just like sitting atop the stairs so many years ago, pooling with blood in and out of consciousness, I felt very much the same that I was part of the sinking ship with my life's past and current trauma. So, if I got off, they could perhaps breathe and float for the first time without my baggage weighing them down. And to alleviate the pain I was in, well, that was a risk I was willing to take. I shut the phone and then shut the drawer. What was this whole "giving your life to Jesus" madness if nothing changes was the tone that rang through my thoughts as I felt a swell of a panic attack begin to rise. Tears flooded the back of my throat and the tenseness in my body was unmistakable. Then, almost simultaneously, my cell phone rang. I was in no position to talk to a bill collector, or anyone for that matter, and I didn't recognize the number, but I felt compelled to answer. "Hello?" "Hi Nicole!" the voice was a kind female on the other line. "Yes, who is this?" "Hi, my name is Celeste and I'm calling from the church where you clicked the surrender button on our live-stream. I wanted to personally call and congratulate you and tell you how proud I am of you!" I fell to my knees and started to sob. I thanked her for calling and explained to her that just earlier I was planning to not wake up the next day. And her reaching out was a clear intervention from the God I that my story isn't over yet. We spoke for a while, and I explained our situation and she prayed for me that God would intervene with a miracle. And I promised her I'd stay. She kept in touch with me to make sure. I guess sometimes you must take the risk despite it all and push the button.

There was no sign of a job or even an interview, and we had no idea what we were going to do. But I prayed to a God I couldn't see every night for a miracle. Not understanding that I was a walking, talking, breathing miracle; yet I felt like anything but. I went through the motions of packing the various items we had accumulated over the years and found myself sitting in the memories they held. A box of cards collected from birthdays and various celebrations. Baby hats and pacifiers, random photos of moments in time that I could feel as if I was there reliving it all. Perhaps that's what I was being shown, what I prayed for, a miracle. Each thing I picked up was a small miracle that occurred. And I was being reminded of that, despite feeling as though I was losing everything. The weather was starting to get warmer, and the kids were nearing the end of the school year. Cliff and I were still taking our trips to a storage unit while pretending everything was going to be okay. When neither of us knew that for certain. I attempted the best I could to not impose my daily depression on the kids. But hoped that a new job for either of us would allow us to stay and leave their lives uninterrupted. Unfortunately, that did not happen, as we were out of options. Except one. One I dreaded facing with every fiber of my being. One I fought internally with my pride until there was none left. I had told our landlord we were in fact moving out, and why. She was understanding and allowed us until mid-July to vacate. The panic set in as potential homelessness loomed nearby.

Over the course of the years of chaos that I was living, my mom had left Delaware and moved to a remote town in Texas, again, for a man. She said she knew him from some mutual friends who did missionary work, and they connected. I didn't know this man, just that she packed up her life again and moved; I can't say I was surprised. She was able to leave her kid behind years ago; what's a couple of grandkids too? I was very resentful, and it was a continual burning ember that churned in me that I could not extinguish no matter how hard I tried. But, despite my best efforts to not have my family living on the street, she was the only option I fought long and hard to avoid. Cliff and I sat in the Target parking lot on the way back from the storage unit and parked. We were physically sweating and so tired, but more tired of sitting in the unknown. We stared out the windows for what felt like hours when it was only a few heartbeats of time. I had nothing to lose at this point. I was full of shame and my courage was fleeting. I didn't understand in that moment how a God who was supposed to be so good allowed me to feel so utterly terrible. Why did He want me to continually suffer? Why didn't He just let me die when I had the chance? Thoughts flooded my mind, and I was almost in a trance of my own self-pity when I heard Cliff say, "Just call her. The worst she can say is no." I contested with that internally more than he will ever know. I reluctantly picked up my phone and put it on speaker. I lived in a constant state of defensiveness, understandably so. But Cliff brings a calm to every situation and can speak for me when everything in me wants to cry and scream. So, I knew the moment she answered he'd help keep me and the situation from spiraling. She answered in a cheery voice, "Hellooo!" almost in a singing-like way. "Hi, Mom, Cliff is here with me, and we wanted to talk to you." "What's wrong?" she replied, as any parent would or should. We went on to explain what had been and what was going on, and she put me on speaker to include the man she was now sharing a life with. He was kind, asked us a few questions, and we were honest about how dire our situation was. With no hesitation, they both said that we were welcome there for as long as we needed. They would make sure the kids had what they needed as they had the space for extra beds and would be sure the kids felt comfortable. As I contended with my pride and shame to hold back the resentment-filled tears, I thanked them. I said we'd be in touch as we still had a few weeks and a lot to still pack. Their voices rang with enthusiasm, but my heart sank at the thought of Texas stretching before us like an endless desert. How do I sell this to the kids? To avoid the street, we must drive halfway across the country, and we need to stay with their grandmother who abandoned them. Hadn't the older girls been through enough? Hadn't I? Now I was going to have to ask them to move again. Leave best friends and boyfriends behind and not give them any assurance we'd be able to return. The thoughts continued as the panic grew in me and tears that wanted to flow as if an ocean was again trapped inside me. We drove back in silence, each taking in the inevitable. Unlike our past hardships, this one had a name, a face, a timeline. We could touch it, measure it, and wrap our minds around it, even as it wrapped itself around our throats. And what was to come felt like an emerging giant I could not see, no matter what rose-colored glasses I attempted to see through. And I was terrified.

We packed what we could in a waterproof roof rack bag. It held only things that were necessary while our whole life and memories were held in a storage unit. We drove for 3 days, stopping in random hotel rooms to rest, that my mom and partner graciously paid for. The little kids thought it was a fun trip while Cecelia and Ava barely spoke the entire way. Unless it was to voice their hatred towards me and the situation, as if somehow, I purposely caused it. We drove to what felt like the middle of nowhere, but nowhere was everywhere. The sun was setting and all of me wanted to crawl out of my skin never to return. We arrived to see a ranch-style house set back off the road and my mom waving to us at the end of the long gravel driveway. We drove in as I offered a lowly wave. As I heard the pops of the gravel on the tires, a back-and-forth glance showed me this was really, nowhere. Her partner met us at the top of the driveway by the garage. He was a larger man with white hair and a flushed face, which I had assumed was his normal hue. We got out and Cliff immediately shook his hand, and my mom hugged us and said how happy she was that we were there. Those of us who felt the heaviness of what was left behind hid behind fake smiles. We didn't want to spoil what appeared to be her sincere joy, though a voice inside me whispered that she'd never shown such concern for my happiness when I needed it most. We were led into the garage and were told there was a deep freezer and to help ourselves to anything. The freezer was stocked with pizza rolls, chicken nuggets, and ice cream sandwiches-comfort food calculated to win over reluctant grandchildren. We walked into the house, which was decorated nicely, very much my mom's doing. The décor was like her Delaware apartment. Bookshelves held photos and trinkets, and a wall of her grandchildren's artwork that she had framed. Her absence from their lives made the framed artwork feel like a museum of moments she'd missed as if preserving their creativity could somehow substitute for not being present. The kitchen was spacious with a small table to sit and eat, and beyond that, a laundry room, and a bathroom. The living room was simple, a TV and couch, nothing extravagant but a nice place for the middle of nowhere. We were all so exhausted, but she was chomping at the bit to show Olivia and Xavier their rooms. She had a room for them with bedding that fit them perfectly. Xavier was full Paw Patrol, and Olivia's bed had a purple headboard with princess bedding. Even a little table in the middle with a light they could use to store their few things they were able to bring. They were excited, and it felt like it was their room, which left a pit in my stomach as nice as it was of her. She brought Cecelia and Ava to their room, two white-framed day beds that also held a trundle bed underneath. She had found nightstands on consignment and painted them to fit the décor. As for the bedding, one was a light blue, the other a coral color. They showed their appreciation as the pit in my stomach grew even bigger. She took us to the room where Cliff and I would stay-it was a very shabby chic decorated type of room. It had floral bedding and knickknacks on the nightstands. An antique doily was strewn across the dresser. In the corner sat a chair, likely from a consignment shop, and some sheer curtains. It was a very pretty room, seemingly like a cottage Air B&B, even with fresh towels on the bed. I thanked her but was told to leave things where they were as it was *her* room to which she was giving up to us. I asked where she was going to sleep; she said the couch. The pit in my stomach was now a gaping hole. I thanked her again and she told us to get some rest. I stayed with the kids till they fell asleep. Then I crawled into the foreign bed with my husband already asleep and stared at the ceiling. As tears burned my eyes as they fell to the sides of my face. I tried to contain the sea of them by closing them tightly in hopes that when I woke the nightmare would be over. My eyes fluttered open to the vast sunlight that the sheer white curtains did nothing to shield. I sighed deeply in a defeat of despair. I needed a shower, but I didn't know the rules or even where it was. So, I chose to throw on shorts and a t-shirt and just wash my face in the bathroom. I used the towels she left for us and slung one over the door after I dried my face. I froze, suddenly unsure if I'd broken some unspoken rule of the house. Maybe there was a designated hook for towels, maybe she had a system. I hadn't been in the same house with my mom in nearly three decades and I wasn't sure what the rules were, even though I was a grown woman with four kids. That thought screamed at me louder than any had since my arrival. You are a grown woman with four kids who are all living with your mother. You have barely any money, and for no other reason than you'd be on the street otherwise. Some would say it was a blessing to be able to "go home" safe to your parents when you fell on tough times. I didn't feel any of that, and these aren't my parents. I didn't feel like I was in a safe place, nor "home," and I felt like I was an utter failure. I sat in the chair in the corner trying to wrap my head around what was happening. What would happen, what could happen, and what if nothing happened. The kids flung open the door, allowing my brain to be unclenched from the fury of doom that I was under. They said they were going to 'pick stuff' and pulled my arm to come with them. I walked out to find coffee made and my mom perched on the corner of the couch reading some uninspiring crime mystery novel. I greeted her with a simple good morning, and she told me there were coffee and mugs in the cabinet above. I poured a cup while the little footsteps ran through the house and giggles to match. I was glad Olivia and Xavier were young enough that they had no idea the real reason we were here. They asked excitedly, "mom-mom when are we going picking?!" I looked at her puzzled. She told me they were going to the garden to pick vegetables and watermelons before it got too hot, and I was welcome to join them. She said to wear pants and a long- sleeved shirt just because of bugs and spiders. Bugs and spiders. Awesome, can't wait. I got the kids covered, myself, and wore my hat I usually wore running and got ready to head out. I walked outside and was immediately hit with an oppressive heat that I had never felt before. Why is it 10am and 100 degrees? We followed her to a giant garden that sprawled beyond my eyes' reach. Tomatoes grew on tall vines, watermelons that grew on vines but were much lower on the ground. Zucchini and squash plants, and green beans in droves ready to be picked. Although quite impressive if that's what you're into. I knew if you grew your own produce in this capacity that there wasn't a grocery store nearby and we were, in fact, in the middle of nowhere. I helped pick what seemed like a never-ending supply of green beans, and we threw all the harvest into a bug bucket to take back to the house. I had just driven for 3 days, hadn't showered, and I was now dripping in sweat while laboring to gather their crops. The kids were over it, tired and needed water. We went in the house and guzzled all the water we could consume, all of us reddened in the face. I changed the kids into fresh clothes while giving them a snack of goldfish and tablets to play on. I peeked in to see if my mom was okay, but she was out counting how many of each of the crops were picked. I just stood there knowing I was vehemently opposed to ever doing *that* again. I checked on the older girls, and they were still in bed, in no rush or shape to do anything, but I couldn't blame them; I hurt *for them*. I did this to them, and my heart broke a bit more in that moment. With phones in hand, probably scrolling through the places and friends they were vying to go back to. When I asked if they were okay, they just stared blankly at me and said to leave them alone. I shut the door while tears stung and built in my eyes as I hung my head in shame. I found the shower and managed to find what I needed to wash off what I hoped was a bad dream or a living nightmare. I pulled off my sweat-laden clothes and stood there in the beat of the water on my head and cried. The ocean of tears had released in what felt like an upheaval of waves that were just waiting to escape from me. I could no longer stand, and I sat as the water beat on my back, muffling out the sounds of me crying. I was trying to hold it together for everyone. But I was facing years of old demons I had buried and never wanted to confront. Time feels as though it is standing still even though the days tick by. I was constantly scouring the internet and applying for jobs. Hoping somehow, someway this wouldn't be our permanent residence much longer. Despite the beautiful sunrises and sunsets, I was living in a constant state of hidden anxiety and panic. I had gotten good at faking my way through things because I knew if my kids saw I wasn't OK, they wouldn't be OK. We would take drives here and there to break up the boredom and became quick fans of a Dairy Queen we spotted about 25 minutes away. It was well over 110 degrees each day, so being outside was not conducive to anyone's health. But ice cream could eliminate not just the heat but put a pause on the broken hearts I saw in my kids and in me. We'd sit in a booth made of slatted wood, so it was bound to leave marks on our already heat-swollen skin. The kids would get Oreo blizzards, Cliff usually a sundae of some sort, and I, always a chocolate-dipped cone. Who knew you could get a soft serve ice cream cone dipped in some magic chocolate that formed a hard magic shell around it? I can still feel the refreshing wave of A/C as you walked in, escaping the Texas heat. The floors were sticky, and the air was a mix of fried food and ice cream. Those moments everyone was OK...laughter and a slight sense of joy. We'd eat slower, letting everyone finish. A deep dread would cover us like a heavy blanket when we knew it was time to leave. We'd get back to the house as if we were guests and not family. I'd lived on my own since I was 19 years old, so the awkwardness I felt was palpable. I needed to do something that made me feel some sense of who I was despite the world imploding around me. There was a very long gravel driveway that I had been surveying each day, wondering how many times I'd need to run up and back to equal a mile. I was used to running several miles a day, competing in various long-distance running races. After nearly a decade of training in all types of weather, I found comfort in the thought that, yes, this was monotonous, but the task was within reach. The only difference is I never trained in this type of stifling heat; well, everything is stifling now, so why not include this too. I never looked at things like they were too hard, or I might fail. Okay, maybe this time I might pass out from a heat stroke, but there is a first time for everything. I got dressed, laced up my sneaks, and headed outside as if it were any other run. But, despite my training and my tenacity, I was unprepared for what I was about to endure. I stepped outside with caution as I shut the garage door, hearing "please be careful" lingering behind me. I was so angry and bitter at my lack of control over this situation, and I needed to channel that energy somewhere. Running was always my go-to; it helped me clear the clutter and think more clearly. And I walked out in the blistering heat of 115 degrees wafting in my face, I stood there bewildered, my faith suddenly a stranger to me. A Jesus I gave my life to allowed this to happen, not just to me, but to my whole family. Isn't He supposed to be good? I started the activity tracker on my phone and started to warm up with a walk down the driveway and back; down was easy, back was uphill. I contemplated for a few seconds how crazy this was and almost retreated. But we were in the middle of nowhere Texas and the only things that drove on the road were 18-wheelers, going about 90 mph. So, I'll stick to the driveway. Plus, I'm so stubborn that I don't give up *that easily*. Up and back, I went, over and over. Cliff brought me cold water, asking me to rest. I scoffed at him, and I'm sure he knew my reaction before I even could wave him away. Twelve times up and back, that was my mile. I was sweating, and the sun was scorching my head despite my dry wick hat. I guzzled some water, even poured it on my head and face, and continued. I was determined to not have this situation take every ounce of who I was away from me. My mom came out to check on me, Cliff again, and now the kids. I assured them I was fine, as I headed back down the driveway as tears began to build behind my eyes and I held back the choke in my throat. I am not going to allow this to win. I forced myself to fight back up the driveway. I finished three rounds of twelve-three miles total in now 120-degree heat. I sat on the bumper of our truck, sipping cold water, catching my breath. It was a heat I've never experienced. And I felt dizzy from pushing myself so hard, trying to prove I was still in some capacity not just a shell of myself as I so often felt now. But in that moment with my lungs burning and sweat stinging my eyes, I could only feel contempt for my own existence. I looked up at the merciless Texas sky and silently demanded answers from a God who seemed to have abandoned me; why keep me alive through all those years when death had extended its hand so many times? The question hung unanswered in the scorching air, though someday I would understand His purpose.

Playing Uno and eating Cheetos became a nightly routine my mom did with the little kids. Eventually, the older ones joined in and for a moment, I heard that laughter and joy just days ago while they ate their Oreo blizzards. I joined a game or two but mostly watched. I let her be with her grandchildren by letting them stay up late, eating snacks, and enjoying their company. What I didn't know is that would be one of the last times anything like that would ever happen. A few days passed and Cliff's phone rang from the State of NJ. He'd normally not answer calls he didn't know but I told him to answer it. He obliged as I saw a shocked look come upon his face, then a smile. Then a "yes, absolutely, thank you so much" as he ended the conversation. I stared with a concerning hesitation... He exclaimed "I got a job!" smiling ear to ear knowing the time here was in fact temporary. I had applied for so many jobs for him and myself over several months and he even had interviews, but nothing came to fruition. Until now. He had an interview back in April with the State of NJ but never heard anything, until today. They offered him a full-time accounting position, with pension, benefits, you name it. The catch is he needs to start on August 14th. That's less than a month. So, the good thing is that meant we were in fact moving back to New Jersey; the bad thing, where to? We had no money to rent anything and no matter how much of my big brain I used, I couldn't make sense of anything. I had been texting Celeste, just checking in from time to time wanting to know how I was. I filled her in on the whole saga-of our Texas exile, Cliff's unexpected job offer, and our desperate scramble to find housing back in New Jersey. She understood our impossible situation and promised to ask God for divine intervention on our behalf. She also told me they were holding baptisms on the main campus on the 12th of August, it was a Saturday. I thought about it for a long minute. The idea of baptism is you leave your old self in the water after going under and you are a new creation in Christ. Out with your old crappy self, in with your new self. It seemed easy enough, but I didn't know how water was magically going to leave all the awful parts of me in a pool of water to never be seen again. I'm not just willing; I'm desperate. I talked to Cliff about it being so close to his new job start date, but he was ecstatic and said absolutely we would make it work! I went to work talking to the realtor who helped us with rentals in the past. I asked if she could find something for us and what would be required to move into any of the places she found. She kept in touch with me, sending me listings that were way out of our league. Then she presented me with an option of going to a person who had a house for sale for over six months. There was no activity, so she was preparing to negotiate to see if he would consider renting it to us. He bought it from some elderly woman, and he gutted it all and redid the whole place. In the photos, it was beautiful, more than I thought we deserved. It would require some contingencies and some of her master negotiation tactics, so I didn't push. In the meantime, Cliff got in touch with his sister who was living in his parents' house. He explained the situation, and she, without hesitation, said we could stay if we needed to until we got a place of our own. But I rejected this notion entirely. I was so tired of living in someone else's space-the constant feeling of being a burden, tiptoeing around unfamiliar routines, but then I'd feel guilty for my ingratitude when these people were saving us from homelessness. We had no other option, and I hated that I couldn't make peace with it. But we would have several weeks in nowhere Texas, so I tried to make the best of it. My mom and her partner sustained all our bills for us so we could go back with a clean slate. Even paying for the storage unit that I couldn't wait to empty. Celeste asked me to join a women's fellowship group that met each week. They supported one another in whatever was going on and prayed for one another. This was all very foreign to me, women who met on Zoom, had no judgment, and just wanted you to be successful and know you were valued and loved. What's the catch? I have always waited for the preverbal other shoe to drop, but this time, no shoe, and no catch. I met some of the most amazing women there, with whom I'm still friends to this day. But during this time, the leader, Dee, and Pam heard my story, and I could feel their hurt for me, even though it was through a computer screen. They were all on a mission to make sure I could get the help I needed. They went so far as to go to that very church, and one person's response was, "Could we just put them in a shelter?" Dee about lost her mind and told me that was not God's best, and she'd do whatever *she* and the other women could do to help. I also met a young woman, Bree, in that group. She was kind and funny, but her work schedule made her inconsistent. But she would later become a constant presence in my life even up until today. She truly is the Meredith to my Christina. I continued to try to find some peace in the last few weeks in nowhere Texas, and for the first time, I could see why God did what He did.

He was trying to get our attention, probably mostly mine. I'd talked to Him and said how I didn't understand why all this bad had to happen. But the Bible says all things will turn out for good and in my favor. I had to believe that, even if I was holding on to a thread of faith and hope I couldn't see. But the peace I tried to find turned into a perpetual anxiety that grew with each day we got closer to leaving. I didn't want to stay, but I didn't want to go either. We needed to get an oil change before we left, so my mom and her partner arranged for us to get to a shop, but it was some ways away. He was away on business, so my mom went with Cliff, and I stayed back with the kids. It wasn't like I had anywhere to go anyhow, but I was grateful for the time to myself. Where time seems to stand still when you're in the middle of nowhere. About an hour or so later, Cliff called me and updated me on our truck. He said not only did it need an oil change but new tires, as the metal was coming through the one entirely. Wait, we drove all the way here on that?! Had that come off we could've gotten into a severe accident, or possibly worse. He rattled off some other work that was needed but I heard none of it. I was stuck on the fact that we had been driving for days, thousands of miles in all kinds of weather. We had to have had a fleet of angels protecting us. My mom reluctantly paid for the work to get done, knowing we had surely worn out our welcome. Later that day, I could tell Cliff was deep in thought. Part of me wondered if he felt the shame and weight of the situation as I did. But this was different. Something happened on that ride with my mom, and I wanted to know what it was. Did she make him feel guilty? Make him feel like a failure? Whatever it was I was determined to find out. Though the Texas heat lingered, I liked to go outside at sunset and regroup my thoughts. Except now my thoughts were only on the future I had little knowledge of or faith in. Cliff found me and stood next to me, not saying anything as if my energy was speaking volumes for both of us. But what he said I was not expecting. "Your mom talked to me on the drive to the shop about your life growing up, saying how truly horrible it was." I turned to face him, my eyes narrowing, searching his face for a minute...where was he going with this? "She said she feels terrible and she's sorry for all you had to go through. I'm not sure why she told me. She feels terrible about all the abuse. She said a lot more, but I don't want you to relive those things again. We're going through enough right now." *Again?* I live with those things every day as if they happened yesterday. And they've taken up space in my adult life and shaped me into a person I very much don't like. "I told her she should tell you," he said. As tears pricked my eyes and a constricting feeling of panic and anger erupted throughout my body. It's as if I was outside of myself, outside of time, trying to comprehend the words relayed to me. Anger took front and center as I asked curtly, "why would she tell *you* and not *me?*" Did she think I'd let him in to every dark moment of my past? At the least of what she knew. Not the dark collateral mess of a past she knows nothing of, not even aware of the destruction of her decisions that caused it. "I'm not sure, I wasn't even sure how to respond to her when she was talking. Her apology to me doesn't convey into an apology to you, and you deserve that more than anyone else." Cliff gently replied. I was seething with anger. A rage that tingled my entire being wanting to storm into the house, state my grievances and search for answers! But my legs felt like cement, and I was affixed to the ground with a darkening sky as the sun set in the distance. And that's how I felt, just an inevitable darkness that came with a past I have tried to bury so deep that it would never haunt me again. I couldn't have been more wrong.

Chapter Thirty-One

We left with much happier kids than when we arrived in Nowhere, Texas, as I'll always refer to it in my mind, that nameless speck on the Texas map. Everyone said their goodbyes and prayers for safe travels. We pulled away knowing that would be a place I'd never come back to; I don't know how I knew, but I knew. We headed towards home, but first, making the pit stop for my baptism. I had been communicating with the women in my group up to my arrival. As they awaited my next step in faith with great anticipation, although I felt like I lacked everything except that. We stopped at a hotel close to the church because I needed to be there around 1 p.m. the next day. It was no small feat to get a family that had traveled halfway across the country, and they needed rest. I was still reeling from my mom's bombshell: she acknowledged my traumatic abusive past and spoke of it, but just *not to me*. I was still trying to process that and where the heck we were going to live when we got back. All while putting on a brave smiling face for everyone, again. We arrived at the church, not your typical white steeple church, but a building that resembled some sort of resort. We sat in the parking spot for a minute as this was a bit intimidating. I had to collect myself before I entered those large silver doors not knowing what was behind them or who would greet me. Dee texted me to ask if I had arrived yet, showing concern for the drive we had endured and ensuring our safety. I replied to her, yes, we just arrived and were heading in. I touched up my makeup as best I could in the heat that didn't seem to leave this part of the country. As I walked towards the doors, feeling like Dorothy when she traveled so far and finally arrived in Oz, not knowing what to do. I pulled open the doors and there was a gathering of people who were awaiting my arrival. My eyes locked in on one, Celeste. She walked towards me as I rushed to meet her. As we embraced with a hug, knowing she had been sent to save my life that dark junk drawer afternoon. We cried tears of joy as she hugged my family, and I saw others whom I'd only seen through a screen. Dee, Pam, and the other ladies in the group were all there for me! They flew in from all over the country to celebrate my new life I was embarking on. Hugs and tears flowed as my heart swelled with gratitude. The online pastors were there to also greet me. They asked me if I'd be willing to take some photos and talk about how my encounter altered my life. I was in a slurry of emotions, so I agreed with the contingency that my family stayed close. They asked me a few questions in front of a camera, took a few photos, then escorted me and my family outside for some shots. I wasn't sure what was garnering the attention in that moment, but it felt a little surreal. All because I said I was going to take my life and a phone call shifted that. I overthink everything so this must be one of those times, but I let it pass and joined the others. Baptisms weren't until after the 5 p.m. service, so we had a few hours. And Dee then suggested we get lunch at a local pizza place since it was a large group. I gulped internally realizing we had no money for a restaurant; we barely had enough for the journey home. We tried to pass, but she was insistent. The kids were beaming with joy. Slices of pizza made their way around the table as they eagerly reached for seconds, cheese stretching between their fingers and tomato sauce dotting the corners of their smiles. But Cliff and I kept it minimal. We talked with the people who joined us: some volunteers, some staff, the women from the group, and their partners. Celeste and I chatted as she asked me if I'd heard from the realtor on the house. I hesitated, then said I did hear from her, and the guy agreed to rent to us. But we needed to meet the criteria and pay a deposit and the first month's rent. And, since we didn't have that, it seemed we would have to use Cliff's parents' house as a base until we saved up from Cliff's new job. By that time, the house might not even be available. She was always very good at telling me if it was "God's will" that He would make a way. I agreed and finished the crust of my pizza, reveling in a slew of thoughts I had tried to put aside but somehow kept creeping back in. What were we going to do? Where were we going to live? Would the kids be able to go back to the schools they loved? The server came over with the check, and I quickly came out of my haze to see how much we were going to have to pay. But Dee put a card in and handed it back immediately. I let out a huge audible sigh. She said, "I asked *you* to lunch," then winked as if to know I was in my head trying to calm my spirit. Now back at the church, since we were guests, we had assigned seats in the auditorium. I'd seen it on TV but somehow in person it looked like a stage and not a pulpit for any sermons. As the "experience" started, I was in awe of not how loud it was but how I felt in that moment. I was overcome with emotion and looked at the people who surrounded me wondering how I could have ever thought to leave them. I'd never see this moment and I had no idea how the trajectory of my life was about to change. As the worship team played, I got an alert on my phone that money was deposited into my bank account by Celeste. I looked at her, my mouth gaping. She just smiled and grabbed my hand in hers. The sermon started and even though I remember the title I don't remember much of it. Not only was I about to be baptized, but someone who barely knew me was depositing money into my bank account. As the sermon ended and we headed to our tents and tanks, my phone buzzed again. More money had been deposited into my bank account. I looked to Celeste, and I embraced her fully, she said to me over the rumbles of voices leaving the auditorium, "now you have the money for the house!" She left me speechless as she laughed, put her arm around me, and led me outside. When we reached the outside area where the baptisms were being held, the coordinator was spewing off instructions and handing out drawstring bags that held T-shirts, shorts, towels, and some basic post-hygiene items. I approached the woman handing out the bags. She asked my size, not knowing who I was at first. But I knew exactly who she was. I answered, "Medium please." She looked up and met my eyes, knowing the last time she spoke about me, she wanted to 'just put me in a shelter.' She realized in no time who I was and rattled off some nonsense about how happy she was to see me, and she was glad I was there. Some Christians give the rest of us a bad rap because she was as fake to me as the highlights that were in her hair. Celeste also grabbed a bag, and I looked at her puzzled. She said, "Surprise! Did you think I'd let you do this alone?" In that moment, my heart felt like a glass overfilled decades of hurt and hope suddenly colliding with this unexpected kindness, making my chest ache in a way that felt both painful and cleansing. I became convinced that God assigned her to me to ensure I left behind every buried thing and every gravesite in that water. They had makeshift dressing areas with some pipe and drape as we changed and headed to our assigned tank. There were a lot of people as it was a weekend baptism offering, so there were three tents to hold the various people. They all wore the same shirts, all looking for where they should go to find the redemption they desperately were seeking. The day was shifting rapidly into night as the smell of chlorine wafted in the air as we entered the oversized outside tent. There was a line and the sounds of conversations and cheer swirled around me as if I was standing in the middle of a place I did not belong. As we approached the tank, my heart quickened and became a rapid pounding in my ears, trying to give myself every reason to back out. But the weight of shame and pain I felt weighed me firmly to the ground. I tried to clap and show my support to the other people who went before me, but my brain wouldn't allow me to be in this moment, for them, or for myself. Celeste was in front of me, and she was next grabbing my hand pulling me along, yanking me out of the daze I was in. When suddenly everything became so very loud. I heard music and cheering from families. Then, I heard splashing water as people exited the tank. I watched with adoration as Celeste so bravely walked on the platform down the few stairs into the tank. The pastor who was conducting the ceremony was one I was familiar with; he was one of the people who met us upon our arrival. I watched as he prayed for her and baptized her as she came up out of the water and hugged him and exited. But not towards the outside as the ushers were guiding everyone, paying no mind to them. Soaking wet, she moved to the side of the tank waiting for me to step in, to witness what I had promised her I'd do. Live. I stepped on the platform as so many had done before me, but from this vantage point, I could see my family, people who cared if I lived or died. People I didn't even know applauding me. Then I noticed how many people were surrounding this tank that were not there before. Men and women of all ages…or were they always there and I was too caught up in my fear to notice? But all of them provided an encouraging look or smile almost knowing I needed to muster up every ounce of courage I had to do this. I took a deep breath and entered the tank. The water was only waist high, but it was warm, and the smell of chlorine was now thicker than it had been earlier. The pastor's hand settled on my right shoulder while Celeste's found my left, their prayers washing over me like the water I stood in. I held my head in what seemed like prayer, but I felt held down by shame and humiliation. I looked up and tears flooded my eyes as if to release what felt like toxins trying to escape my innermost self. I heard the people quiet down into a whisper as the pastor grabbed a clean white washcloth that he would use to cover my nose with. I felt the panic erupting. What was I *doing*?! How was *this* supposed to help me? A million thoughts flooded my mind, but before I had a chance to circumvent them, he held my back and told me to hold his arm. He blessed me in the name of the Father, the Son, and the Holy Spirit and pushed me backwards until I was under the water. I heard nothing but silence except for a rushing gurgling sound in my ears. Maybe this was it; maybe this is how I go. I drown in the baptism tank, how fitting. He lifted me up, and I took a long, gasping breath as if I had been held underwater for what felt like hours. Then I heard cheers erupt as I regained my bearings. I instinctively lifted my arms up in victory with my eyes still closed as if I had won a battle against myself. The self that I left behind to drown in the very water I stepped out of. Unsure how to feel, except heavy in my wet clothes, I managed to pose for pictures with strangers whose faces blurred together, their arms around my shoulders as if we'd shared something profound. But lingering made me anxious, and I needed an escape route to collect myself. I changed in the makeshift dressing rooms back to my regular clothes and saw the sun starting to find its setting place. We had a long drive ahead of us, and we needed to get going. Everyone was staying in town, so they all made plans to go out to dinner and celebrate. So, we said our goodbyes and got a few more prayers for safe travels and for my "new life in Christ." Dee gave me a card with some cash for gas, hugged me, and whispered in my ear how proud she was of me. My hardest goodbye was to Celeste. I found out she lived only a few hours away. The church preferred to keep volunteers' contact information private for security reasons, which is why I never knew how close she was in proximity to me. And come to find out, she lived in the same state as me, which was no coincidence. I told her I'd keep in touch along the way, and I thanked her again for her generous gift; she hugged me and said it was not from her but from God. I understood what she meant, but it was still more than generous. We all got back into the car, waved to those still close by, and drove away as if the day was a book that opened and closed in less than six hours. I didn't *feel* any different, but Cliff said he was so happy I followed through and told me I was the strongest person he knew. I gave a half smile, knowing that I didn't feel any stronger. That's the thing about endorphins and dopamine. They are short-lived in your body, and even though I felt that coming out of that water, I could conquer anything. But I was nothing but a scared, anxious little girl inside who felt disassociated from what had occurred. And nothing but apprehensive about what was to come. But I gave my life to Jesus and proclaimed my faith in front of everyone to see. Then why did I feel so awful?

Chapter Thirty-Two

After what felt like a never-ending car ride, we finally arrived back in New Jersey at my sister-in-law's Denise's house. But as far as I was concerned, it was and will always be their parent's house. I had replayed the last few months in my mind and tried to remind myself that I was now a "new creation". Whatever creation I was, every fiber of my being rebelled against staying at my sister-in-law's house. We'd already imposed on my mother, and now here we were again, dependent on family charity while I forced a brave face for my children who somehow still believed everything would work out. We weren't waiting for a house to be built or having renovations done; we were, in fact, homeless. I was grateful, don't get me wrong, but I was now a 41-year-old woman who had lived a life filled with abuse, trauma, and discord. So why would a God that supposedly loved me allow this to happen? I felt like I kept asking myself this same question over and over and not getting any answers. I just braced myself for whatever tsunami of misfortune was already forming on the horizon. Everyone exited the truck excited to be back, and I sat there looking at the house while a fire stirred inside of me. I was slowly burning from the inside out. I knew I had to eventually go in or Cliff would soon come looking for me. But I was frozen in place, my heart pounding as I could hear the swooshing of my pulse in my ears. My breathing shallowed. Panic. I contended with it, tried to will it away. But I couldn't stop the onslaught of emotions that were preparing to erupt like a volcano. I saw Cliff walking toward the car, looking for me as I predicted. I moved around, pretending to look for something. I didn't want him to see I was in a full-on panic attack, *again*. Why was he with a mess of a person like me anyway? I came with an eighteen-wheeler full of baggage that followed us everywhere we went. I didn't feel worthy of a man like him and I sure didn't feel worthy of his unconditional love that he so willingly gave. In fact, I felt unworthy of anything at all. He opened the door and asked me if I was coming in. The fire that was burning inside of me was now an inferno as I replied, "No! I don't want to be here! Leave me alone!" I might as well have been shooting flames from my mouth like a dragon I was so angry. But this wasn't me talking. It was the panic and the emotions I hadn't had a chance to let process because another decision was made on my behalf that I had no say in. The emotions I had kept so tightly wound inside of me for everyone else's sake had reached a level of rage and ferocity that I feared anyone who crossed my path, but mostly my own. My breath still shallow and the sting of tears in my eyes and the shame that gripped me like a vice. I took a breath and walked courageously into the house. I smiled and thanked Denise for letting us stay there, all while my jaw ached from clenching, my shoulders hunched toward my ears as I tried to make myself smaller in someone else's space. Every "thank you" tasted like copper pennies in my mouth. The kids were all reunited with their cousins, and that occupied them for a short while. Cliff's new job started the following day, so I knew that meant he'd be taking the truck. This meant that I and our four kids would be left in the house all day long. There was no Wi-Fi, no TV, and no form of mindless entertainment to at least occupy the time. At least they had phones and tablets, and I could hook them up to my phone as a hotspot. We made the best of it, but inside I was sinking back into the dark realms that had consumed me so many times before. But what truly pushed me to my breaking point was watching my kids sleep on couches and fold-out chairs, while feeling both crushing guilt for putting them there and shameful relief that at least they had somewhere, anywhere, to lay their heads. Each night I'd tuck them in, whispering reassurances I half-believed myself, torn between gratitude for the roof and resentment at our circumstances. I hadn't heard anything on the house we intended to rent so yes, again, we were homeless, and Cliff hadn't seen even his first paycheck yet. Over the past six months, I applied for hundreds of jobs, only to receive a generic reply of "Thanks, but no thanks". The kids became anxious and questioned me more on when we were leaving. I never imagined that continuously facing opposition would be the response to giving up everything to follow Jesus. "Have faith. Stay in the Word. God will show you how. It's His timing." All the phrases said to me meant nothing. I fought demons in my own personal hell each day, as I'd been doing since I was old enough to remember. I was to have faith in something I couldn't use my senses to comprehend. And that warped my very logical mind as something I committed to do. I was even given a Bible at my baptism, but I didn't know what any of it meant. I felt not only dejected, rejected, but very, very alone. My kids were looking forward to going back to their usual schools, seeing their friends, and we were in late August now. And I had no idea what we were going to do. I was used to putting all the pieces together, doing all the hard work to make all things go, and nothing I did made anything move or go. Sometimes you can do everything in your own strength you know how to do but be met with defeat each time. But it's strange to me that no matter how hard we try, one text message, a phone call, an email, or a conversation can change the complete course of your life. The realtor who was going to do her best to negotiate with the guy who couldn't sell the house and rent it instead? I thought that was a lost cause as weeks had passed with no contact from her. Well, when she called me and said, "The house is still on the market, and he's agreed to rent it, but you must view it first. And now that you're back in town, when can you come look at it?" Panic and excitement commingled in my mind as I tried to wrap my head around what she was saying. The next day was Saturday, so I agreed to meet her at the property at 10am. I kept the news to myself since Cliff was still at work. The new position was demanding so much of him already. He was commuting to and from Trenton which was an hour each way and he was not even coming home to a place of his own. Instead, he returned to a home filled with both good and bad memories. When he got in, I told him the news and we agreed to keep it discreet as to not get the kids' hopes up, especially the older girls. The house was completely redone, and it was perfect for us. The attic had been made into livable space and covered the length of the whole house; it was perfect for Cecelia and Ava. I could already see us there, but I didn't want to get my hopes up until I knew what the qualifications were. She said, "a credit report and they want to meet you". Cliff and I left, and there was an eerie silence between us driving back to his sister's. Our credit has taken a hit since we initially lost our jobs, so we couldn't look good on paper. We hadn't touched the money Celeste graciously gave to us, so we knew we had that to move in. There was no way we could pull this off on our own as we had just had the worst year of our lives happen in mass proportions. If this was going to work, it was going to take a miracle of equal proportions. I pulled our credit, and to my surprise, it wasn't as awful as I'd anticipated. It wasn't great, but I sent the pages that *mattered*, considering I *did* pay for it, and sent that to the realtor, whom I assumed would pass it on. We were meeting with the owners in 2 days, and we were already past our welcome point, again at my sister-in-law's. This wasn't my first "interview" with a landlord, so I knew the drill, but my gut felt more of a desperation than it had in previous times. The house was built by a friendly middle-aged couple for their daughter, who is a medical student, as they shared during the conversation. But she decided to do her residency in New York, so they were stuck with a home no one wanted. God works in mysterious ways because we weren't *no one*. We briefly explained the situation, leaving out the gory details. We told them Cliff had a stable job with the state and we had the cash for the security and first month's rent, (thanks to a woman who barely knew me but saved me from un-aliving myself). After a beat, or what seemed like many later, they agreed to rent and said if we wanted the place, it was ours. I could hardly contain my internal shock! He said he'd have the realtor write up the lease and it would start September 1st.... wait, that's only a few days from now. The only caveat is no inspection on the property, which is standard on all houses in Jersey. But I didn't care why, and I hastily agreed as school started in a week, and I needed to prove we lived there. The kids would be ecstatic; I was sure of it. We met at the property to sign the lease a few days later, and we were handed the keys. I thanked them, and they went on their way telling us to enjoy 'our new home'. I had no idea what weight that statement would hold years later. We brought the kids over and they ran and claimed their rooms, excited to be somewhere other than anyone else's house. But Cliff and I still needed to get all the things from storage and make this place a home quick, fast, and in a hurry. We may not see eye to eye all the time, but we were a good team when times called for it, and this was one of those times. We arrived at the storage unit and as soon as we were loading the last haul of our things into the truck, I spotted a giant rainbow in the distance. Not a half bow of a rainbow but the entire thing! It had rained earlier, but I was so focused on everything else that I missed even the weather around me. But I had to believe that it was directed at us, or me, letting me know God had it all worked out. Did I enjoy the 11:59:59 time marker? Absolutely not. But it seemed to be the way things had been playing out in our lives now. We finally moved everything in, and I wanted nothing more than to take a breath. The problem was, we threw out all the beds as the storage unit couldn't hold them, so all we had were air mattresses. It didn't matter; we had our own house, which meant I could no longer say we were "homeless". I told my mom the news despite the still distress I felt with her, merely to let her know we found a house to rent, and the kids were okay. She asked if we got everything out of storage and if the kids had their things all together and settled. I winced at the shame I felt yet again while I talked to her. I explained that we couldn't salvage everything, so we left the beds behind, but we had air mattresses and would be fine. She battled and protested and asked me why I'd do that and so on. This is why I tell her nothing as it's always met with contention. And I had no energy for explanations to anyone, so I ended the call. I had way too much to do to make this house a home. But within days, my mom's partner rented a U-Haul and drove all the way from Nowhere, Texas. And my mom, driving behind him, pulled into the driveway. They brought all the beds they bought for the kids, nightstands, bedding, and all. Then my mom took us to a big box store and filled our fridge, freezer, cleaning supplies, and of course all the snacks the kids could ask for. They stayed for a few days in a local hotel, but he had to get back for work. So, we said our goodbyes, but she no sooner handed me half of next month's rent. She said, "God always provides." I was speechless, which wasn't a part of my being, so I hugged her and thanked her for all she did for us. Holding back my inevitable ocean of tears, they left, and I sat on the couch stunned, as if I had entered a different dimension. Glimpses and flashbacks of all that had happened since I professed my faith to a Jesus I couldn't see or hear just months earlier ran through my mind. I like to think He was so proud of me that all the events up to this point were like looking at a masterpiece of art or music that He was finally able to watch come to life. I fell to my knees and cried. This was a guttural cry from the depths of my soul that was awaiting release. I thanked him; a man I couldn't see, or touch, but I could feel His presence as if He were in that very room with me. A million broken pieces I left on that floor and told Him I could no longer see a way to put them back together. The thing about giving your brokenness to Him... He takes those broken pieces and turns them into a beautiful piece of mosaic art that only He can create.

Chapter Thirty- Three

The kids were able to start school again without missing a beat. A different house on the other side of town, but for everyone, but this place was still home. The bus came for Olivia, and Cecelia's friend took her and Ava to school. Xavier was too young to go to school, so he was home with me. The me that was both grateful and resentful that I didn't have a job, and now Cliff had to get another one just so we could make ends meet. We'd been homeless just a few months prior; I should be nothing *but* thankful, and I was. But I never saw my husband since he worked all week and now all weekend, and I was handling everything alone. We were both drowning in fatigue that seemed to seep into our bones. But while his eyes were tired, mine flickered between gratitude and resentment. One moment softening at his sacrifice, the next hardening with the shame of my own uselessness. I had worked since I was 15 years old, and I had no idea what to do with the amount of rejection I was receiving daily. I craved simple human interaction, not a child's demand for something; and then hated myself for even thinking that, for resenting these innocent little beings who needed me, who were the only reason I got out of bed most mornings. I also longed for someone to see me. Not just as a mother or caretaker, but as the woman beneath the exhaustion, with desires and needs of her own. As I watched myself spiral yet again into the darkness, part of me fought against it while another part welcomed its familiar embrace, leaving me suspended between desperate clawing toward light and the perverse comfort of surrendering to the void I'd known for so long. Xavier and I would wait for Olivia each day on our front step as she got off the bus. It came right to our door as we were now directly on a main road. It was so loud. Ambulances streaked by, wailing their sirens as police cars followed. Why didn't I notice this traffic and noise before? They were so excited to see each other that I didn't need to entertain them for the rest of the day. I just had to grab a snack or two as they were fast in the world of being best friends. They'd endured so much in their short little lives and had no idea of the impact of it all. They believed in us as parents and trusted us unconditionally. The faith of a child is so pure I am almost jealous. I never had the chance to experience that, or for that matter, never really experienced being a child in its truest sense of the word. I'd spent the afternoons scouring the internet job boards like it *was* my job. I was desperate to find something that would take me out of my racing thoughts that I battled each day. Each day started and ended the same. Cliff left for work; I handled all the kids and all that came with teenagers, down to toddlers. Although we lived through a very hard season, on the surface we seemed like we'd turned it around. Except we were having two very different experiences. I felt like an anchor was weighing me down further underwater until I could barely keep my head above it. I didn't know where God was that showed His power and grace towards us as He seemed elusive now. And I didn't know if that was all part of some bigger plan, but if it was, it didn't mean I had to like it. The holidays were approaching, and we barely had money for food, let alone find a way to have Thanksgiving dinner and Christmas gifts. The schools were good about knowing which kids were receiving free or reduced lunch because as if I didn't already feel enough shame in that; they offered via email to me a Thanksgiving meal kit. Fully stocked with a turkey and all the trimmings, even dessert. I had sunk further down the well of shame as I stared at the email on my screen. Letting the tears pass down my face when I closed my eyes, hoping this was all a bad dream. I responded "yes" to the form that was attached and hit send, my chest aching. I promised myself I'd be the parent I never had, and I'd never let my children suffer in a way I did. But I was failing and failing fast. I swallowed every ounce of pride and made my way to the school at the scheduled time, with a two-year-old Xavier in tow. I walked as if I had a shred of dignity left, took a deep breath, and buzzed the doorbell to request access to the school. No reason for request by the speaker before me. I was let in and met with a smile by the young sweet guidance counselor otherwise known as Miss Bee who immediately bent down to talk to Xavier. She said she'd heard everything about him from Olivia and that he's her best friend. He beamed with pride looking around as if she'd suddenly appear. The form asked how many were in my family. A regular dinner for 6 was too much, let alone a holiday one. The food is donated by anyone at the school who wants to take part in helping needy families for the holiday. They went all out on donations and there was plenty of it, but I wanted to feel anything but "needy". Reusable bags were lined up filled to the top with canned goods, stuffing mix, cranberry sauce, gravy, cornbread, and even aluminum pans were accessible if needed. Turkeys laid out from large to small, and pies ranging from apple to pumpkin in all sizes. Miss Bee was in tune to human psychology being a counselor so she could see I was visibly trying to hold back tears as they pricked my eyes waiting to erupt. She grabbed a giant turkey, moved several bags of food and two pies to the side of the table. I looked around as she moved. I thought maybe our name would be on a bag. But she placed her arm on my shoulder and said, "You're ready to go. Can I help take it to your car?" I looked at her with a puzzled brow. The food she'd been moving around was for us. All of it. It took me a beat before I responded, "sure, that would be great!" seemingly unsure of why we'd been given so much un-judgmental generosity. Miss Bee helped me bring and stack everything neatly into my trunk, and as I closed the door after putting Xavier in his car seat. Then let out a sigh of relief as if were exiting from a deep place in my chest. Without a word, Miss Bee embraced me in a hug and whispered, "enjoy Thanksgiving with those amazing little people we all love so much." I thanked her, and she waved as she went back into the school to greet the other families coming in. Before the encampment of tears that I was holding back with the force of an army for so long, I drove toward home so I could allow them to finally be free and escape their captivity. I pulled into the driveway and attempted to keep my emotions locked up a little longer, but there was no more holding them in. I sat in the car and cried. I didn't just cry; I sobbed. Unshed tears that have been bottled up for years were coming to the surface, fighting to claim their way out. I placed my head on the steering wheel, watching the water fall from my eyes in rapid succession. The God I had been crying out to, that I couldn't see...saw me. He was providing for our family, and I was grateful. But years of shame and unspoken sheer survival were like streams of acid that flowed through my body and came out in a waterfall of tears. I had a trunk full of food, a home to live in, a beautiful family, but just a few months back, I was homeless and about to take my life, again. I didn't understand how a loving, good God could allow not just the recent past, but all I had endured up to now. Grateful but angry. Happy but sad. Understanding but confused. Surrounded but lonely. I was conflicted in every way there was. My tears slowed as if to tell me even they were tired of being sad tears and wished they could change to tears of joy occasionally. Me too. So much so.

Thanksgiving came and went in what felt like the blink of an eye. The hours of preparation that went into this meal, only to have everyone ravenously eat in fifteen minutes flat. Clean-up was if not just as long as the preparation, but we'd have enough leftovers for days, so for that I was thankful. But, like clockwork, the moment was stolen. I couldn't enjoy my family's togetherness. I kept worrying about how we would have Christmas. I still wasn't working; Cliff was still working two jobs and that was barely enough. You'd think up to this point I wouldn't worry as we had just eaten an entire free Thanksgiving meal! But the last time I checked, there was no mention of a man in a red suit with a white beard leaving free presents for all the kids. I have always done what I needed to do, even working many jobs at one time to make ends meet in another life.... but I couldn't even get *one* now. It's astonishing to me how one good moment is stolen by a slurry of negative thoughts that haven't even happened nor can you control the outcomes. But, when you're a product of abuse and survival, that's how you cope. At least that's how I did. I didn't allow myself to feel any happiness as I was constantly waiting for that other proverbial shoe to drop at any given moment. I prepared for the worst-case scenarios, so I never had to be disappointed. And went over every contingency plan until I had the entire alphabet covered.

Chapter Thirty-Four

I kept in touch with Dee, Pam, and of course Celeste about our life. They were all so happy we were finally settled in a home. They had prayed for a miracle, just as I had so many times before. I told them reluctantly that I was still looking for a job but met still with rejection. I have heard it said, "rejection is redirection," perhaps, but it still doesn't take the bite or sting out of it. It would be nice if you reached a certain quota of rejections, you automatically got your redirection email showing you exactly what to do. I went through the motions each day of applying for jobs like it was *still* my job, but I wasn't giving up. I haven't given in up to this point and I sure wasn't starting now.

Christmas was looming on top of the existing stress I was carrying. Cliff and I could barely make ends meet, and I didn't have anyone who could be the stand-in for the man in the red suit so my kids weren't disappointed when they woke that day. Or so I thought. Dee had contacted me and asked me to ask what the kids wanted for Christmas, and I thought she was just making conversation, but she then asked if she and her husband could "adopt" my family for the holidays. "Adopt my family for the holidays?" I repeated back to her as a question. She explained that since they don't have any children of their own, they adopt a family each year that is facing difficulties and get all the gifts for the kids, so the parents don't need to carry the burden of that. They only needed us to hand her over a list for the kids. I sat on the other end of the phone in silence as that burn in my eyes I've felt so often lately arose. She said, "please email me the lists for all the kids; we'll make sure they have a great Christmas." I was still silent, now just the muffled sounds of faint sniffles trying to fight the lump in my throat from escaping into a full sob. I just replied, "OK. Thank you so very much." We hung up, and I sat on the couch almost in a fog of disbelief. I was grateful but ashamed all at the same time. It felt like a never-ending year of people having to bail us out, and I was sick of it. Whatever this plan was that God had for me was working on me from the inside out, but I didn't like it one bit. Various packages started arriving from all different carriers at least every day. Come to find out once Celeste found out about Dee's "adopt a family" and it happened to be mine, she wanted in. Dee said she got most of the big asks, so she went to work on the rest. I wasn't told this until after all was ordered and shipped that they were both the secret Santa's this year for us. I was overwhelmed at the generosity as this woman just gave me money to get into this house and she's still giving. I haven't seen many angels in my lifetime; Gram and Aunt Gio were real-life angels for me in my life. But Celeste was one that I know God only gave me for a season, but then she'd move on and find her next assignment. I know this because that's exactly what happened. After unpacking all the delivery boxes that each contained a generosity that I still to this day cannot put into words, we wrapped everything and distributed the gifts in separate areas near and under the tree. It was an old fake tree, but somehow, we made it work with random ornaments we accumulated over the years. Including the red ones from Gram's white tree that stood so tall in place of the lamp all those years ago. Except this year they had a little extra something to them, a bit more wear, felt a bit more fragile, but still shined in the light. That's how I felt. Worn, tattered, fragile, but the only thing I was missing was the light.

Christmas morning came, and the kids were elated as they tore the wrapping paper and threw it aside, as they ripped into the next one. This year, we could only fill their stockings. But God ensured the kids felt pure joy all day. He sends Himself through people, and for this occasion, He chose Dee and Celeste to do that. I sat back, taking in the joy on my children's faces as they proudly displayed each treasure that had appeared as if by magic under our tree. Cliff helped by unpacking the dolls and putting batteries in the toys that needed a boost to help them go. I cooked Gram's traditional Italian Christmas dinner. It was a big pot of gravy, meatballs, and sausage, plus trays of baked manicotti (if you're Italian American, you know to properly pronounce this dish!). All were homemade from scratch. Even the shells and ricotta cheese filling. It took hours, but the house smelled delicious, and everyone ate until they were stuffed. And there were plenty of leftovers to be had. I'd like to think she'd be proud as I've kept her alive in the meals, she made for me and the hours she spent in the kitchen. Now, her legacy lives on through my hands as I create these moments for my children. As the day wound down and things were cleaned up, everyone was in the living room watching TV as the kids were playing with their new toys. As I stood there observing them, I almost felt like I was standing outside of myself looking at me and all the people around me. And the thought occurred to me: how do you go through fire after fire and not come out smelling like smoke? Because not one of these people, including myself, had an ounce of soot on them.

The holidays came and went, and I was thankful a new year was now upon us. Maybe this was a year of new beginnings and rebuilding for not just our family but for me too. But there was still this looming fact I still didn't have a job. But as I worked my job of looking *for* a job, the phone rang. Bill collectors were coming at us like we stole something, and most of them I didn't answer. I could do nothing to ease their accounting reconciliation until I had the money to do so. As a result, I normally let the calls go to voicemail. But this call felt different. It was from a local number, and it just said Mountain Hills on the caller ID. I don't think collection agencies are in the business of naming their companies after something that sounds lovely. So... I answered. "Hello?" The voice on the other line was a woman with a kind voice. When I asked her what she was calling about, she replied, "I'm calling about the job you applied for and wanted to see if you would be able to come in for an interview this week." The job I applied for? I have applied for so many jobs I couldn't remember them all, even if I had tallied them into a spreadsheet. I felt a surge of excitement at getting a call, but my mind was racing, desperately trying to place which "Mountain Hills" this could possibly be among the hundreds of applications I'd sent out. So, I waited for a beat to respond acting nonchalantly, "sure, thanks for calling—what time did you have available?" as if I had *so* many other offers lined up. What I assume is an HR person on the other line said the hiring manager is only available after 5 p.m. and could I do a 5:30 p.m. that week. I'm not able to turn *any* job down right now so I agree and decide I'll figure out the logistics later. She said she'd send me an email confirming all the details and I thanked her for her time and hung up. Staring back at my computer screen filled with various job boards, I pause and think it's probably prudent to look up Mountain Hills and their open positions, hoping it would ring a bell. Maybe I can cross-reference in my email when I apparently applied for a job there. I open their webpage to be met with what looks like a grand hotel based on the photos. Chandeliers, marble floors, various areas of space, even a pool table, a library, and a movie theater. A movie theater?? I go on to read, *"At Mountain Hills, we are an Independent Living, Assisted Living, Memory Care, and Enhanced Care Services. With spacious one-and two-bedroom apartments, exceptional care, resort-like amenities, and engaging programs, we offer just the right blend of personal attention and assistance. Discover a world where luxury meets comfort at Mountain Hills, your loved one's sanctuary of peace and elegance."* Assisted Living. Interesting. I go to their job board and peruse the various openings until one catches my eye. Community Relations Counselor. I open my email and search for that. Bingo! *"Thank you for applying for the Community Relations Counselor at Mountain Hills. If your skills match the job requirements, we will be in touch. Thank you for considering Mountain Hills!"* So generic, it's probably why I didn't think anything of it as I didn't hear anything back, so I assumed it was in the rejection pile. I applied for this job well over a month ago, and it totally makes sense now why I'd have considered that. I read the job description. It was about helping elderly people who lived in this place.

Those with memory issues, and families adjusting to caring for their loved ones. Wait, I have *all* that experience. I see a flash of my Gram's face in my mind and recall each of these moments I did exactly those things with and for her. What I thought was scary and awful and hard, God was training me to not just help one person like this but potentially many! I went in for the interview and was offered the job on the spot given my history and real-life experience in those areas. Not only did I need a job, but I loved people, specifically elderly people. They are full of wisdom and stories you can get lost in. It would take a few weeks to run your typical background checks and get the onboarding details out of the way, but I was given an official start date for orientation. And all I could think was how excited and terrified I was at the same time. I was getting tired of these conflicting feelings. But I had to chalk it up to the past year we endured and just needing to find my footing again. I needed stability, an income, and to feel purposeful, plus this meant Cliff could quit his weekend job, *finally*. So, after all the logistics of our life's ecosystem were finalized, the day came that I'd been waiting for. Cliff gave me his standard "you've got this and do your thing" pep talk, but this time I needed more than a pep talk. I pulled into the parking lot and holy smokes; this did resemble a full-on resort. It really looked like a luxury hotel. I sat there in my car for a few minutes pretending my makeup needed touching up, only to look at myself in the mirror to see a woman. But the reflection looking back at me was not of a woman. It was a scared young girl who was about to see her beloved Gram in all the faces she was about to encounter. I took a deep breath, smoothed my dress, and walked in with the confidence of a lion, but the timidness of a lamb. I approached reception, told them who I was here to see, and they told me to have a seat. There were all kinds of people milling about the lobby, some cleaning, some residents who passed by and waved. And a woman who sat in the chair next to the one I was ushered to. She immediately smiled and introduced herself as Jess. She was taller than me, had a sweet smile, a kind spirit, and was *so* friendly. She was asking me if it was my first day too, giving off sort of golden retriever vibes. I reciprocated with an introduction and said it was, and I was pleased to meet her. She asked what I'd be doing, and I told her, and she was stunned because she said excitedly, "that means we will be working together, yay!" as she lifted her hands in the air slightly as if in a cheer. I didn't know her, well, at all, but something told me she and I would be fast friends. We attended the required orientations by various staff and HR on conduct, and so on. As we listened and took the handouts provided, we started to have a little fun as the day went on, as we started asking the questions. "Why do you like working here?" "What about this job keeps you going?" "What keeps you up at night about it?" Jess and I took turns coming into a tidal wave of synchronicity as if we were performing in the Olympics. Eventually we high-fived when someone finally left us alone. She said, "I knew I liked you," and I simply responded, "nothing but a great team already." We were shown our office, and by office, I mean two desks facing each other with fluorescent lights above. The shelves were full of cookies, tea, coffee, weird candies, gift bags, and who knows what else. It looked like TJ Maxx or Marshall's had thrown up on it. The next-door office was a woman who was older than both of us, and she introduced herself as Hope. We eventually learned that Hope was never at her desk, or in the building for that matter. On the wall hung a giant whiteboard of all the residents and their rooms. I guess in the event we needed to help them, we'd know the floor and where to go. I was totally wrong. This was the death board. This was the resident who was no longer with us, how quickly can we turn that room around for profit. We stared for a few silent breaths looking quizzically at the board. Until our boss, of Indian descent, Amir, greeted us at the doorway of the office smiling. "Are you settling in okay? How about some lunch, we can order in. Indian or Chinese? Or pizza if you want, whatever you'd like, let me know." Dude, take a breath. He left as Jess and I just stared at each other and giggled for the same reason: did we share a brain? Was she my long-lost sister? Over time, we got acclimated, but we were initially sold a bill of goods that we'd be helping people. As loved ones of a potential resident visited several assisted living communities in the area, we tried to convince them that ours was the best. Yet, I was expected to sell those rooms to those who inquired and came to tour the grounds. This didn't feel like selling to me. These people were caring for loved ones at the end of their own ropes at times and needed just that: help. I cared more about people than I did about filling rooms. And it came as naturally for contracts to be signed because I could relate to them, as I had been where they were. You don't need to be a salesperson in this line of work; you need empathy, and I was full to the rim with it. Each potential resident got a small token of thanks for coming to visit. But it was up to you to discover what that little thing would be to push them over, knowing you'd take care of their mom or dad. This was Jess's area of expertise. I'd share notes, and she'd find the perfect gift. We were supposed to take it to their homes, but that was very invasive. So, I'd go and leave it on their porch with my card like an Amazon delivery tailored just for them. This went on for months. We worked with nurses on home visits. They checked if patients could come to our facility or if they needed round-the-clock nursing care. We built relationships with the staff, but also the residents. These were amazing humans. Like Kate, who was a Carnegie Hall violinist, or Sarah, who was a WWII veteran nurse, or my favorite, Mr. Gennaro. The Italian accent was thick and comforting; I never knew my Pop, and I'd like to imagine he'd be very similar. He was such a gentleman, and he loved coming to see us, inviting us to join him for lunch in the attached restaurant. The cost of food was included in their stay, so we'd oblige here and there, letting him take both or just one of us to accompany him for a meal. He had blue eyes that shone tired, like he'd lived a thousand years, and someone dumped him here. But we made it our mission to bring light to not just his but all the residents. They especially got sad on weekends and holidays when family didn't arrive as expected. One man, Mr. Joe, waited all day for his family to pick him up for church on Easter. He refused to leave his perch by the piano looking out the floor-to-ceiling window, for fear he'd miss them. They weren't coming. They never did. Because we had to work alternating weekends, we made sure to distract the residents who were always waiting for someone to come with games or by sitting and listening to them talk about their lives. They just wanted to be heard and seen. I embraced as many as I could with hugs, letting them know I saw them. They all took a liking to me, including the residents who were behind a locked door in the memory care unit. This was hard, so I didn't frequent it often. But some of the people that came in needed to be in there, so it was my job to show them what we offered for their loved ones' care. Miss Doris would be standing perpetually at the door as if to make a run for it, but only wanted to show you her bedazzled hat or new baby doll she got. Different therapies helped the residents there who were stuck in a place they couldn't get out of. Like when they were a mom, allowing them to care for a doll as their "baby." Or a room designed for a person who could sit at a typewriter because they were used to working each day. Even though these events were decades prior. They loved to see me, and I embraced them all as I had everyone else. I told them I'd be back to check in, making sure they were listening to the nurses and eating. I annoyed those nurses initially, but I told them I took care of my Gram who had dementia, so this was not me placating them; I knew exactly how to handle them. They eased up and gave me what I'd like to think was a pass to visit anytime. Each time you'd fill a room, because it was vacant, and by vacant, I mean cause, well...death. Or someone moved to a more skilled nursing facility. But you got a bonus once contracts were signed. And I was making bonuses left and right; this place was full, and everyone seemed happy. Until one day the Volturi themselves made an appearance. I call them that because, if you've seen Twilight, you know the ominous feeling when the Volturi appeared, and you knew something bad was about to happen. And that's exactly what they were. These were top vice presidents or directors or whatever they were called that month, who came around whenever they smelled anything abnormal. Kitchen staff, state reviews, but they never came to our area, ever. Until now. We can hear the clicks of heels on the marble floor getting closer until they reach the areas of offices and stop directly in front of our office door. Now Jess and I have built a great, fun relationship, and we work well together and even listen to the occasional gangster rap playlist. We even got a took an old Tiffany lamp from the storage unit for the desk instead of the overhead fluorescent helicopter lights. This time, we stared at each other in horror. We wondered, almost telepathically, what they wanted with us. Immediately, the helicopter lights were turned on, blinding us both. Here we go…let the "how am I keeping your building full when you couldn't" interrogation begin. Besides being the Volturi, these women were tall, almost statuesque. One blonde, one brunette, and trying to be intimidating. But meh, holding your venti Starbucks pink drink isn't giving me intimidating anything, sure not for me or Jess. They asked how we were liking the job and some other obscure nonsensical questions; lady, get to the point. They implied we were not keeping things generic when dealing with the families and pulled up a list of items we gifted them that weren't on the throw-up shelf that was behind me. I stood. They cocked their heads in question. But I stuck my ground. "Those residents are not treated as your brochures portray. But they do get kindness, a listening ear, and empathy from me, and I will not be challenged if my methods are, in fact, working". Jess sat there speechless. So, I said, "if there is nothing else, Jess and I have a job to do as we are meeting with a family to give them a tour of the community. Hopefully to add to the waiting list that we now have". I turned the helicopter light off on my way out and motioned for Jess to join me. The Volturi were left speechless and in the now dimly lit room, alone. When we returned, they were gone. We told Amir and he was shocked and said it was unacceptable. Yeah, some help you are. I'm giving up weekends with my family, rearranging my whole house's ecosystem, and you say it's unacceptable? A week later, Jess gave in her two-week resignation. "No, you can't let them win, don't you see? That's what they want." She was adamant, said a better gig, more stable, came along with no Vultori in sight. On her last day, we had a party for her with her favorite foods and cake to wish her well. I played the part, but inside I was crushed. I finally had a friend. One who got me, one who was silly and just as weird as I was. The tears I held back eventually released when we were walking back to the office. I stopped to look at her, and we hugged for what seemed like forever.

I opened the office now, only occupying one seat, but I kept the Tiffany light on to remind me of her. I went through the motions and continued to get grilled like a sandwich by the Vultori. I was spent. I loved my job, I loved these residents, but this was bullying and abuse. And I had gone through way too much in my life to get pushed around by Satan dressed up in high heels and a designer pantsuit.

Chapter Thirty-Five

Scrolling mindlessly through social media while I sat in this office alone, I dreaded looking for a new job again. I saw a church in Philly that started to follow me, Faith Church. I'd never heard of them, nor had a church ever followed me. I clicked on their page to find this was not some weird cult but the complete opposite. It showed what looked like a big family of all ages, both old and young. I needed to feel like I had some community since the one I'm working in is anything but. Dee, Celeste, and Pam had all gone about their lives after Christmas, and I hadn't heard much from them, if at all. That's how I knew God was only using them for a season. And what a season it was. I talked to Cliff about visiting this church one day and he was fully on board but said we'd visit first. He didn't want to take the kids to a place that might only be temporary. They'd had enough of that. Service was at 10 am, so after a quick drive over the bridge, we saw their teardrop street signs pointing to the church. I don't see a church; what I see is a well-known comedy club transformed into a makeshift meeting place for people to be with God. Their branding was everywhere. It was on the tent, the pipe and drape, and the signs, except for the bar. That was a dead giveaway we were not in your typical "church."

We were 30 minutes early, but I'd rather be early than late to anything, especially church. We walked up as we were met by a woman, Miss Debbie, who was in her mid-60's and had a smile that could fill your joy cup to the brim. She greeted us with hugs and made us feel welcomed. We told her it was our first time here, and she was elated. Not even thinking she would bring us in and introduce us to as many people as she could, even the pastors who were talking to someone at the time. Everyone was kind, and she showed us where the coffee was and told us to help ourselves. After a few minutes, the pastors came over, and introduced themselves as Elias and Lia. Their enthusiasm and positivity overwhelmed me that I was taken aback. They were both tall, in their mid-thirties, and a husband and wife who only planted the church a mere three months ago. It seemed there were only about 30-40 people there, but it was understandable considering it was new. We told them a bit about ourselves and that we had four kids, but we wanted to check out the church before we brought them too. They were elated to hear this but also had a guilty "you should've brought them" in their pastoral tone. They took us over to the kids' ministry and introduced us to Miss Katt, who too embraced us and said how happy she was to meet us. She said she was a teacher in her real day job, and teaching was her purpose. So, when she heard we had four kids, her eyes lit up wondering where they were. I told her next time, and she just smiled while her attention was diverted to a child pulling out all the toys from the prize box. Elias pointed out two kids, a boy and girl, and said those were their kids and boy did they spit them out. I thanked them for the tour, but they excused themselves to get ready for service. Not before making sure next time, we came we'd go to lunch after church to get to know each other. Food will not make me come back, but I gave the obligatory *"sounds great!"*. We entered the church area which was literally the comedy stage. The same round tables and chairs that were used for every audience while they watched a wannabe rising comic hoping to catch a break. Even the floors had a slight stickiness to them from spilled drinks from the night before. The house lights were low as the stage lights were illuminated brighter. It held a drum kit, guitars, a keyboard, and a few mics just waiting to be played. We took seats at one of the tables in the back as people filed in, whispering greetings and hugs as faint music started to play. The band, or worship team, was made up of a Benetton-worthy group of people who didn't sound all that bad. They did covers of various other groups' songs but nonetheless gave it all they had. Once they were finished, Pastor Elias welcomed us and said the reason we sit at tables and not rows is to build community. Um, it's because it's a comedy club and one floor, and you needed that to accommodate handicapped people. I digress and stop letting my thoughts get the better of me. The sermon was good, and it ended by 11 a.m. After, we exited to the lobby, or rather, the bar, people kindly said they hoped to see us again as we headed towards the door. Pastor Elias made his way to us, shaking Cliff's hand and hugging me. He said hopefully we would see him next week and he couldn't wait to meet our kids. Cliff grabbed my hand and escorted me out the door as I was welcomed with a breath of air I desperately needed. We got into the car, and both just couldn't understand if this was real or fake because we were new. We chatted about this and that on the ride home but decided we would go next week with the kids.

I continued to work for the Vultori while looking for another job anywhere else but here. The stress I was under was palpable. While reviewing my chapters of worst-case scenarios, my phone rang. It was the realtor, Christina, who helped us get into the house late last year. I answered cheerfully, hoping everything was okay and they weren't kicking us out. Because I had a worst-case chapter for that one, and it was ready to go. But no mention of the house was made other than how we were doing and whether everything was going well. I told her I was at work, and I only had a few minutes to chat, so I got to it, asking if everything was okay. She chuckled and said yes, all was fine except she was too busy to handle her business. She wanted someone to do the admin work and schedule house showings for her. She asked if I'd be interested in a full-time job to help her grow her business. I hesitated for a minute thinking...wait, you want me to do what now? She went on to say how much the pay would be, which was "ok" in my opinion, but she sold me with that I could work remotely from home. That meant no more childcare costs, no commute, and no gas. I'd have my freedom and be free of the Vultori for good (or so I thought...). I thanked her and told her I'd talk it over with Cliff and let her know by the following day. It wasn't like I was making any more bonuses as we were totally full; it was just a waiting list. A waiting list of waiting for people to die. I called Christina the next day, accepting her offer. I told her I had to give two weeks' notice, and she understood. I'd start working for her at the end of August 2018. That's a memorable date because what came after that was another path to alter the already shaky trajectory of life we were on. I gave my notice to Amir; can't say he was surprised and asked if there was anything he could do to get me to stay. Only if the Vultori get fired, or somehow spontaneously combust, no, there isn't. He knew what I meant to the residents, and it was breaking my heart to do this to them. Some wouldn't remember me after I visited them, but others came looking for me in my office to see if I was okay. I had copious amounts of grandparents who made sure I was not just okay, but I was eating, and if they could do anything for *me*. What they didn't know is they had no idea how much they already had.

We continued to attend Faith Church and our kids blended into this existing family as if we always were. Our kids were loved, cared for, and taught the Word of God, but in a way they could understand it. Miss Katt made up raps and affirmations, so they knew they were in fact God's perfect creation. The older girls served in various areas, including the kid's ministry and the online platform. Pastor Elias and Lia's kids were the same age as Olivia and Xavier, and we became fast friends and looked forward to Sundays now. Cliff and I built a relationship with the pastors as friends, not just the leaders of the church, and we shared time outside of church, cultivating that bond. We let them in on the things we'd been through, and the look I saw in Elias's eyes when he heard this was the same I had at Christmas time a year before. Wondering how you went through so many fires and not come out smelling like smoke. Mountain Hills will be a place I'll always cherish. And I know God put me there, even for a season. It was to see that, despite all I'd been through, I could help others with immense empathy. He gave me both friends and too many grandmoms and grandpops to count. But the one thing He did was allow me to see a parallel of my Gram in other people. Where in one world she was as big as the sun and coherent, and in another where she didn't know who I was. Each resident was an angel sent by God himself to help me heal from such a brutal season I just passed. I'd have gone directly to my Gram at times like that and sat on her love seat with her telling me 'tomorrow is another day'. But believe me when I say there were many others I sat with who were able to be her stand-in and tell me tomorrow is, in fact, another day.

Chapter Thirty-Six

When living in a constant fight or flight response for what felt like forever, I was finally able to come down slightly. Being able to work at home and be there for the kids again was a huge lift off my weighted shoulders. Christine came over and gave me a crash course on what I was to do and explained what she wanted to have done in the future to help grow her real estate business. This was stuff I knew, as I had worked in this world for so long, so I didn't consider this necessarily difficult to grasp. She gave me a document listing all the websites and credentials, and she'd check in later as she had many showings to tend to. There are only a few weeks left until school starts, and the kids were spun up waiting to get their backpacks and clothes and the like. It was a distraction having them there while I was trying to learn a new job, but I wouldn't have had it any other way. As the house would soon be eerily quiet as Xavier was starting school as well. We would have to make a budgetary change with me starting a new job, but I was now going to be paid weekly. And on any of the homes that were shown and chose Christine to represent them, and they closed on a house, I was given a cut of the commission. It was sort of a bonus, but at least I wasn't waiting for anyone to die.

The first day of school was upon us, and the girl's process was the same as last year. Except not for Xavier. There was no more waiting for Olivia to come home while we sat on the step waiting for the bus, as she was in school for a full day now. This time he too would be go to school just like his big sister, and his best friend. She hugged him in her squeaky voice and said he was going to do great and make lots of friends like her. She held his shoulders and looked him square in the eyes and said, "Don't be scared. Okay?" He shook his head timidly. "I promise you will love it!" she replied, then gave him another hug before hopping on the bus. I had to drive Xavier to school as they didn't offer transportation for Pre-K as it's not a prerequisite but beneficial all the while. We exited the car as I strapped his oversized Batman backpack to him, grabbed his hand as we walked towards the school. This is a moment I feel I've mastered with the other kids, but I keep my emotions locked up until I am at least home and in the privacy of my own bathroom before I ugly cry over another "first" moment. I fought to keep the lump in my throat enclosed and smiled and swung my arms with Xavier's to ease his evident anxiety. As we approached the doors, the kindest, sweetest woman was waiting there for her class. She approached us and said to call her Miss G. She bent down and spoke to Xavier in her sweet sugarcane voice. She asked if he was excited and some other questions he feared answering. I think the anxiety was permeating from both of us as he squeezed my hand a little harder and nuzzled to the side of my thigh. Finally, all the kids arrived, and she was able to get them into a line, all while the parents all formed a barricade of sorts around the outside. She held out her hand and Xavier took it, and I leaned down and whispered, "you got this, I love you. I'll be here when you're done waiting for you." He gave a half smile. Miss G. winked at me and whispered, "I'll take good care of him, there is something special about him." Yes, there sure is. I watched him enter the building with the other kids until he was out of sight. Then, the lump in my throat decided it was time to escape. My eyes stung and I needed to leave before I started sobbing in front of everyone, leaving my only son on his first day of school. I've been here before so many times; why was *this* time so hard? I heard it's been said boys and their moms have a special bond, so I'm going to believe that's the reason for the water leaking from my eyes that I can't seem to control. I go home to an empty, silent house. The last time I heard this type of screaming silence, I was sitting at the top of my stairs in my apartment all those years ago trying to end my life. It's funny that way, life. The extreme perspectives and polarity from one time vs. another. I don't find humor in it, just the way those vying moments seem to have no coincidence to them whatsoever. Just when you think you've seen the worst, an even worse storm comes along only to be bigger than the one you just left. But somehow, we get through what we thought we wouldn't and the one after that too. But if I'm honest, I'd like to reach land, preferably with a beach and a waiting cocktail. I put my headphones in to drown out the deafening silence. I worked for a while figuring out systems, seeing where processes can be put in place for efficiency. But I found myself drifting to the various faces of the residents at Mountain Hills. Wondering if they are okay, if they miss me, if I hurt them. Do they even know I'm gone? I heard my alarm go off, shaking me out of my haze. It was time to pick up Xavier. The school is on the other side of town, and this day I think I hit every red light that there was. I quickly parked and practically ran to the door as I promised him that I'd be there as soon as he walked out. I saw him running out with a huge smile on his face, wearing a paper crown saying, "First day of Pre-K!". He was holding a red helium balloon, and Miss G. was coming up behind him. He saw me, almost knocked a few kids down on the way to get to me and wrapped his arms around my waist. After a moment or two, Miss G. came up smiling, saying how great he did. He warmed up and played so nicely with the other kids. She told me he is so kind and sweet, and she can tell he's loved. She has no idea how much. I thanked her and took Xavier's backpack from him, and then his hand walking alongside him asking how his very first day of school was. He beamed not letting go of his balloon for fear it would fly away, so I tied it to his wrist. He thought that was pure magic. Mom magic but still magic for a 4-year-old, nonetheless. He beamed as he told me about his day, "It was so fun, they have Legos, and trucks, even a supermarket! Oh, and I did circle time and got to look out the window to see the weather! Oh, and they even have their own potty too, did you know that?" I just listened and smiled as he ran through his day and gave the occasional "wow really that's so cool, I'm so proud of you" responses. We arrived at the car, and he was now sweating from the adrenaline coursing through his veins over the whirlwind of a day he had. I gave him his water and we headed home. On the drive back, he asked if he could go back tomorrow. I just replied, "Of course you can". He gave a quiet "yes!" of victory under his breath. And all the air I had been holding in all day came out in a giant sigh as if my lungs were holding in tanks of air that needed to be released. We got home, fed him lunch, he'd watch TV, have several snacks, and he'd count the minutes until Olivia got home while I worked. Olivia got home, hardly containing herself to see her best friend. They hugged, and she asked him how his day was. He just replied "awesoooome!" with an extra emphasis on the letter 'o'. She said, "see I told you!" They both scurried away into their little zone until Cliff got home, and they'd greet him at the door. Both taking turns spewing off what happened today. He just walked in, hugged them, and said how proud he was of them. This was it, the new routine. It was solid now and ran like clockwork each day. Then the holidays, as they always do, approach again. This time we could give our kids a good Christmas without having to be "adopted." I was settling into my new job quite easily despite Christine's moments of misdirected anger at another agent. But I was somehow the punching bag. I was getting paid, and I was making her job easier, and she was making money hand over fist. I have been through worse. I'm not letting this get to me yet. Thanksgiving comes and goes, and we enter December. Cecelia is now working at a local assisted living community as a server and loves it, go figure. She spent three years there building relationships just as I had. I loved hearing her stories and when she'd show genuine concern for someone who was ill. I don't know if it's the shifts and pivots that I've been enduring, but I'm feeling pretty wiped out. The last two times this happened, mononucleosis reared its ugly head. This time was different. I did come down with a cold a few weeks prior, so maybe I just didn't let my body rest enough. My periods are the most predictable thing I have in my life since, as far back as I can remember. Every 28 days, not a day sooner, not a day later. But they had been off the past several months. Most likely from all the change and stress; sometimes early, sometimes late. Christmas was looming and maybe that was an added stressor, but here we are again with a late period. But like I did every month before during this stretch of what felt like climbing uphill with no water, if I was late, I took a pregnancy test. They'd always come out negative and by some divine intervention my period would come the next day. So, this time was no different; I'll take the test, it will be negative, and we can move on. Except this time, I wasn't just late; I was pregnant. Wait, I am 43 years old. How can I be *pregnant*? We weren't trying not to be pregnant. But, at my age, I thought it was impossible. After Xavier, we had never thought this would happen. Oh my gosh, I'm pregnant! Wait, I've been here before; let's not get ahead of ourselves. I'll buy another test and try a different brand. Five tests later, all confirmed even in words "Pregnant". I sat on the bed and stared at the floor, slightly shaking. Probably from adrenaline, but my age puts me at such risk for genetic issues or worse. I can't think like that. If God has known what He was doing with me all along, who am I to argue now with a gift that He's giving me? I called the doctor immediately and told them I needed an appointment to confirm the pregnancy and make sure all was okay. They said they don't see anyone until 7 weeks, so I made an appointment for the very beginning of January. I think the receptionists could hear the fear in my voice. My track record with pregnancies and birth wasn't the best. And I needed to make sure I was in fact looked after properly by the doctors, all knowing my history. I wanted to tell Cliff, but in a creative way since I never had. So, I went to the dollar store, bought pink and blue Hershey Kisses, and put them in a box with the note that read "Pregnant" in words on top. I left it on his nightstand as that's usually the first place he goes when he comes home to unload his pockets of his wallet, and keys. That night after the barrage of attacks by the kids on him was finished, he went into the bedroom as he always did. Except this time, he called me into the room with him. He was sitting on the bed holding the open box. I tried to read his face, but I couldn't tell if he was happy or worse, angry. He put the box down and wrapped his arms around my waist, holding me tightly. He stood and kissed me gently and asked if I was sure. So, I took out the other five tests and threw them on the bed as confirmation that I was, in fact, sure. He smiled and hugged me and said, "here we go again, let's do it" as he squeezed a little harder. I don't know if it's because I had many kids before, but I started not being able to button my pants rather quickly. I wasn't telling anyone in our family until we had confirmation of a viable pregnancy and proof from the doctor. I wasn't telling anyone outside of them until well past the first trimester. You never know what can happen, as it's the most crucial time. I tried to distract myself by getting ready and wrapping Christmas gifts. By this time, the kids were on holiday break, wreaking havoc on each other. Christmas came and this was finally one we could give the good gifts we wanted to all the kids. Chromebooks for Olivia and Xavier so they could play Roblox instead of on our phones. A new phone for Ava because she's perpetually destroying the ones she has. And a real film camera for Cecelia. She was taking photography in school, and they were teaching them how to develop film and she loved it. So, all in all, it was a pretty good Christmas. New Year's Eve came and went with a small party for the kids and some music and fun. I didn't drink, obviously, but I didn't normally drink around the kids, so it wasn't questioned.

Finally, the day was here for my doctor's appointment. This time the kids were back in school so I made it early enough that I could still pick up Xavier. Cliff took the day off to be with me and to surprise Xavier at pick-up. He will be elated; his dad is his hero, still is even till today. We pull up and I take a breath as if to prepare myself, skimming the worst-case scenario chapters on pregnancy and birth in my head. Cliff squeezes my hand and assures me everything will be okay. He's always so calming. I'm so envious of how he can just be cool as a cucumber in every situation. We sign in and wait to be called back to the next waiting room to seal our upcoming fate. The nurse calls me and brings me to a room with the standard exam table, but an ultrasound machine is also in the room. She takes my vitals and tells me to have a seat on the table and hit the call button on the wall when I'm ready. I do as she says, and moments later, I hear a door open. Dr. White enters the room. She is the very doctor that delivered Olivia, so I was so happy to see she was the one who was doing this scan. She laughed, asking, "How many more are you all going to have?" She did an ultrasound and, of course, the screen wasn't facing us until she confirmed what she needed to. She spun it towards us, showing us a moving little 8-week-old baby bean. I gasped in a breath. Then she turned on the speaker, thump, thump, thump, thump, thump...I know that sound. It's the sound of a tiny fast heartbeat. As I closed my eyes for a moment, holding my breath as if she was going to tell me something was amiss. But instead, she put her hand on my leg and said, "breathe...the baby looks perfect." My eyes welled up before I could stop it, and I let the tears fall down the sides of my face, wetting the paper that was beneath me. Cliff wiped them away as she handed us a few souvenir photos to take with us. I had to come back in two weeks for testing, then again in two more for another ultrasound. I felt good knowing I had a team of doctors that was going to not just take exceptional care of my unborn baby, but of me.

Chapter Thirty-Seven

Getting a new job and suddenly becoming pregnant was not how I intended things to go, but God doesn't make mistakes. And I had to know everything was okay not only before I told a new employer, but anyone for that matter. At ten weeks is when they do all the genetic testing. I'm not only a "geriatric" pregnancy, but also a high-risk pregnancy now as well. If something is amiss or not viable, I suppose they give you options. There was no option for me no matter what the markers or outcome were of these tests, other than waiting ten days for results. Also, "geriatric" is a term that should be revised in the obstetric and gynecological textbooks. But I digress. I got the tests done, then, I did the intake of all the catastrophic things that "could" go wrong. Eventually, it became just a midwife talking. I heard nothing of what she said. It was just noise and I merely nodded at the brochures she was giving me. She could see I didn't feel well, because of hormones now flooding my body to build a human, again. And my blood pressure was a bit low but comes with the territory. She stopped talking and said, "Drink extra fluid, take a B6 and half a Unisom, it works like a charm for that pesky nausea". She smiled and stacked the tree of papers for me and told me to come back in a month unless we needed them earlier, and someone would call me with my "genetic results" soon. Super fantastic, can I go now? Can someone please show me the exit before I vomit all over this just buffed floor was all I could think. I still had four kids I was raising, a new job, and now a baby to grow. I was tired, but I made the appointment-see you in a month. Then, a week later I got a call from the OB's office; I'd programmed it into my phone years ago with the whole Olivia fiasco. I take a breath, wait for a moment, and answer. I listen intently to the person on the other line bracing for some unbearable news. But nothing came except good news all around; a perfectly healthy baby, genetically speaking, but still a win. I had a whole high-risk pregnancy ahead of me. She asked if I wanted to know the gender. For a split second I thought maybe we should be surprised, and as fast as that thought came in, it left. "Yes. Yes, I do," I replied, what seemed so confident, but I was pacing the floor because this means it's real, a real connection now. "It's a girl!" she joyfully said. When I replied, "Oh wow," she said, "Do you not have any girls?" "Actually, I have three, this makes four." She laughed and said, "Well you must be an expert then! Congratulations! Take care!" And she hung up. I was extremely happy, but this meant a little person inside of me was now not just a person but my daughter. And I was in mama bear protection mode all over again. There is a bond that I believe is immediately created when you find out what you're having. You give it a name, it's no longer "the baby" or "it." I told Cliff and the kids, and they were over the moon happy and patiently waited for their little sister to make her arrival. A month later, I wake up feeling something cold and wet surrounding me. Daylight is starting to peek through the blinds so I pull the covers down not to wake Cliff, and I am covered in blood. Me, the sheets, and it's coming *out* of me. I immediately panic with "oh no" and "what's happenings". I wake him immediately, and Cliff is super calm by nature, but even now he turns a bit pale and tells me not to worry that I am okay. I am convinced I am having a miscarriage. High risk, geriatric pregnancy, what was I thinking? I immediately dial the doctor's office, and they tell me to come right in. I stand in the shower trying to clean the dried and still wet blood from me. Cliff strips the sheets and does his best to clean the mattress. I apologize profusely to him, and as much as he tries to center me, but it is useless. I am still bleeding, but it seems to have subsided slightly. We arrive at the office and are immediately whisked back, meeting a doctor who is ready with a giant ultrasound machine. He squirts some warm jelly on my abdomen and moves the wand around my lower belly as he asks questions while he's scanning. I say I did nothing but wake up like this. He looks some more at the screen, and I can't see even if I try. He says, "the baby is fine, except you have placenta previa". Again, doctors start talking and I zone out because all I heard was the baby is fine. He went on to tell me what it was and that the placenta was covering my cervix entirely and absolutely not supposed to happen. And how crazy is it that a woman can make an organ that's full of blood and all the nutrients a baby needs? I'm not just growing a human; I'm growing new organs, no wonder I'm tired. But I got it, this was bad, and that's not supposed to happen. He said it usually moves up as the baby grows, but he put his hand on my knee and said, "This is serious. It will require bed rest for at least a month and no activity until the next scan to see if it is moving up as it's supposed to". Here comes the worst-case scenario rolodex whizzing in my brain. "What happens if it doesn't move?" I asked. He replied with the scariest things I have ever heard: "Maternal hemorrhaging, shock from loss of blood, fetal distress from lack of oxygen, pre-term birth". He attempted to continue but I put my hand up as if to say please don't say anymore. "I got it, full bed rest". Cliff grabbed my hand and squeezed. I was trying not to let the burn of my eyes and the lump in my throat come out, but one tear escaped. Damn hormones. The doctor showed me the screen, and I saw a little person in me having no idea what was going on outside, just cozy and squirming around. Another tear escaped. The doctor looked me straight in my eyes and said, "It's going to be okay. We know everything there is to know about your past pregnancies and deliveries, and it's understandable you're scared. But we will do all we can to take care of you and bring a healthy baby here". Then all the tears just escaped their cages, snot and all. Cliff took me home and immediately put me in bed. He gave me snacks, books, my laptop to do work and I had everything I needed. Including him. My month passes without incident, and I go back in for an ultrasound. But this is lined up with my 5-month anatomy scan, and I'm praying for good news all around. Yes, thankfully, no more previa, but I still must meet with the doc to give me the OK to come off bed rest after the scan. I had noticed I felt much bigger in the belly than usual; is this a giant baby is all I could think, not anything of what I was about to hear. The scan was completed, and we were given our obligatory souvenir photos to take home. The tech led us to a room and said the doctor would be in shortly. I wrung my hands pacing the room, as Cliff was telling me to sit down, not knowing if I was supposed to be walking around yet. The same doctor entered, greeting us and smiling, but I can't read his face as that's what he did the last time. He said good news is I'm off bed rest, well halle-frickin-luiah! But…why is there always a "but"? Can't it just be everything looks good, have a great rest of your day? No, it's like I'm cursed, and nothing can just be simple; one pregnancy, all I'm asking. "You have very high amniotic fluid, it's called polyhydramnios". I think polyhy-whats the issue here, doc, spit it out. He goes on to say that "This just means your baby is in a lot of fluid and although no distress now, this can cause your water to break early. That means pre-term labor is possible." Oh. Come. On. I'm waiting for Ashton Kutcher to come out and tell me I'm being punked. He droned on about how my body may just absorb the fluid but now I must come in every 2 weeks for ultrasounds to measure the fluid. Additionally, starting stress tests at 26 weeks. This child will not be coming that early into the world, doc, no matter how many tests you throw at me.

I'm still working but have *not* disclosed my pregnancy to Christine. On occasion, she requests I meet her at some local breakfast place to "go over the status of things". Translated to, are you doing anything to make my business better? I wear oversized cardigans to close and cover up my growing belly, but this can only go on for so long; I'm increasing in fluid at a rapid pace. I leave the breakfast meetings with my excuse that I must pick up Xavier, which is true, but I know I must come clean. She calls me the Tuesday before Mother's Day to tell me she will be going out of town. She is letting me know in case the sky falls while she's away. I follow her instructions and tell decide to tell her flatly, "Christine, there is something you should know. Due to health-related concerns, I wanted to let you know I am pregnant." There is complete silence on the other end, almost as if thinking the call disconnected. She says an obligatory "Oh my gosh congratulations, I had no idea". Of course, you didn't; you only think of yourself and how all things benefit you. I explain I can work up till I have the baby and I'll take family leave for 12 weeks as the state offers. She took an audible gasp, "A few months! What happened to the standard 6 weeks?" I rolled my eyes at the ignorance that is her entire demeanor right now. How do you employ people and not know the laws? I respond, "Again, there are health-related concerns not just for the baby, but for me. So, I'm being treated as higher risk than normal. I will have more frequent doctor visits and in case anything, God forbid, should happen, I didn't want you to be unaware. But I haven't been able to say anything until now for those very reasons, and I needed to know we were both going to be ok. But monitored heavily for the rest of this pregnancy". There is another very long pause of silence. So, I just say "Ok well have a safe trip, all will be fine while you're away. I'll be sure to document everything so you can stay informed should you need to be". She says nothing but "Ok, talk to you later". Ending that call I breathed out a considerable sigh. All that and she says nothing, nada, zilch. Not "oh I'm so sorry you're going through this", no, "whatever you need", no "oh, how can I help?" She was only thinking how this will affect her, not whether I or my unborn child are healthy, or worse, if we aren't. I go about the week, excited for Mother's Day. Not because I have four children and a husband who will make sure I'm given the customary hand-drawn cards made from construction paper. Or that I'll receive the obligatory supermarket flower bouquet that will eventually stay in the vase far too long while watching their dying leaves fall. But because this time I have another child growing inside of me. And I have at least a few days of peace without Christine texting me every 30 minutes or micromanaging me from afar. The same week, now three days before the one day a year I am celebrated as being a mother, Christine calls me nearing the end of the day. I thought she was just checking in per her usual obsessive-compulsive need to control things. But what she was about to say I was not prepared for. I answer in a friendly tone, quickly asking if everything was okay on her trip. She wasn't due back, so I figured it was the polite thing to ask. "Yes, everything is fine, but I wanted to talk to you about our conversation the other day. After looking at the landscape for my business, I've decided to cut back on some things". I'm thinking she's going to stop paying for so many website portals or for her very unused office space she has at the parent company. Nope. Not even close. "Unfortunately, I'm going to have to let you go today. I can't afford the expense any longer and it will hurt me more than help. I hope you can understand with your condition and all". My mouth gapes open. She rambles on about how I'll be paid for the next two weeks in the month. And she will approve unemployment and something about how my family is important. And I have no idea what else because all I could hear was a quiet ringing in my ears. She is laying me off because I told her less than 48 hours ago, I was pregnant! That's the only reason, and it is complete discrimination. I am not only hurt but I am livid. But keeping calm is necessary not for the situation but because this baby is going through enough stress. And I'm not going to let *her* add to it. I hear "Are you there?" I'm brought back to the moment, and take a breath, still seething. I just respond, "I'm sorry to hear this but I understand you must do what's best for your business. Please be sure to provide my last check via direct deposit as I will not be able to pick up a physical check with me being in this *condition* and all" I say condescendingly, throwing her words back at her. "If there is nothing else, I wish you the best and take care". I don't wait for her to respond; I hang up and toss the phone on the bed. I open the computer and go directly to the unemployment website to file a claim. I never thought I'd be here doing this again. How am I going to tell Cliff his high-risk pregnant wife just lost her job, oh and not to mention right before Mother's Day. And to top it off, next month is Cecelia's high school graduation. I believe evil spirits can attach themselves to people. And those people can pose as people you work with, your bosses, your friends, even your family. What does the devil know that he would send his cronies to mess with me for my entire life that he wants to prevent? It must be impactful. But vengeance isn't mine, it's God's And the last time I checked he doesn't like it when his kids get messed with.

Chapter Thirty- Eight

One amazing high school graduation of my firstborn and a few short, very hot summer months later, I am at the doctor each week. Every visit is no less than three hours. Between non-stress tests, ultrasounds, results with the doctor, I'm now on a first-name basis with the staff. They are even giving me baby gifts and trinkets awaiting her arrival. I'm given the okay to walk each day trying to sweat out this fluid which hasn't increased but hasn't gotten better. When my water breaks, I imagine I'll flood wherever I am, which is hopefully in a controlled environment. I'm still unemployed but have decided who is going to hire a giant pregnant woman only to have her leave. I chalk it up to a blessing because unnecessary stress would be to the detriment now, and who am I to argue with what God does or doesn't do. It doesn't mean I don't try to, because it never works; but I'm now learning to stop trying to do God's job for Him and that He knows what He's doing. I get a random call one day and from the caller ID I can tell it's the same boss, Jay, I worked for just a few years back. After I'd gotten laid off the same day he did, I hadn't spoken to him. I answer happy to hear from him and we exchange pleasantries for a bit until he gets to the point of the call. He has a job open and wanted to see if I was looking for a new role. Of course, he does. It's a job I need, and probably pays well too. I don't tell him we just lived through homelessness after the last time I worked for him, nor do I tell him all the unnecessary details in between. I just thank him for thinking of me but tell him I'm 8 months pregnant, so it's probably not a good idea, but I do thank him for considering me. He was very excited and congratulated me, as the last time I was pregnant he was the boss I returned to after Xavier was born. He wished me well and would keep me in mind for anything in the future. Sigh...

I'm woken up in the early morning by what I think are just cramps, Braxton Hicks contractions-like pain. Except this time, it wasn't subsiding. I had a planned doctor's visit and Cliff was going to go with me for this one. Since it was summer, all the kids were home from school, and it was becoming a lot for me. Plus, he hadn't been at any of the multitude of visits with me yet. The older girls were home and they agreed to hang with the little kids so he could go. And I figured I'd mention the pain when we arrived for our appointment. There was no sign of bleeding, but every few minutes I was doubled over in pain. I still have almost a month to go; this must just be my body preparing for the baby's arrival. We get to the office, and I'm whisked as usual to the non-stress test room, hooked up to the monitors while I wince in pain. The tech asks me if I'm in pain and I just look at her as to say *isn't it evident?* She shows me the screen and it's covered in a roller coaster of ups and down peaks. It's clearly showing I'm having contractions, so I am taken off the monitors and brought to the office to await the doctor. A midwife appears in the doorway asking if she can come in; she was filling in today for some of the doctors who got called on emergencies. Her voice is calming, she has a kind smile and asks me if I'm in any pain, and when I say yes, she asks for how long, then all the standard questions you'd ask to understand a course of action. She said the non-stress test still looked good even though she can see I'm having contractions but typical for how far along I am. She asked if she could do an exam to make sure I'm in good shape, and this is all just par for the course. I oblige and she prepares by washing her hands and drying them, putting on her purple gloves. Why are all doctor gloves purple or blue? Why not pink or black? She checks and immediately takes off the gloves and tosses them in the trash. She puts her arm on my leg and says "You're about 4-5 cm dilated, which is why you're in pain; you're in labor, so head to the hospital as soon as you can. I'll let them know you're on your way." I just lie there in shock. I'm in the middle of my 36th week; I have almost a whole month to go. Why is this happening, *again*? I get dressed and I look at Cliff, who is as cool as a fall day, and says, "Not our first rodeo babe, let's go have a baby". I see the midwife as I'm leaving, and she stares at me and says, "Good luck, they will take good care of you". I felt an urgency to hug her; as if she didn't intervene, I might have had the baby on the kitchen floor or worse. I embraced her and thanked her quietly while I imprisoned the tsunami of tears that was desperately wanting to escape. I already have a bag packed so we make a quick pit stop at home to sit the kids down and tell them what's going on. Excitement gleamed on their faces. I tell Ava and Cecelia they are responsible for the little kids, and I need them to step up for me. I know I can count on them when it's absolutely needed. But to go out on a date, or to dinner, forget it. I hugged them all and we drove to the hospital as quickly as possible. They were already waiting for me, so I was immediately brought up to Labor and Delivery 'High Risk Unit.' Ugh, just seeing that churned my very empty hungry stomach. I'm hooked up and IVs are administered, along with a nice midwife checking me again, telling me I'm halfway there now, asking me about epidurals. I feel as though I just got here but I can start to see the sun's piercing glow through the blinds knowing it's nearing the end of the day. I'm in active labor and I've gotten this far with no pain relief; won't the baby just pop out now? Nope, no such thing will happen but it's moving fast so I agree an epidural is best in the event a C-section is needed. Yeah, yeah, I know the drill. I breathe through each contraction as they increase in intensity. I don't see a NICU unit on standby so maybe she will be okay. I see feet in sneakers start to enter the room. A man's legs are in scrubs, and the privacy curtain is drawn back, and I see the same doctor who delivered Xavier four years ago. The imprisoned tsunami of tears has escaped. He comes to my side sits next to me and hugs me, telling me he's happy to see me again, then shakes Cliff's hand. I said, "I'm scared, she's not ready yet". He said gently, "I'll tell you the same thing I told you last time…do I look worried?" I shook my head no. "Then you have no reason to be either," as he shakes my foot. He says he's going to break my water as they are on their way to administer the epidural and hopefully this will speed things along. Oh no, I'm going to flood the floor! I said, "With all the excess fluid I have, am I going to burst?" He laughed and said there's plenty of padding to absorb it and I should feel a big relief. It doesn't take long before I feel a giant gush of fluid escape me. It's not stopping. The nurse changes pads quickly as he gently pushes on my belly to expel the remaining fluid. I feel lighter, like a dam that broke, and the water was released. I see the anesthesiologist enter and glare at him pensively. By this time, nurses' shifts had changed, I had a great night nurse. She was kind and gentle and helped me breathe through the needle as it entered my spine. It's like a cold liquid at first but soothing as it passes through the appropriate channels in my body. The contractions start to quicken, and the epidural has yet to take its effects. But I feel an intense pressure building soon thereafter. I buzz for the nurse on the bedside call button. Another nurse comes in, and I tell her what's going on, and she lifts the sheet. She stares at me wide-eyed and says, "Whatever you do, do not push," and rushes out of the room. Within minutes my doctor and nurse are in the room with me, dressing in scrub coverings and gloves as they enter. He said, "Do you remember how to push?" I look at him blankly. "Cause it's time to have a baby!". With Cliff watching in wonder and encouraging me, I pushed and it felt like I was on fire. Then a little girl emerged crying, as if we'd awoken her from a warm slumber. She's placed immediately on my chest with a hat and a blanket over us both. I'm shivering in shock but there it is, the warm feeling of laundry right from the dryer next to my skin. Stella Mae was born at 6 lbs. 3 oz, even early she was a good size and needed no intervention, and she was beautiful. Mae is Gram's middle name. I found it appropriate since Stella means "star" she'd be named after the very star that shone so brightly in my life. I lay there savoring the scent of this new person, still in shock at how quickly she wanted to make her grand entrance. I let the nurse clean her up and look over her while the doc finished up on me. "Listen, I'm very proud of you. Not many people can do what you did and stay calm and focused despite the epidural zonking out on you," he said, chuckling. "You're going to be in some pain, but it should all heal in a few weeks. I'll check in on you in the morning; get some rest. Oh, and someone will bring you food; please eat, you need your strength." He gave me a hug and just like that, my hero doctor was gone. And in a heartbeat of a moment, I was now the mom of five beautiful kids. I *had* to stay here, *alive*... and keep going or I'd have missed all of it, and God knew it. I was brought to a recovery room and gently put into bed. But by now it's well past 11 pm, so Cliff had left to go home to be with the kids once he saw I was settled and met my recovery nurse. She told him to get rest and she'd take good care of me and Stella. I'm convinced that labor and delivery overnight nurses are angels sent from heaven. They work a job caring for others overnight while leaving their own families. That takes not just sacrifice, but they have a calm presence to them no matter what the mother is facing, good or bad. Several doctors came in to look at Stella to make sure she was still doing okay since she was early, but they didn't see anything to raise any alarm bells. Stella would eventually go on to raise several alarms, but for today, she was perfect. My nurse gave her a sponge bath and washed her hair, and once she was clean and swaddled back up, she handed her to me. I held this little person who was now peacefully asleep and just stared at her thinking. I must be favored because no matter how hard I try to find it, so far, I still do not smell like smoke and there is no soot anywhere. I didn't sleep too well as I was in a lot of pain, but I also was woken up when I did drift off to either a tech checking my vitals or Stella. I lay there sitting upright in bed watching the sun start to rise so slightly through the blinds. And I heard the door open with a faint knock. My hero doctor kept his promise and came to see me before his shift ended. I smiled and thanked him for checking on me. He peered over at Stella and smiled. Then he said, "You did good, kid." I closed my eyes for only a moment, just savoring the phrase of someone telling me I did something good. My nurse had entered the room not expecting him to be there, but he said he couldn't end his shift without seeing me and making sure I was okay. He asked her about my pain, and she responded that what was being given to me to manage was only ibuprofen. He looked at me with his tired eyes and shook his head, then said, "You're tough". My nurse nodded her head in agreement but paid me a compliment and said I've been nothing but easy and a pleasure as a patient. He took another look at Stella and sat next to me on the bed. He told the nurse it was okay to take out my IV and my labs were normal. He said, "You're one brave woman. And from what I can see, as tough as they come." He chuckled slightly. "I am honored to welcome another of your children into your world. You should be very proud of yourself; you did amazing". He reached down to hug me goodbye. The sea of tears I've held back let a few out. They trickled down my cheeks. I quickly wiped them away, fearing a Niagara Falls-sized waterfall might erupt. He walked and tapped my foot saying, "I'm only a phone call away if you need anything; I'll see you in a few weeks for your checkup." And just like that, my hero doctor was gone again, as I heard the click of the door shut behind him. I don't know if it's my now empty belly that held the person next to me for so long, the pain, the hormones that are trying to readjust, or the fact that someone who knew nothing of me or the life I have lived and almost ended said they were proud of me, and I was brave, and I was tough. Right on cue, that waterfall of tears could not be contained any longer. Sobs of every imaginable emotion came out full force. I let them wash over me and fill me with gratitude and appreciation for all I've gone through that has led me to this moment. I pick up Stella and held her close. I don't know if she knew I was crying, but she opened her eyes and locked eyes with mine, and my tears stopped just as quickly as they came. The kids came to visit, enthralled by their new baby sister, taking turns to hold her. Babies bring a peace even amid chaos. We are living on one income and my unemployment checks, and barely scraping by. But now that will require diapers, formula, and all the accompaniments that come with an infant. I have no job to return to and no job prospects. But, as I looked at the family I built from pain and perseverance, none of that mattered. This family is all I have, and I will push through every dark thought that comes my way to ensure they have what I didn't.

I was preparing for discharge and the same nurse as the day before, who I took a liking to, saw all the kids and she said she'd be back with my forms and instructions. Although I was showered and put my makeup on the best I could, I was exhausted and uncomfortable. She arrived what felt like an hour later, carrying the discharge folder with all the details of who to call and what to look out for. Lady, this is not my first kid, but I let her give me her rundown. I noticed she was carrying several large "patient belongings bags" that seemed very full. I had all my things in a backpack, so I looked at her puzzled. She started apologizing for the delay, but I stopped her mid-sentence, figuring out what she'd done. I could see the outline of diapers and bottles and who knows what else throughout the bags. I hugged her—she held me as if I was her own daughter and whispered, "I've been there. Enjoy your beautiful family and go home". She left the room as we stared down at what must have been almost a dozen bags we were somehow supposed to leave the hospital with. Thankfully, you leave through a separate entrance than you entered. And everyone carried a bag or two, so we didn't draw attention to the fact we had half the baby supplies in tow. No one so much as glanced at the people behind the visitor counter as they waved goodbye. They just hauled the bags into the back of the truck. I stood there with Stella sleeping snugly in her car seat just waiting for someone to remember to come back for me. We pulled away and breathed a sigh of relief, for now.

Chapter Thirty- Nine

Summer is winding down and we try as best we can under limited income to get the kids ready for school. Cecelia teetered with going to community college for two years but decided to hold out for the school she really wants to go to. An art school in Philly. She missed the application deadline so she will apply next year and just work till then. Both she and everyone seem to be adjusting to the newest member of our family. Our church even started a meal train, so I didn't have to worry about cooking cause food would get delivered, mostly pizza shop food. And one day Pastor Elias even came by to hand deliver marinated chicken and sides we could just throw in the crock pot. It was all very generous, and they were good people. But while he was there, he blessed Stella and prayed for her. Thanking Him for bringing her here safely and covering her with prayers and strength for us. What I hadn't known at that time is that the prayer for strength for us would come into testing soon thereafter.

I took Stella to all her standard doctor appointments and did all the obligatory things a newborn needed. And even though I did all the things, something was off, and I felt it. She started coughing at about 10 days old. Not just the spitting-up coughing; I mean coughing like she was sick. I was back and forth to the pediatrician three times. And each time I was met with "she probably has reflux; she was early, so giving her this medication should calm down rather quickly." Nothing worked, and I know she didn't have reflux. I'm now entering week two of her coughing, and she's gasping for air when these coughing fits happen. I marched back to the pediatrician at 4 p.m. on a Friday. The last appointment of the day before they leave for a well-deserved restful weekend. The doctor who saw Stella knows all my kids, takes one listen to her, and watches her have a coughing fit where she turns a shade of purple. She placed her hands on my lap and said firmly, "You need to get her to the emergency room as quickly as possible; do you understand?" I stare at her as fear fills my body at such a high rate of speed; she says, "I believe Stella has Pertussis". I respond, "Isn't that whooping cough? There is a vaccine for that, right?" She says softly, "Not until she's eight weeks old, and we have no time to waste; I'm telling the hospital you are on your way". I put Stella back in her car seat and nod my head. She said she'd be checking in to see what is going on. I know, not only is she vested now, but she knows several other doctors failed me when this could not have escalated to this. I call Cliff and tell him what's going on and that I'm on my way to the pediatric ER and explain all the details on the way. He is calm, tells me to breathe and to let me know when I get there. I dump all my fear and emotions on him all while he's home taking care of our other kids, which wasn't fair. I can only imagine what is going on in his mind while we navigate this, but he still must put on a brave face for the kids. Without him, I feel lost, like a part of me is missing. But I know he's doing exactly what is needed in this moment, and it's to be a dad and remain calm. He tells me to call him as soon as I arrive and that he has everything under control at home. This man isn't just my rock; he is my person. I got to the ER and it was confirmed she did have pertussis. But this hospital was not equipped to handle Stella's illness, so they needed to transfer me to a major children's hospital in Philadelphia immediately. This is all happening so fast and I'm completely helpless. I then see two men arrive. One wearing a full Air Force jumpsuit and the other in dark gray scrubs and carrying bags of medical equipment. They were briefed and explained to me who they were. They stated that they'd be accompanying my daughter and me to the hospital. When I asked why he was wearing a military jumpsuit, he responded, "Ma'am, I am Joe Caruso, Captain in the US Air Force. But I am trained as a medical physician ordered to take your daughter to get the help she needs as fast as possible. We were going to fly her there by the Medivac, but it's dispatched out. I will be driving her to the waiting hospital and will do everything I can to ensure her and your safety." I just stared at him. Medivac? Stella is so critical they were going to airlift her. My eyes burn and all I can muster out is "Thank you". They put this tiny human on a gigantic gurney, and they covered her in blankets, stacked papers and bags around her, and hung the IV bag on the hook. I could barely see her. I followed them and heard "good luck" behind me. I didn't so much as turn around. She is hoisted into the back of a waiting ambulance, and I climb in behind, sitting next to her on the cold steel bench. I stare around me, seeing all the lifesaving medical equipment, and it feels ominous. I flash back to the last time I was in an ambulance; it was because I tried to take my *own* life. And that very same medical equipment was used on me to do what it was designed to do: save my life. I hear the whirl of the engine and I'm removed quickly from the ghost of the past trying to make me look into a mirror that no longer exists. We pull away and I am startled by the sounds of the sirens and the rate of speed at which we are going. I look down at Stella and back up to the other man in scrubs tapping gently on her chest. I can tell he sees my eyes furrowing in question. He says with a slight smile, "It helps clear the congestion from her chest and lungs." He checks her oxygen monitor while continuing to tap. "My name is John and I'm an ICU nurse from Children's Hospital; it's nice to meet you, Mom. How long has Stella been sick?" Shouldn't he know this information already with all the papers and charts surrounding the gurney in front of him? But I consider for a moment that he's making sure I'm coherent and not in shock. Which I am, but I normally give shock a run for her money so I'm not about to let her win now. I give him a quick run- down and he just nods as I speak. "And now, after all of that, we are here with you to help". He can tell I'm trying to hold it together as I peer down at Stella and back up to him. "You just gave birth a few weeks ago, and now that very baby is sick. I know you want to sacrifice yourself for her. But she needs you to have your strength through this. So please allow yourself time to recover while the doctors help her to." I nod in agreement just as a few stray tears slide down my face, but I wipe them away quickly. We sit in silence for a while as the sirens ripple through me like molten lava not knowing what will await us at our destination. Captain Joe says over the speaker in the back that we are pulling into the hospital ICU bay. I stare up at John with fear in my eyes. He smiles and says, putting a hand on my knee across the gurney, "Listen to me, we won't leave until we know she is safe and secured". I let out a sigh and thank him. Alone and terrified, I believe God sent me two angels to protect not just Stella, but me too. The back doors of the ambulance open and I stay put until they take her out, and John holds a hand to help me down. Captain Joe shuts the doors, and they push Stella into an awaiting elevator. I look at them with a perplexed expression. Captain Joe says, "Stella is critical, so we are heading right up to the Pediatric ICU where the doctors await her arrival". I feel my stomach turn from that statement and from the speed at which the elevator raises several floors up. The doors' part and I follow them for what feels like a very narrowing hallway until we arrive at a giant open sliding glass door. Inside are a team of several doctors. Some in white coats, some in the same dark gray scrubs as John, and a female nurse who met my gaze and said in a friendly voice, "Hi, are you mom? I'm Theresa, I'll be Stella's nurse tonight." I am listening but focused on Captain Joe and John shifting a very tiny Stella from the ambulance gurney to a hospital bed. They attach the IV to the hook near the bed. They rattle off some medical stats to the doctors and pass over papers and plastic bags. I later find out they are antibiotics and pain medicine they were giving her through the IV. It feels like time is standing still, and I know it's only been a few seconds, but I respond, "Yes, I'm Nicole, Stella's mom, nice to meet you". She has long curly dark hair, and I can see a protruding belly which tells me she's about 5-6 months pregnant. That's like a knife in my metaphorical chest. I was just pregnant a few short weeks ago, and now my daughter is fighting for her life. I stand off to the side letting the team of doctors examine Stella. Listening with stethoscopes, all murmuring words I don't understand while

Captain Joe and John stand on either side of me. John tells me they are assessing her condition. Since she's so small, they must create a detailed medical plan to help her heal. Captain Joe stands there with his arms crossed at his front watching their every move. One doctor in gray scrubs comes over to me and tells me his name. But my mind was not in a place to recount anyone's names in that moment. He explained that Stella is very sick, and this illness is serious. How many more people are going to tell me that, I got it. He says specifically the coughing can and probably has deprived her of oxygen. So, they will be putting her on a high flow nasal cannula. The last time I saw an oxygen nasal cannula was on Gram and I start to see the parallels of my past colliding with my present. The ambulance, the oxygen, and no way am I giving into this ghost that's trying to not just haunt me but taunt me. The doctor also went on that she will be on several medications, antibiotics, and one to help her sleep so her lungs can rest. There is a monitor that measures all her vitals, including her heart rate and oxygen. He said because she needs one-to-one care, there will be only one nurse assigned to her with no other patients but Stella. I watch as they hook her up to the various monitors and the machine that administers her medication at the set dosages. My fists clench at my sides trying to keep every part of me from wanting to lay next to my baby and hold her and protect her. I start to physically tremble not knowing Captain Joe is watching me and sees my panic attempting to erupt. He stands clear in front of me in his very intimidating uniform and places his hands on either side of my shoulders. My breath is shallow, my heart is racing, as my eyes go back and forth watching machines being attached to Stella as he says, "Look at me." I am startled by his stern but calm tone and stare at him, shaking. "Breathe," he commands. I close my eyes for a moment and take a few deep breaths waiting for the panic to pass. It's not leaving but I still aim to look around familiarizing myself with the room. John is watching intently to what is going on. Then looks over as Captain Joe is still shielding me or maybe protecting me from what is happening. I guess they've been in this place long enough to know what parents should or shouldn't see. I see from the corner of my eye as Nurse Theresa sends Captain Joe a look and he nods his head. He moves back to my side. The doctors are gone. Only the sounds of beeping and wires from every machine are connected to a three-week-old baby, who just happens to be mine. I was frozen in place, like my legs were made of cement. Why can't I move? I'm in shock. Shock won, then she took my money and ran. Captain Joe and John spoke to Nurse Theresa and then walked over to me. Still standing in the same spot I was affixed to minutes ago. Just staring at the room that feels like a cacophony of overgrown wires and noise. John spoke quietly, "It's time for us to go." My eyes widened. Captain Joe spoke in a low tone, "She is in good hands, and so are you." I know they only told me they'd stay until they got Stella settled but I didn't want them to go. I was scared, and they brought a sense of comfort and protection with them. I held back the lump in my throat and said to them both, "You have no idea the impact you made tonight. If it wasn't for you, my daughter would not be here, and if she weren't, I might not be either." Captain Joe hugged me as I whispered, "Thank you," he just responded, "This is one I won't forget. Thank you for letting us serve you, ma'am". When I let go, he was visibly shaking off whatever emotion was trying to come out and stood by the door. John hugged me tightly and said, "Your daughter is beautiful and has the best mom she could ask for". He let go misty-eyed and he met Captain Joe at the door. I said, trying to break the hovering emotion that was enveloping all of us, "Time for you to go save someone else's life. And don't forget their moms too". They both smiled and held out their hands to wave. And just like that, they were gone. I walked over to the oversized bed that held my sweet little newborn who was attached to machines, IV tubes, a feeding tube down her throat, and a nasal cannula taped to her face. I felt like my heart was inside my chest cracking into another million pieces. I bent down not to disturb the lifesaving equipment and kissed her on the head. I stayed there for a while just stroking her head, wanting so badly to hold her, and let her know I was there. But what I needed was to hear my husband's voice telling me everything would be okay. Nurse Theresa turned off the overhead fluorescent lights. She left the dim recessed lights on. It helped the room not feel so sterile, but it didn't help the sound of the machines, though. She came over to me asking if I needed anything. I asked if she could get me some hygiene products, a toothbrush, toothpaste, some soap, towels, and some sanitary pads. I had rushed over to the hospital, so I didn't stop to gather anything from home. I'm only just at three weeks postpartum, so I'm still bleeding, cramping; my stitches haven't fully healed. And I have no medicine to take, great. I call Cliff, and just hearing his voice brings a well of tears to my eyes. But I don't want him to hear me cry as I know he's dealing with this too in his own way. So, I tell him all that's happened thus far, having to pause in between so I can keep it together and not give him my fear to carry too. After I ramble on, he stops me and says, "Babe, I know you're scared, and you have every reason to be, but God has it all handled." I thanked him for being with the kids and making sure they were okay. He scoffed, "Come on, we are a team, that's what we do; I got this, and you have it covered there; we'll figure it all out along the way." I let out a big sigh, but in that sigh was nothing but gratitude for this man. He assured me he would be there in the morning and to send him what he can bring for me, and that I should try to get some rest. The hours until he gets here can't come fast enough. Nurse Theresa comes back with a bag of things she collected, and I was so grateful for her and her kindness. When I asked how far along she was, she beamed with a smile and said 5 and a half months, and it was their first child. I listened as she talked about her family being excited and her husband can't wait. I told her if she was half as good a mom as she was a nurse, her baby was in good hands. I grabbed the bag of items she brought heading into the bathroom, and she said she'd go get some blankets and a pillow for me. I thanked her again as she slid the glass door shut. I took one look at myself and boy, did I look like hell passed over me and back again. I washed my face, brushed my teeth, and cleaned up as best I could. I was exhausted, but wide awake as thoughts came in and out like rapid fire. As my brain started to settle and my eyes drifted closed, I was awakened by the intense sound of Stella coughing. Nurse Theresa was already there administering another dose of meds to keep her calm and rested. She smiled and said, "she's okay." The same as a few weeks ago, the day after Stella was born, I watch the sun rise through the blinds. It brought me back to a moment of peace.

All I hear now are monitors beeping and no peace to be found. Today, a lovely doctor, who referred to herself as Dr.

Jaz, came in to check on Stella. She let me know she was the attending physician for the day. Just as Nurse Theresa came in to tell me she was heading out. My face must have told on me because she assured me she'd be back tonight. Dr. Jaz said she'd like to try to wake Stella up a bit and see if she can sit in a chair and even take a bottle. I was ecstatic! She said it would take a few hours for the meds to wear off. But sitting her up might help the fluid pass through better than lying down. The daytime nurse also came into the room and introduced herself as Chelsea and that she was briefed on all things Stella. Dr. Jaz told her the plan, and she said she'd arrange for the items to be brought over. They both left, and I looked at my phone and had a barrage of notifications and voicemails. Pastor Elias, my mom, friends from church, and who knows who else. All looking for some update on the little girl who was fighting for her life, and the mom who was fighting for hers. I sit there slumped on the very uncomfortable small couch with my hand on my head, and I hear "Hey". I look up and see Cliff standing at the doorway holding my backpack. I guess I didn't really prepare him for what he was about to see. He put the bag down and hugged me. All the tears that I have been holding in that were weighing me down erupted like a volcano. My hormones were trying to regulate themselves, but in this moment, they have taken over and cannot be stopped. I sob into his chest as if it's perfectly designed for my head. I hear the door slide open, and Nurse Chelsea is here with the infant chair, a few bottles of formula, and a little whale with a speaker on it. She said it plays classical music, and it's helpful for the 'littles' that are in the ICU. Stella starts to stir and coughs with gasping breaths; she recovers but is not in the clear. Cliff and

I stand there as I clutch my hand into his, as Nurse Chelsea calls Dr. Jaz, and within a few minutes, she's arrived. Dr. Jaz and Nurse Chelsea lift Stella and all her accompanying wires and tubes into the chair. She is semi-alert but looks puffy and tired, and nothing like the baby I took home just a few short weeks ago. My concern must have been evident because Dr. Jaz said, "She looks puffy because of the IV. But her diapers are always wet, so she's passing the fluid fine." She let her sit there for a while as we talked to her and let her hear our voices. Dr. Jaz said she appeared okay, and we'd see what happens if we try to feed her. She grabbed a bottle and rubbed it over Stella's lips, and she latched on just as normal. She only gave her a bit because she's got the feeding tube as well, but she said she'd be back before her shift was over to check in. By now, it's nearing the end of the afternoon, and the older girls had been home with Olivia and Xavier so Cliff could be with me. But I knew as he looked at the clock he was preparing to leave. "I wish you could stay," I said softly, "Me too," as he made an audible sigh. I could tell he was conflicted with leaving me, but I replied and moved closer to him. "It's ok. You're being an amazing dad to these kids. You're meeting all their needs. I'm here with just one of them. No one can care for them better than you. We are a team, remember? You said yourself we'd figure it out as we go. And that's what we're going to do". Thankfully Cliff has very understanding bosses who told him to take as much time as he needs off. He just looked at me and embraced me as if it was the very thing, we both needed. He kissed my forehead and said he'd be back tomorrow, and I just nodded my head and could only say "Ok". I was missing him and the kids so much, but I know he's torn. He's sad and helpless watching his new baby sick in a hospital, then, he must be a happy, easy-going dad when he opens our front door. I had been calling the kids since I got here letting them know Stella was ok and getting the help she needed, and that I was ok. Not allowing them to keep asking when we were coming home to switching asking them about what they have been up to that day. They'd fight to take turns and go on about how someone ate the last of the goldfish crackers or how they were playing with daddy. He was big on "play time" with them where he truly plays with them and lets their imagination run in every direction. From making up games, playing the kiddie versions of instruments, and creating an entire band. Art, coloring, and even creating masterpieces just out of play dough. I know he's carrying a lot for our family's sake, so I hope spending time with the kids like this will lift his spirits. I want him to disconnect, if just for a little while. As I sat there thinking of just missing the smell of him and the hugs of my kids, I got a text from Pastor Elias. Who I had been avoiding just because I was tired of talking to people really, but asking if he could come by and if he could bring me any food. I happily took the offer mainly because I was starving. He showed up around an hour later with a hoagie (aka sub sandwich,) some snacks, candy, and a few drinks. Stella was still in her seat, and he talked to her in baby talk like anyone would a three- week-old and said a prayer over her for healing. He was surprised to see her sitting up, and I said the doctor thought it would help with the fluid. Stella was still coughing, but she should be in soon to tell me next steps as I peer at the clock. He asked if I needed anything else as he had to get home, and I said I was good and appreciated the food for sure. He assured me everyone was praying for us and to let him know of any changes. I was glad when he left as I housed the hoagie and stuffed my face with chips and cold iced tea. Dr. Jaz came in about 30 minutes later and suggested we try a bottle again. But his time wasn't so successful, so she suggested I try in a few hours. I was brought in a rocking chair that was set next to the monitors, and they showed me how to pick her up to not disrupt anything. They took her out of the chair and laid her back down, and she drifted to sleep. Nurse Theresa was back, and I told her how the day went, and she was so excited for the progress. The night droned on to the sounds of monitors beeping, and now a little whale playing Mozart quietly on the table next to Stella. I prayed for God to heal her body every chance I got despite the sheer lack of peace I felt. It was about 10:30pm and the time Dr. Jaz told me to feed Stella. I lifted her gently and placed her delicately on my lap. She didn't take much, but it was good to hold her even if it wasn't close and attached to tubes and wires. I laid her back down and Nurse Theresa said she was going on her 30-minute break. I had no idea what her fill-in nurse's name was, but she waved through the window letting me know she was there. About 10 minutes went by and Stella started coughing. I saw the nurse looking into the window and I tapped her gently like they showed me when she started to cough. But this time she was turning purple. I looked up to the window and waved for help. Stella was now turning blue as I smacked her on the back pleading for her to breathe. Suddenly the monitor made a long steady flat sounding beep... Stella was limp and not moving. The nurse hit the code button on the wall and a swarm of doctors and nurses invaded the small room. They moved chairs into the bathroom and the hallway to accommodate the amount of people in there. As they surrounded her, trying to revive her, I felt like I was in a medical TV show. In shock, I shrank back into a corner watching the room close in on me. A tall doctor came over to me and said, "I need to put a tube down your daughter's throat to help her breathe," as if he was asking permission. "Okay", was all I could get out. I was met by a nurse who suggested I wait outside with her as she guided me out of the room. She explained they would be intubating Stella and attaching her to a ventilator to help her breathe. I heard her faint cry, a monitor beep slowly, then I didn't hear anything. I stood in the narrow hallway as I slid down the wall and sat with my hands on my head. I heard from down the hall Nurse Theresa say, "I was only gone for 30 minutes; *what happened*?!" After the other nurses told her what occurred, she slid the door open and shut it behind her. The same nurse who hit the button leaned down and said she was so sorry, and she'd check in to see how she was. I'm guessing she had to go back to whoever she was taking care of; I bet they are at least alive. I was completely alone in this stark white hallway and not one person was seeing if *I'm* okay. Where is Cliff? He always knows what to do! Where are Captain Joe and John? They promised they'd stay to make sure she was okay! They are all taking care of people who need them, and I know this, but I need someone, anyone. I feel my chest is heavy, enveloped with pain. Nurse Theresa exited the room and bent down next to me. She explained, in a reassuring voice, that Stella was without oxygen for some time. They stabilized her, but she is very critical. She went on to say she's not breathing fully on her own, but she is getting assistance from a machine. Also, her lungs are very damaged, and they will be doing daily x-rays to see if she's contracted pneumonia from the fluid. They will treat her with all the antibiotics they can to help her. I just looked at her vacantly because the one thing she couldn't tell me is if my daughter was going to live or die. She said they were bringing in a team of physicians and respiratory therapists that were going to take over. And she has no doubt they are the best ones to take care of her. I just listen and stare at the wall emptily as if I'm outside of myself looking into someone I don't know. She asked if there was anyone I wanted to call; I can't even speak, how am I going to talk to anyone? I asked her to please call Cliff as I didn't know what to convey to him. I don't even know how this little human got this sick or how, she just *got* here! I feel like an elephant is sitting on my chest, and why is everyone *still in the room*? Cliff doesn't answer as it's well after midnight, but she said she'd keep trying. I start to see people slowly file out of the room and I look up waiting for someone to acknowledge me, but they don't. I see the tall doctor who told me he had to put a tube down Stella's throat take his cap off and walk down the hall. I look at Nurse Theresa for something, anything. She goes in and once the final person leaves, she shuts the door behind her. "Listen to me". She says trying to get my full attention while pulling me up off the floor. "This will be hard for you to see but I want you to know she is still Stella just with a few more tubes and machines, OK? "I stare at her blankly, "Okay". Why is that the only word I can get out of me tonight? She holds my hand and leads me into Stella's room. I freeze when I see the enormous ventilator and hear the swishing sounds it makes pumping air in and out. Nurse Theresa says, "Hey it's ok, take a deep breath. I'm going to show you everything but first your daughter needs to hear your voice, so she can fight".

CHAPTER THIRTY- NINE

She keeps my hand in hers and brings me to the oversized bed, and I was not prepared for what I was about to see. I gasp as my hand covers my mouth. This little person has several tubes in her mouth, throat and nose. They are taped to her face. A long, oversized tube is attached to the machine beside her. Nurse Theresa says informatively and calmly, "They had to put her into a medically induced coma so her lungs can heal. She may cough from time to time, but this tube here acts as a suction to take any gunk out that we can. I know it's hard, and it doesn't look like the baby you came in here with, but she's in there, I promise". I just stare and nod my head. I bend down to look at her face, and all I can smell is antiseptic and the food I ate hours ago fights to come back up. I reach over to her with trembling hands, and I place my hand on her head and stroke her hair. Nurse Theresa puts a hand on my back as if to comfort me and encourages me to talk to Stella. They say people can still hear when they are in a coma, medically induced or not, so I do just that. I tell her how much I and her daddy love her, but she needs her rest to get better. Her sisters and brother want her to come home and play. Nurse Theresa brings me a chair and I sit down not taking my gaze away from her. Still talking, telling her about all the things that have been going on that she's missed. I hear a door slide and click. I'm alone with the whooshing sounds of the ventilator, the beeping of now several more monitors and even though I love my daughter, I want to be anywhere but here. Nurse Theresa comes in around 4am, I've not slept, and I'm in the same position she was when she left. She tells me she talked to Cliff and told him what was going on and he was going to call me. I have no idea if he called, I felt like I was in quicksand and I needed someone to pull me up. My

313

legs are heavy, and I'm beyond exhausted, but I call him, and he answers right away. I try to hold the tears in, and I ramble. I apologize for not calling him, but I couldn't even speak let alone talk to him or anyone and that it all happened so fast. He could hear in my voice I was in shock but holding it together as best I could, and he'd be there as soon as he could. That means coordinating with Cecelia or Ava to watch the little kids, but I couldn't just not acknowledge that. He stopped me from talking and told me to let him worry about that and that wasn't my concern today. Cliff, being the calmest person I know puts everything in a positive light, and this time was no different. Before we hung up, he told me that when the nurse called him, he prayed. He said God told him immediately that 'the child will be ok, and she will not die'; and to this day he stands by that word. I am sitting with my phone in my hand in a Pediatric Intensive Care Unit praying that this is all just a bad dream. I must have fallen asleep as I'm startled by a tech wheeling in a giant portable X-ray machine. She apologizes for waking me. I just wave my hand as if to say don't worry about it as I see the peeking of the sunlight start to shine through the blinds. Except this time, it doesn't bring any peace. Doctors and nurses come in checking her vitals and nodding to me as if there's nothing new to report. I get up off the very uncomfortable couch and open the blinds slightly. I now see a daytime view of the vast array of machines and wires as if they are in 3D, especially the tubes extending from Stella's mouth. The tape seems to be pulling at her skin, but I remember it's because she's swollen with fluid. Then Nurse Chelsea walks in, face in shock. She comes to Stella's side and looks at me and says, "What the hell happened last night?". I sigh as I know that's a rhetorical question as she can see in the chart what happened. But what she meant was she left with Stella sitting up drinking a bottle, and now she's intubated. I shrug my shoulders all while thinking I watched my daughter die last night, that's what really happened. And no one can tell me if she's going to live if you want to get technical. She asks if I need anything and I just shake my head and say, 'No thank you." She checks a few things on the machines, and I head into the bathroom. I am met in shock to see the chairs piled in from last night's events. But I'm too tired to fight with my emotions; so, I take them all out and place them back in their proper places. I go back in and brush my teeth as I stare at my swollen red eyes wishing I had some Visine. I brush and pull my hair back and open the door to see Pastor Lia standing there waiting for me at the foot of Stella's bed with tears in her eyes. She embraces me and I'm about as strong as a wet noodle. I said, "Wait, aren't you supposed to be in church?" She said she rushed over here from church as soon as she heard what happened from Cliff and God wouldn't want her anywhere else. She asked me how I was, and I again just shrugged in what felt like defeat. She asked if I wanted to get a coffee downstairs and we'd come right back so Stella isn't alone. Chelsea came in to do her standard vital checks and said, "It's ok, go get some coffee, I'll stay here till you get back." I reluctantly agreed because maybe with a warm cup of coffee in my hands, will wake me up so I can do something else but say "okay" or shrug in response to people. We got our coffee and headed back up and Pastor Lia sat for a bit to what I presume helped me feel better. But as much as I was appreciative of her, I was in desperate need of Cliff to arrive. After about an hour, he stood at the doorway as he had a few days prior. But this look was what I can describe as shock as he tried to stay calm and play it off. I hugged him, putting my head in the space just made for me, soaking in his smell, comfort, and the peace he exudes. He brought me some things from home, snacks, and drinks, and sat them down gently on the chair. Then he stood at the end of the bed, taking it all in. I'm the one with the most experience here, so I'll give the grand tour of all the bells, whistles, and upgrades Stella received overnight. I show him each machine and what it does and the tubes they connect to, including the ones she is intubated with. I showed him the monitors and what each beep signifies as if I am showing him a new car. I ushered him over to Stella and said exactly what Nurse Theresa said to me. "I know this doesn't look like her, but she is in there, talk to her so she can hear your voice". He obliged and sat in the same chair I did. Pastor Lia hugged me goodbye and said to call for anything. I thanked her and then put a hand on my husband's back just as Nurse Theresa did for me the night before. In silent prayer, I asked God to show His miracle-working power and bring her back to life. But when, was not up to me. I only knew in my spirit that I had to stay and fight on her behalf, and that is exactly what I did.

Chapter Forty

I met a new team of doctors who were making their "rounds" on the floor Stella was on. They walked with their rolling stands that held their laptops. There were the medical doctors, the fellows, and residents all in tow as it's a teaching hospital. They slid open the door so everyone could peer into the teeny baby who I was unsure was alive or dead and just getting the help of a machine. However, a woman named Dr. Alexis O'Conner led the charge, or so her white coat said. She asked to come in and speak with me. She introduced herself. I said, as you would expect, knowing the care of your daughter rests in her decisions, respectfully, "It's nice to meet you, Doctor O'Conner. Thank you for helping my daughter". She was a bit curt, but I didn't take offense; just a no-nonsense, I-must- teach-people-how-to-be-doctors vibe to her. She replied, "Just Alex. No 'O'Conner' needed. We are going to see a lot of each other, so I want you to feel comfortable when around me. My students and fellow staff will refer to me by my title, but I want to always be honest and up front with you and keep you informed. We come each morning around this same time 10am, to do rounds of the floor. The night nurses will inform us of how Stella did and if she had the need for any intervention. Based on that and the additional tests and scans I'm ordering; we will give you a plan of care that we put together for her". I stare at her as if I'm being read an instruction manual. She goes on, "We don't like to keep anyone intubated longer than we must, but her lungs need to rest. I am ordering them to lighten her sedation to see how she responds. If it becomes difficult for her breathing, we increase slowly until she's in a twilight state, but no longer coma induced. I am also going to dedicate a respiratory therapist for Stella. If, and when she shows improvement, their jobs are to reduce the amount of air the ventilator is giving her and see if she can do some breathing on her own. They are great and are fully capable, and I'm sending you all the best people I know to help her. Many parents have no idea what is happening until they ask, and that is not how I operate. With that said, your daughter is very sick, and she needs a team of people for her care. But I am going to do everything I can to help her heal and get on the road to recovery, which will be a long one, but recovery, nonetheless. But your role in this is critical because as sick as she appears, she won't fight without knowing you are here. The sound of your voice, your touch, and even your smell." My eyes sting with tears. "I understand this is all very sudden, and it is okay to take breaks, eat, get some fresh air, and take care of yourself. You just gave birth to her only shy of three weeks ago; you are also healing, and she needs you to have your strength. I understand you have other children?" I reply, trying to take in all the information she's giving me, but my brain is on overload. I simply reply, "Yes, they are home with my husband." She responds in a slightly less abrupt tone, "Okay good. When she is in a more stable place, they can visit her if they'd like. This may increase the speed of her healing, listening to the voices she's heard all around her while you were pregnant. And of course, we have a team of people who help younger kiddos not fear seeing their sibling sick, and all the beeps and machines. It's overwhelming for an adult, let alone a child. But when that time comes, I'll let you know. For now, you're doing exactly what you should be. If you need me, the nurses can page me; otherwise, I'll see you tomorrow morning". And she turned on her heel and walked out to the rolling laptops outside of the room. I sat down and felt not just overwhelmed but overstimulated. Hadn't the past 24 hours been enough for my brain's capacity to comprehend and how is it still be functioning? But before I can sit in that thought too long, which is probably a good thing, a young pretty what I think is a nurse enters the room. She's in blue scrubs, not the typical dark gray. She says, "Hi! Are you Stella's mom?!" I cautiously respond, "I am." She goes on in a very chipper tone, which is a little over the top… "Cool, I'm Brooke! I'm the respiratory therapist for Stella today, it's great to meet you!" She went over to the ventilator pressing buttons and looking at what I assume is acclimating herself to the limits of flow Stella is on. She walks over to where Stella lies, so still, and she says, "Wow, she's beautiful." And she adjusts some wires and says she is going to change the tape. With a swift move from her pocket, she pulls out tape and scissors, cuts the pieces she needs. She pulls off the old tape without disrupting a single tube or wire and applies the new tape. She admires her work "Now, that's *much* better! Come see!" I walk over to where she is standing and there is no more pulling of her face, and she looks like Stella. Still puffy, but no longer a version of her I didn't know. Brooke said in her chipper voice, "See! If she let me do that, she's a fighter and she's going to do just fine! I'll be back a few times a day to check in."

The days felt long, and it seemed like the beeps got louder on every machine as the days grew into nights. But I waited, ready every morning for the rolling laptops to come by to tell me something, anything good. Just that Stella remains critical, and they are doing all they can. I'd walk back into the room filled with the noisy machines and just sit back on the uncomfortable small couch in defeat, every time. What we needed was a miracle, and fast. I prayed every day looking for a way that somehow, I could convince the God of the universe to stop all His worldly plans and heal my daughter. My mom just flew in from nowhere, Texas, to help with the kids at home and to stay at the hospital with Stella. This way I could go home and be a mom to the rest of the humans that needed me. Which I had to go kicking and screaming to do. All I could think of in the worst-case scenario chapter was what if I left her and she woke up, or worse, and I wasn't there. It wasn't until Dr. Alex came in randomly one afternoon to do a check on Stella. Listening to her intently with her stethoscope, both her heart and lungs. She then covered her back up in her slight swaddle and said, "She sounds a bit clearer but not out of the woods yet." My eyes widened, taking this as an encouraging statement, but she said, "She's got a long road ahead of her." I exhaled audibly. She asked me from across the bed, "When is the last time you went home?" I told her I hadn't since we were admitted and that there was a shower and food. Almost trying to convince her I'm not leaving her, so lady, don't ask. She put her stethoscope around her neck and stared at me with more gentleness in her eyes than I was used to. "Go home. Get a good night's rest and be with your other kids. They need you too. Stella has an entire team dedicated to her. And if something happens, I will personally call you myself, but I have confidence she will be okay. And this isn't negotiable, doctor's orders." School was starting the following week, and I thought to myself I can't *not* be there for that. Plus, I could use a shower in my own house and sleep in a room that doesn't constantly have the sounds of whooshing beeps of machines. "OK, fine. But if anything happens, I am holding *you* responsible." That wasn't reasonable, but she just responded, "Fair enough." She smiled and walked out, sliding the door behind her. I paced the small room, wringing my hands together, wondering how I could be in both places at once. I plopped down and put my hands in my head as I could feel the stinging of tears start to well until I heard the door open again. I looked up from my hands to see my mom and Cliff standing there. I don't think my mom was prepared for what she was walking into. That seems to be the running theme here. But before she acknowledged Stella or the various machines, she hugged me and whispered, "I'm so sorry I didn't get here sooner." Those tears that were stinging and my eyelashes I fought to push away just moments ago came out in a flood. And into a deep cry that this situation is so dire I might not leave this hospital with a baby at all. I tried to compose myself and told her to go meet her granddaughter. She immediately began talking to her and rubbing her head just like I did the first time I saw her. A mother's maternal instinct is so palpable; there is nothing like it in the world. I thanked her for coming and for offering to help with the kids. We stayed for a bit, and I told them I was ordered home for rest, so I'd go back with them. My mom immediately said, "I'll stay." I looked at her perplexed, and she said, "It will give me time to get acquainted with my new granddaughter. I will be fine, and I'll call you if anything happens." I explained to her where the kitchen was, the coffee, and she stopped me. She said kindly that she knows how to find her way around in a hospital. Of course, she does; she left me to move to another country with a man she met while working *in* a hospital! Damn, that ghost of the past tried to rise again, but I quickly pushed it away, and I just thanked her. I kissed Stella and told the new night nurse, Jenn, that my mom was going to stay tonight. She said she'd put her name with security and get her a bracelet. Then she smiled and said, "Go home to your other babies, I'll see you tomorrow." I got home and the kids thought something was wrong, but I assured them I was there for them and just to rest. Cliff took them out a few days before to get all their school supplies, backpacks, and lunch boxes to which they couldn't wait to show me. I said 'wow and oh cool' more than a dozen times, and then they told me mom-mom made them dinner too! I was thankful. Because when it comes down to it, this family, the one I created, will go to the far ends of the earth for me, and I was full of gratitude. I promised them I'd be able to take them to school on their first day and they were elated, jumping in a happy dance. I took a long hot shower hoping the water would wash this terrible dream I was living away; it didn't, but at least I was clean. I climbed into bed-my body so heavily laden from trying to deal with the current circumstances. But I was still postpartum and trying to heal and everything hurt, head to toe. Cliff made me a cup of tea and gave me some strong ibuprofen and I must have drifted asleep soon thereafter. But I was startled awake seeing the light of the sun peeking through the blinds. And each time this happens something strips that peace it is supposed to bring away. When things like this happen, you should be able to put on those rose colored glasses I wore of Grams to bring you back to center. But all they do is mask what's real. But I'd give anything for them right now. I look at my phone and see a text from my mom that Stella's IV came out and they had to replace it. Dammit! Why wasn't I there! She assured me she was fine and not to worry. Then WHY TELL ME AT ALL? I got dressed and took the long drive back to the hospital, dreading what may await me. I called my mom and told her we were downstairs, and Cliff would take her back to the house. They left as I headed in, bypassing security as they already had me on a first-name basis. I saw Jenn and ran up and asked what happened. She brushed it off and said babies' IVs fall out all the time, so they just put it in her other foot. This kid is going to look like a pin cushion! But she said that I just missed rounds and smiled, so that meant no noise from Dr. Alex. But she said she'd be in later this afternoon. I looked at her puzzled. "She's really invested in her, that's a blessing. Take it and don't ask questions because she doesn't do this for everyone." I smiled and walked in to see a less puffy Stella and then Brook bubbles in behind me, chipper as ever with her now sidekick Chen. He was a young guy who was surely way more chill than Brook. She saw me in the hall and wanted to introduce me to him since they'd be taking shifts with Stella. I shook his hand, and he nodded, just studying Stella and the machine she's connected to. Brook said, "Well, good news, Mom, we are titrating down as she is starting to breathe more on her own. But if she's struggling, we can always move it back, but Dr. Alex OK'd it." I must have had a shocked look on my face as Chen spoke up and said, "Mom, this is a good thing, I'll be watching her so no worries." All I can reply again is "Okay". Dr Alexis came in as expected and said she has good news and bad news. The bad news is Stella had a slight fever, and a test result showed she had a staph infection. Probably from the intubation, and they are giving her more antibiotics to treat. She suggested I call my doctor and the kid's pediatrician and I should get a cycle of antibiotics in case I caught something and brought it home. I said, "So, what's the good news?" She said with a smile, "I'm going to try, and I mean try to extubate her this weekend *if* she clears this infection. She's still very sick, but we will watch to see if we can continue to titrate her down on the vent because she's showing her lungs are healing. It's Monday. A. Whole. Additional. Week. I hid my racing mind, spinning through worst-case scenarios. Then, she said, "Brook will help you hold her, wires and all. I think the touch will help with her healing." How am I supposed to hold what looks like a baby connected to everything in this room and not damage her? I replied hesitantly, "Are you sure?" She said "Yes, I'm sure- Brook will be in again later today." I thanked her, and she smiled and nodded and walked out as quickly as she came in. Sigh…maybe God did hear my prayers but isn't answering them how I think they should be. Isn't that the way though, telling God your plan? I imagine He chuckles to Himself when if we only knew His plan would blow our minds. I called Cliff, and he said he was in route and tried to give him as best a synopsis that I could. He said this was great news and he was not too far from the hospital and assured me that God has it under control. This man is dealing with not just the kids and teenagers, but now his mother-in-law, and a fair weather one at that. There is a special place and title in heaven for people like him; they are called Saints. When he arrived, we were waiting with bated breath for the therapists to arrive. I used the time to call all the doctors and told them what was going on. And before I knew it, six antibiotic prescriptions were called in, waiting for pickup. I knew I had to be home tomorrow to get the kids ready, so I'd deal with that then. My breath hitched when I saw Brook and Chen slide open the door. She says, "Hi guys! Well, are we ready to hold your baby?!" She is so happy and encouraging but slightly annoying, but I don't dwell on that too much; she means well after all. I wash my hands and sit in the rocking chair Chen rolled in. They unhooked a few things and picked her up gently and placed her in the crook of my arm. I held her bottom if not to break her, as they draped the wires along the sides of the chair. They couldn't leave in the event something happened, understandably. I was so nervous but started to talk to her and tell her how great she is doing and I'm so proud of her. Not knowing if anything I'm doing is working as she's unconscious. But Brook bent down to my knees and quietly said, "She knows it's you. Her heart rate slowed down to normal range; maybe Dr. Alex was right." as she winked at me. Before they must take her back, I hold her tightly to me and take a quick swift sniff of her baby head. One stray tear falls from my face onto her blanket and then another, then they settle her back in bed. They turn to me, and I can't muster anything through the swirl of emotions other than "Thank you so much." Brook hugs me and says, "I love that baby. She's made so many people love her too. Watching you guys fight for her is so inspiring. We're going to get her better!" They leave, and I turn to Cliff as he just sits and holds me and lets me process the happiness and the grief I am holding on to. I don't deserve this man. He signed up to be with a woman who still has that 18-wheeler of baggage parked in the driveway. This would have sent any man running for the hills. But this man, he's not leaving me, or any of us. This just makes him stick his heels in and not just stay with us, but to fight *for* us.

As promised, I was there to see the kids off to school. Ava left early as high school starts at 7:30 am. Her friend picked her up and still had a few more to get. So, she rushed out the door hugging me while a puff of whatever smelled like sugar cookies and vanilla perfume followed her. We took the obligatory outside photos with the little kids as they beamed and smiled with first day excitement. Their backpacks still seem giant on their small frames, but I cannot argue with Shopkins or Spiderman as they suit them perfectly. I have their small army's worth of school supplies in separate bags to pass off to the teachers at drop-off. I hope they have help because if every kid brings this much, there better not be a request for boxes of tissues or a glue stick come the middle of the year. We pull into a street that's filled with cars while I watch parents and their children walk towards the school. Some are dressed to head right to work, some maybe took the day off; either way, we all know "firsts" are hard for kids, good or bad. We get to the playground and all the classes are lined up a little chaotically. But at least there is no beeping or swooshing of machines. Just excited elementary school kids all wide-eyed, although some tears are being shed, but all wondering what their day will bring. We hugged them goodbye and told them daddy would pick them up; I squished a little harder knowing I wouldn't be with him. We watched them walk into the building until they were out of sight. Cliff grabbed my hand, and we started walking back to the car. As we walked in silence, I couldn't help but think they almost didn't make it either. But I just dropped them off at school, so why wouldn't Stella pull through this just the same? Would God not show the same grace He showed to them, or even to me? We got coffee and drove again to the hospital. It always feels like impending doom the closer you get to it, like no one goes to a hospital like this unless they are sick. And this hospital is full of sick children and parents who hope to bring their children home healthy. But some never do; and that makes a pit heavy in my stomach. I push it aside for now as we park in the garage and head in quickly hoping I make it in time for rounds. It's Wednesday, only a few more days until she's free of that tube is all I'm thinking as I head in a quickened step towards Stella's room. Nurse Jenn, who I'm surprised to see, is there tending to her medicine machine. She hears me enter and gives me a small smile. "The antibiotics weren't working so we are trying something different; Dr. Alex will be in to talk to you soon." And just like that my mood from optimistic from seeing my kids off to school is now thwarted by anxiety and worry. Cliff is so positive that I think his face is next to it in the dictionary, but it isn't positivity this time, it's faith. Faith that we serve a God who knows all that we are facing but is doing a work inside of us at the same time. He wants us to trust Him as a child would a parent. If I'm honest, that's harder to do when you're in a storm and you can't see three feet in front of you. But He doesn't give us all the steps I finally had to learn, just the next one to take. Dr. Alex comes in and I brace myself from the top of my head to the bottom of my feet. "She hasn't been able to clear the infection so we will have to push out our plan and see how she is next week and reassess." I stare at her, my eyes filling. I say, "You said..." She interrupts, "I know and I'm sorry, but she still has some fighting to do. We are also giving her steroids to help reduce the inflammation. I'll keep you informed of everything; you have my word." And just like that we are at another week stuck in this place where I'm beginning to think no one leaves, ever.

Chapter Forty-One

Fight or flight is defined as an automatic physiological reaction that occurs when a person perceives a threat to their survival. Sometimes it's good for us. Like when it prevents us from a dangerous situation. For example, slamming on the brakes to a person who stops short in front of you while driving. Or being faced with a growling dog, or grabbing a weapon if you feel unsafe in your home in the middle of the night from a noise you heard. Nope, not me; I'm stuck there 24/7 and it is exhausting. I can't tell if something is a threat; I just see red all the time. Growing up in such trauma and not dealing with any of it allows it just to store inside of you like an overgrown field of weeds. So, when a plan shifts or a change happens, my body's subconscious reaction is to fight or run. But the reality is the only person I'm fighting or running from is me. I need order, routine. I thrive on logic and reasoning, and cause and effect. Then I'm able to cope with the red because I'm in control of it and it makes sense. This situation... I'm not in control of any of it. And I am struggling in my core with panic, anxiety, and depression. Because I'm now processing the grief I pushed down, and I start to blame myself that Stella is here. It's ridiculous and I *know* this, and my brain does too, but my stories always have a villain and there is no one to blame here but me. She lies there hooked up to machines to keep her alive and I run through all the different scenarios of how this happened. If I did this differently, or that. Or maybe it's because of my age. Just finding someone to put the blame on. Cliff knows I'm spiraling and says, "Stop, you had nothing to do with this. God knows when it's time, not a doctor, nor a team of them. He will give them the evidence they need to take her off the machines, but you must let Him work, and Him take this burden from you. It's too much for you to carry." I lay my head on his chest knowing he always has the right thing to say at the right time. As I close my eyes briefly to hear Chen come in with his usual nod, or is it a bow? I don't know, but he said he was titrating Stella down slightly, but he's keeping an eye on her. I nodded my head in thanks. Everything seems heavier now, like a helium balloon that was flying high is suddenly losing air and slowly deflating. I know Cliff needs to leave to pick up the kids, and an idea popped into my head. "What if we had my mom pick up the kids for the rest of the week from school so you can be here with me?" He looked at me like he'd rather choke on nails but said he'd think about it. "I can't be alone in this place with my thoughts; they are dark and scary, and when you're here, they aren't so loud." I love this man for taking a woman who is broken into a million little pieces, then he makes it his mission to pick up each piece and place it back together. He hugs me and says he will have the kids call me when they get home. He walks out and I'm here with the singing whale, the whooshing, and the beeping is as if it starts to make the strange sound that they are in sync with the others. Or I'm probably delirious and need medical intervention myself, or maybe just some sleep. My mom is more than willing to pick up the kids from school. But Cliff has her go with him for a few days, so she has it down and knows how to get home. I have no concern with her at home with the kids. Even the older girls, she doesn't ask many questions about their comings and goings. She doesn't ask many intrusive questions, like where they are going, who they are going with, who will be there, and when they will be home. All the questions that I would ask. So, she's probably a welcome break for them. She cooks, does laundry, cleans, and does anything she can to ease the burden of that missing part in all of us. Doctors and techs file in and out of this small ICU room, which has now doubled as my temporary living space. And I don't even bother acknowledging them anymore. I haven't turned rigid to the people caring for Stella, but it is not a feeling I can describe in words how helpless I feel. I'm supposed to be protecting her from the world, and I can't so much as pick her up. As I'm wallowing in my own self-pity, Nurse Jenn, who has now changed to day shift, comes in. I've been here so long I know the damn nursing schedule; that's sad. I greet her with a smile, but she asks me to help her as she's carrying a bunch of things in her arms and if I can then shut the door. She's carrying the items as when we say we are going into the grocery store to grab one or two things, but you wind up carrying seven or eight. And you wind up stacking things on top of things because you're too far from a basket or a cart. I take the items, looking perplexed, and she walks over to the side of Stella's bed and says, "You're going to help me give her a bath." My mouth gapes open. "I don't think I'm allowed to do that," I respond hesitantly. "She's *your* baby, why can't you?" Jenn is different from the other nurses, not that they aren't amazing, but she sees *me*, too. She gently removes the baby hospital blankets but leaves one over Stella; I'm assuming not to give her a chill. Yep, I was right; this kid's legs and feet are beat up like a pin cushion. I let out a sigh just staring at her from head to toe, admiring her little baby feet and hands that I long to hold and kiss so much. Nurse Jenn can tell I'm not fully here, so she starts rattling off what we are going to do to refocus my mind. "These wipes are antibacterial, and since she's in the intensive care unit, she has to be wiped with these and not soap and water." She hands me one, and they are like a baby wipe, just bigger and smell like antiseptic and not, well, like babies. I watch as she wipes her, and I do the same trying to be as gentle as possible to not disrupt the litany of wires and tubes. We go from bottom to top and I see her go into the bathroom, leaving me there like a deer in headlights. "Here, take it and wipe her head with it." She hands me a warm washcloth and she nods her head, motioning me to complete Stella's "bath." I softly wipe the cloth over her black hair and around her ears. I talk to her as any mother would be giving their infant a bath, not realizing how connected and therapeutic this was. But this was Nurse Jenn's plan all along. To give me any moment I could have that would resemble normalcy even under the worst circumstances. I looked up at her and blinked the tears away. "You are a great mom, and few parents even stay with their kids here. You're the exception and we *all* see you." I reply through the lump in my throat, "Thank you, I really needed to hear that." She went on to move Stella gingerly around while I helped change her sheets and put fresh swaddling blankets around her. She added a small pair of bright yellow socks on her feet. Probably to cover up her being poked and prodded, but I decided she just wanted to keep her feet warm. After all was cleaned up, Nurse Jenn left to chart her done tasks, but I'm sure she left out the part that I was her assistant. I hear the faint sound of the whale's music on the table, and I was so sick of hearing it, so I decided to play my own music for Stella. I turned off the poor whale and for a moment I thought I heard it sigh in appreciation; great, now I'm hallucinating. I grabbed my phone with so much music I forgot what I had on it and turned on "Raise a Hallelujah" by Bethel Music. This song was able to get me through some tough moments and it has sort of become an anthem, a fight song of faith.

"I raise a hallelujah in the presence of my enemies.
I raise a hallelujah, louder than the unbelief.
I raise a hallelujah; my weapon is my melody.
I raise a hallelujah; heaven comes to fight for me."

The writers of this song wrote it when their friend's child was sick in the hospital fighting for his life. So, what better song to play instead of a droning whale? I played that song over and over and sang it over Stella while worshiping the very God who can save her. The kids were getting anxious and asked when they could visit their new baby sister. I wonder if the machines and wires and the fact that Stella being purposely unconscious would frighten them. But I knew the person to ask, and I waited for her to come around the corner with her trusty rolling laptop cart, Dr. Alex. After the typical stats that she's healing and the infection is clearing, I ask straight out. "I don't know how much longer Stella will be here, but she has four siblings that haven't seen her in weeks. I'd like to have them visit her; can that be arranged? "The other doctors looked at me with wide eyes as if that was the first time anyone had asked that question. "Absolutely,"

Dr. Alex responds without flinching a muscle or even moving her hands from the laptop's keyboard. "I will arrange for a therapist to put together a care package for them so when they arrive, they have things to do while they are here. Crayons, snacks, things like that. This way it won't be overwhelming, and I'll make sure the therapist stays in case you need them. How about Saturday? I'm here all day in the event you need me for anything or just an extra person to help explain what's happening". I think all the other doctors and I have the same shocked expression. But I square my shoulders with as little courage as I have left and reply, "Thank you, that would be great. I appreciate you coordinating that". She nods as the pack of rolling carts and white coats continues to the next room.

The therapist put practically gift bags, or buckets in this case, of all kinds of things for the kids. And even got the older girls a few things too. She left them in the room and said to let Nurse Jenn know when they arrived, and she'd call her. Visiting hours are limited in the ICU, so Cliff knew he'd have to arrive early and not stay too long with them. When he called to say he was on his way with everyone, including my mom. I made him put me on speaker. I wanted to sound excited and couldn't wait to see them. I hung up and paced the floor. I've done this so much I think I might have worn the tile down. I was excited, but I was also terrified that I'd be consoling four kids who have no idea what I or Stella are enduring. But that's what you do as a mom; you sacrifice yourself for the good of your kids. I heard the door slide open and saw the sweetest faces one could ever see run over to me. Bypassing all the mechanical items and their sister, as they embraced me, telling me how much they missed me.

334

Cecelia and Ava, not so much; they stood at the door like so many others in shock at what they were seeing. I hugged them both as tears welled in their eyes. I understood it was overwhelming, but Ava broke away and went over to Stella's bedside. She started talking to her as if she'd been there all along. The little kids followed. There was a stool next to the couch, and I put it in front, and Olivia, holding her brother's hand, started talking too. They carried little pink stuffed bears to give her and placed them right next to her and Cecelia eventually joined. They all surrounded their new baby sister with love and adoration, completely looking past the beeps, wires, and tubes. I was so thankful, but my heart was breaking again inside my chest because I was so proud of them. For their bravery and courage and absolute unconditional love. They all peered over to me, and I gave them a smile and said I had some things for them. The therapist never came back during the visit, and I'm sure Nurse Jenn had something to do with that. I saw her through the window, giving her a look as if to say did you call the therapist…she shook her head, "no," and just winked. As the kids dug through their buckets of goodies and the older ones went to raid the refrigerator in the kitchen, as they keep drinks and snacks for the families there. My mom just sat next to Stella humming a tune to her, stroking her hair. Maybe it was a hymn or a song about faith like I've played for her, but it was some unspoken language she was speaking to her. The girls emerged holding bags of chips, a plethora of drinks, and even ice cream. Cliff held my hand as we looked at the scene in front of us. As if almost telepathically saying we've made it through so much and this is no different. He squeezed my hand a little harder, so I knew we were in fact thinking the same thing. it was time for them to go and I hugged them all goodbye and squished them "too hard," they said, and they waved bye to Stella as if she could hear every word they spoke. Xavier walked back over and stood on the stool still at the side of the bed. He said in his little voice, "See you soon, Stella and we will have playtime with daddy. Love you," and he kissed her gently on her tiny hand peeking out from the blanket. That moment will forever be etched in my mind. He had so much faith that he'd see her soon that it ignited everyone's in that room that, yes, we will see you soon, Stella. And you will in fact go on to have many playtimes with Daddy.

Stella was rushed to this ICU just shy of three weeks old. She has just hit her sixth week of being on this earth. It's been like the time she has been here has been cut in half. She's unconscious, intubated, and fighting a disease of her entire respiratory system. Plus, the plethora of bacteria that have accompanied her being like this for so long. I was told she was making progress. In turn increasing my hope. Then I was told she's contracted another infection. Then diminishing that hope. It has been this roller coaster of hope rising then falling hard. And as a mother, all I can do is hold on to the mustard seed of faith I have because all of this is out of my control. And the only one that can help me now is God Himself. As I stare into another week of a perpetual groundhog's day, it is lightened by a few visitors from our church family and Pastor Elias. All of them praying over Stella. No one prays for me, which I think is odd, but hey, I'm not the one lying in a hospital bed, so I let it go. I became fast friends with a woman at church named Laura. She messaged me in the middle of that week in the evening, asking if she could visit. But it's well past visiting hours unless you are immediate family only.

But I could really use adult conversation that doesn't have medical terminology attached. And it would be nice to see a face of a friend right about now. She can't come during the day because she works as a nanny for an amazing family, and I haven't seen her since all this happened. I tell her that it's after visiting hours, but did she think she could play the game with me of saying she's my "sister"-she laughs when I propose this to her and says, "Well we kind of look alike." I laugh as we do not resemble one another whatsoever. But I ask her this because security will let her up if she is my "sister," as that counts as immediate family. But I must tell the nurse, whom I do not know tonight, to call security with all her info and ask to allow her up. The nurse happily accommodated my request and called security, and as I told Laura immediately, she was in the clear. About 40 minutes later, she slid open the big glass door carrying a small pizza box and a paper bag. I stood so happy to see her. She dropped what she was carrying quickly and took only a few strides to hug me so tightly. She didn't say anything, but I know she could feel my gratitude within that embrace. Her eyes welled up, and I told her how much I missed her; she chuckled, "You should not be telling anyone you miss them, it's *you* we all miss!" That made me smile knowing I had so many people who truly looked out for us, but she was like an actual sister to me with how close we grew. The lights are dim with just the glow of the machines as it's about 9pm now. She walked to the oversized bed where Stella is being what feels like held captive now. She gently talks to her and rubs her head with a smile as if somehow Stella can see and hear her. She's the only one so far not fazed by all the machines, tubes, and wires, or at least she's not acting like it. I revel in that comfort even if it's only to make me feel better. The pizza box and the bag were in fact for me; she stopped on her way as she didn't know if I had eaten, and as she talked about it, I inhaled it. She laughed and said, "guess not!" We chatted on for some time, talking about nothing medical or sickness, just regular life things. She told me about the goings-on in her life, and I was so grateful for being able to hold a conversation with someone who didn't see me as fragile. Everyone that visits tiptoes around me like I'm going to shatter if anything, but the current situation isn't discussed. Before I know it, it's close to midnight, and the medical team starts peppering in at 6am every morning. She is startled at the time as well, but it was just what I needed, a friend who wasn't afraid to be just that. She prayed over Stella as everyone does, but then she came and prayed *for me*. My already very heavy eyes fight the burn to cry as she prays a covering of strength and restoration over me. She thanks God for me, for my endurance and my will to fight for who I love. She prays that Stella will be made whole, and I will hold her in my arms as this never happened. I am always in awe of how people can pray in the spirit because she took me with her because I believed everything, she spoke over me. We hugged, and she left me with not just a full belly but a full heart.

The team came as expected for rounds the next day with their rolling laptop stands. I remember it was a Friday because they don't do rounds on weekends. This would be the last time I'd see them this week to give me any update on Stella, good or bad. I brace myself as I always do but square my shoulders, feeling a sudden sense of confidence I hadn't felt since we got here. Dr. Alex gave her obligatory good morning and the nurse ran down how Stella was the night before. So far, Stella hasn't needed any intervention for several days now, both day shift and night. I see Dr. Alex type something on her laptop and ask the group of students some questions about what was relayed. They chattered in what seems like another language to one another for a few minutes. I start to grow impatient and it's showing. I look at all of them and say, "Can you relay that in layman's terms for the rest of us who don't have a medical degree?" Dr. Alex swiftly apologizes and moves over to face me. Here I go skimming through the worst-case scenario rolodex in my brain. Then she says, "I am going to *try* to extubate Stella tomorrow-10am." She emphasizes the word 'try' and I raise my eyebrows because we've been here before, but I let her continue. "She has cleared all secondary infections; her blood counts are all normal and she's doing much of the breathing now on her own. So, I will attempt tomorrow morning and if all her stats stay normal, especially her oxygen levels, we will consider it a success. But if for any reason something is the opposite, I will have to reintubate her, do you understand?" I nod my head quickly to let her know I fully understand. "We will reduce all her sedation today and overnight so she's twilight awake when we attempt the procedure. But she will need to go to the step-down unit to continue to heal. Because being intubated as long as she has, been surely doing some damage internally. But we will run all the tests with ENT to identify any issues and remedy that when the time comes. Also, she will need to drink from bottles fully before she can be given the full clear. So, it may be some time you're both still here but no longer considered 'critical.' Again, do you understand what I'm telling you?" I nod again and say "Completely." I walk back into the room, hands shaking as I pick up the phone to call Cliff. My voice trembling, trying to keep a violent wave of tears from escaping. I tell him what I was told and said he knew she would fight because she's just like her mom. He's been back and forth handling so much, and I know weekends are sacred for rest. And his rush to be here isn't usually hurried. But I asked him if he'd come be with me as soon as he could in the morning and there were no questions asked, just a simple, "Yes." Because one way or another, it was a big day. I don't sleep at all; I just watch the hours tick by until I see the sun as it rises peeking through the blinds as if to say, it's time. I clean myself up in the bathroom and when I come out as I had so many weeks before, I see a person I don't expect: Nurse Jenn. It's her week off so I look at her puzzled. She chuckles, "Come on, you think I'd miss *this*?" She's been such a champion of Stella's. And just like she winked at me a week ago when the therapist never appeared during the kids' visits, this was one of those same times. 10:00 am - Dr. Alex walks in with no less promptness than I'd expect. I greet her, and she obliges and asks if I remember what she said yesterday, and I nod. She said to Nurse Jenn to please prepare the necessary items as she'd like to get started. She said she was only here for this procedure and has family plans at noon. Wait, they both came in here to do this on their days off? I take a quick breath, and she notices; she smiles and says, "Did you think I was going to let someone else do this?" I smile and silently thank God, and I say, "Wait! Can I please say a quick prayer?" I see two other nurses and Brook enter the room. She's giving me an internal squealing smile as she passes over to the ventilator. It appears there is a lot of coordination to do this. I say a prayer covering them and that God may lead their hands and angels surround the room. And while I prayed, I silently begged God to save my baby one more time. I finished the prayer, and I heard a simultaneous "Amen."

Not like before, they let me stay in the room this time. And this time it was bright, and the sun was shining as if angels were encapsulating the room with their glowing presence. Everyone took their places as if this were a performance that they had been preparing for and finally got to complete. I heard Dr. Alex say. "One..." my breath hitches. "Two..." I close my eyes. "Three." The tubes are extracted from her throat, and Dr. Alex rubs her gently, waiting for her oxygen to level off. She takes a big breath and turns from ruddy to pink in minutes. My eyes are wide and waiting. "Well, that's the most beautiful shade of pink I've ever seen!" Dr. Alex says to me. Nurse Jenn puts the nasal cannula on her for precaution, and Dr. Alex orders them to 'hurry and give her to her mother'. I felt in that moment like it was life or death if she wasn't placed in my arms. Dr. Alex hands Stella over to me and smiles. She's still hooked to wires to measure her oxygen and heart rate, but when she's placed in my arms. She is wide awake and staring at me so intently as if to say, "I've missed you." I looked up as the team surrounding me made sure she's still pink, and Dr. Alex nods to Brook to turn off the ventilator. The whooshing sound stops just like that. I looked up as it's a sound that has been embedded in my soul, but Brook just smiles, squeezes my shoulder, and rolls the machine out of the way. Cliff arrives amongst all this and is in shock that I'm holding a fully alive, wide-awake, giant-eyed beautiful baby in my arms. We immediately switch as he deserves this just as much as I do, maybe even more. She stares at him with the same intensity as he talks to her, telling her she gave us all a good scare. But she gazes at him as if to know how much protection he brings to her. Dr. Alex is off to the side just observing as I'm sure she's required to do. But I stand in front of her as she has so many times for me and say, "Thank you for saving my daughter." She embraces me and I hug her in nothing but sheer gratitude, but I can also sense her relief. She looks at me, but her eyes are softer this time, "It was my honor to care for Stella. And an honor to know her mother and her family. She's got a road ahead of her, but you'll get her there, and quickly, I have no doubt." I hugged her again and she walked out and slid the big glass door shut. Brook and Nurse Jess surround me giving me their "I told you so's" but from a place of nothing but love. I thank them and the eruption of tears finally comes out and they just hug me. While I watch over their shoulder, Cliff kisses Stella's head.

I held a newborn who was very sick, then I watched her die in front of me. And now we have a child who was resurrected from that very death she faced. God did this. And to think He stopped all He was doing in the universe to answer a prayer like this from a person like me. I asked for a miracle, and He far exceeded what I could have ever expected.

Chapter Forty-Two

Stella stayed in the step-down unit and was monitored via a screen at the nurse's station but didn't have one-to-one care like she did before. This area was uninviting and very uncomfortable. And I was looked at not as a mom who was fighting on behalf of her child, but as if I were a mom just staying *with* her child. Her oxygen had to be at a certain level before they could deem her stable. And she had to drink from a bottle, all of which was explained to me by Dr. Alex. I attended rounds every day as I usually did, but these doctors didn't like that one bit, and I couldn't have *cared one bit*. I was my daughter's voice and her advocate, and they hadn't met the likes of me yet. The head physician had come into the room, and I assumed she was to what Dr. Alex was in the ICU. She led all the rounds and was the one asking all the questions to the students, but she never formally introduced herself to me. When someone makes an impact on my life, the life of my children, or my family, I will remember your name. It's a weird quirk of mine remembering the weirdest of people some would never think to remember. It's the same when you do something good for the wrong reasons, especially with my kids. I won't just remember your name. I'll make sure they never forget mine. Dr. Heather Thompson was one of those people that I made certain would rue the day she challenged me, and quite possibly the day she met me. So, after several days of Stella being there, she finally approached me personally. She stood across from me, on the other side of the bed. She said, "Ma'am, your daughter is very sick. We need to bring in speech occupational therapy to help feed her. Also, since she lacked oxygen for the period that she did, she may be developmentally and mentally delayed. Plus, since she was intubated for so long, she may not speak well, or if she does, it will be very limited." If I could have spit vile in that moment, she'd have had such a lethal dose it would have killed her. I took a deep breath and responded, "First off, please do not refer to me as ma'am. You are not asking for a coffee or picking up your lunch; I am Stella's mother, and I will be treated with that respect. Additionally, she *was* very sick. She is in this area because she was deemed well enough to start recovery. So, forgive me, Dr. Thompson, but despite what your medical education has taught you…I watched my daughter die. And then she was brought back to life. So, I do not receive all your "maybe worst-case scenarios-it's not only Stella that has fight in her, but so do I. And I will *not* have you speak death over my child any further. So, if you would kindly see your way out of here, that'd be great. And please remind anyone you send in here of the same." She stared at me for a beat then attempted to speak. But I stopped her and said, "The door is that way," as I motioned my hand dismissing her towards it. She turned on her heel and let out a huff of frustration and walked out. A few hours later, a speech therapist by the name of Emily came in. She was a middle-aged, nondescript woman who said she was here to help see if Stella could drink from a bottle. I already knew she could, but I humored her and motioned for her to sit as I was holding Stella. I could do this now because the only time she was hooked up to anything was the heart monitor and feeding tube, which was just a bag on a hook. Stella was awake, and she asked if she could hold her to see if she would eat. Raising my brows, I asked, "Are your hands clean?" She walked to the bathroom, and I could hear the water turn on, and she returned smelling like antiseptic soap and hospital. I offered her Stella, and she spoke softly to her, offering her a small 1oz bottle of warm formula. Stella wasn't impressed. Or she'd already has a full belly, lady, because no one turned off her feeding tube before you just showed up. This side of the house was dramatically different than that of the floor above. They were cold, uncaring, and relentlessly incompetent from what I'd been shown thus far. I motioned to give me Stella, and I took the bottle from her. She said, "She's a little tongue-tied, and it's probably hurting her throat from the intubation. Perhaps we can try tomorrow." I scoffed and gently rubbed the bottle over Stella's lips. She took it with ease and finished the entire thing and was looking for more. "Seems that was a good try. We can continue to do this until she's up to a full bottle, but if not, she may have to go home with a feeding tube to compensate for her nutrition. Also, it may be hard for her to develop at a normal pace with all the trauma she's had. She may have a small whisper or possibly not have a voice at all." Not have a voice at all? **Red**. I see only red and the vile is back, and it needs to land somewhere. What is it with these people speaking death over this little baby... well, here I go again. I asked in a very soft but succinct tone, "Emily, do you have any children?" She shook her head no. "Well, she's my *fifth* child so believe me when I say she will finish every bottle she is given. She will not go home with a feeding tube, and she will have the loudest voice of any child you've ever heard. Leave the bottles; I will handle it from here. Your services are not needed or welcomed here any longer." She looked at me blankly, and I flicked my hand just as I had earlier to Dr. Thompson and said, "There's the door." She gathered her things and walked out sheepishly. I lay Stella down to let her sleep. But mostly because I was enraged at the demons of death parading through this place with their *maybe* diagnosis. I miss Dr. Alex, Brooke, Nurse Jenn, Nurse Theresa, Nurse Chelsea, and Captain Joe and John. Like I said, if you have an impact on my life or the life of my children, I will remember your name. These doctors and nurses are nameless faces in a sea of hopelessness. That's what I was missing, hope. Hope that they will never let Stella leave this place, and Dr. Death will try to keep her grips on as long as she can.

I don't let the kids come here, and Cliff comes and goes. My mom switched off with me a night or two. But no matter where I was, I was pacing the floors waiting for someone to tell me this was my daughter's permanent residence. And I was about ready to set the place on fire and run out with her in my arms. My mom said she drank the bottles with no trouble, but she was conscious to go slow; I reveled in this. I was back in a calmer state, all things considered, on the same day Stella pulled out her feeding tube three times by herself. Even *she* was tired of this and was letting out a Bat signal for help. The nurses just did what they were told and put it back in, but this time this nurse taped it to her face with a large tiger sticker. I was tired of tape on her face entirely, but I had a little internal smile at this one.

Irony will show up at times when you least expect it, and when you notice it, it's even sweeter to acknowledge it. I cock my head slightly to the side and say to the nurse, "So, a tiger sticker to hold her feeding tube in…. hmm, interesting choice." She looks at me puzzled, and I say in a calm return, "A tiger is the most feared animal in the jungle; it has no fear and fights to protect itself." She audibly gulps. "Do you want me to change it?" I close my eyes for a moment and say, "Absolutely not, it's very appropriate, wouldn't you say?" She just stares at me for a moment. I raise my brows and smile as I walk over to Stella while this poor nurse fumbles to get her things together. Then she leaves without so much as a word. Maybe it is postpartum hormones shifting, but I am not feeling particularly pleasant when I hear a knock on the door a few hours later. And a nurse poked in to say, "Emily is here from speech and is here to work with Stella; may I let her in? She's just signing in at the desk". Is this the very woman I sent away days before? Oh, the death demon thinks she's allowed to return. I walk to the door and open it wide. "No, as I told Emily previously, her services are not needed here." This nurse with no courage at all says, "Dr. Thompson ordered her to come back; I'm so sorry, I don't know what to do." I look back to make sure Stella is asleep, and I walk out to the charge nurse. Emily is standing to the side and the mousy nurse is basically trembling. I stare at her without a word until she says, "Can I help you?" I pause to respond, "Hello, are you in charge here?" "Yeah, who wants to know?" she says as she looks at me annoyed that I bothered her in the gorging of her leftover food consumption. I retorted as I looked at her badge, "Well, Nurse Janis, I understand Dr. Thompson ordered speech to come back. But I gave specific instructions that their services are not needed or welcomed for my daughter." She responds back with a mouth full of food, "Who's your daughter again?" I can feel the heated blood coursing through my body, and my heart is pounding at an accelerated rate. My words come out in a curt tone, "Stella, room 221, *right* there", as I point to the door directly in *front* of her. She stops chewing and puts her fork down. "I am only going to say this once, Nurse Janis… please let Dr. Thompson know her death demons are no longer welcome near my child, and that includes her." The mousy nurse is wide-eyed, and a hush is now heard as I look around and all the nurses are looking at me. "Do I make myself clear?" She just nods in return. I say, "Good, now that goes for all of you too." As I motion to the rest of the gaping nurses with my hand like I was Vanna White showing a solved puzzle. "If anyone so much as breathes near my daughter unless you're trying to save her life, don't. I expect ENT in here tomorrow; now *that* you can tell your boss." I peer over at Emily and say, "Have a nice night, ma'am,", as I walk by the mousy nurse, I see her looking at the floor hiding a smile. She looks up for a second, and I wink at her as I walk back into the room with my daughter and let the door click behind me. The thing about the tiger is, the female is extremely protective of her young and would kill anything in the way of her cubs. I should put a sign on the door for warning, "Enter at your own risk; it's a jungle in here." The next day I hear another knock at the door…yep, I should've put up the sign. I open it and there are two tall men carrying large bags with them. They tell me they are from ENT from the ICU, and can they assess my daughter. I gladly motion them in. They show me a small tube they will put in her nose and her throat that has a little light attached. They can see it on the small handheld video camera they prop on the table. He disinfects everything and asks me random questions about how she's been. I respond to what happened and how we are in this pit of a floor. He nods as if he understands even what I don't say. "So, you've been here a while huh?" I respond, "That's an understatement". Suddenly it clicks, "Wait, did you say you were from the ICU?" He smiled and said, "Dr. Alex and I go way back. She called and asked if I could check on a patient, she thinks is ready to go home." He smiled at me. My heart does a full leap inside my chest. I have Stella laying on my legs as it's the easiest and calmest position for her to get poked and prodded again. "Yeah, her throat is a pretty red but that's expected with intubation. Her nose is clear, and I don't see a heaviness of mucus entrapped which is good, but she may still cough just to get whatever is still there out. But nothing to be alarmed of. Just use a bulb syringe to help her out." he says. Ok, yes, bulb syringe I have like 10 at home this isn't my first rodeo. But Dr. Alex sent him and he's the first competent doctor to help since I got to this floor filled with death demons. His assistant is making sure the video feed is recording as he works and before I know it, they were packing up. I stare at them looking for some answers. "I see no reason to keep her and allow her to recover at home. Should she relapse you come back is the worst thing that can happen. But we don't discharge we just recommend and it's up to the docs to give the final call." I thank them and walk them to the door. "I'll be sure to bring this right to Dr. Alex for review," and he squeezes my shoulder.

A few hours later, a doctor I haven't seen brings me paperwork. I brace for the worst. But, she says, "Your daughter is being discharged today. I need you to sign some papers." My heart did a complete 360 in my chest and swelled by a thousand with relief. She droned on about this and that and if this and if that. Yeah, you're another death demon too. As I sign the papers, she removes the monitor, the feeding tube, and my daughter, for the first time in seven weeks, is not hooked up to anything. I immediately pick her up and inhale her smell, her sweet baby head smell. The doctor says, "You must keep her indoors and not take her out as her immune system is still compromised; do you understand that?" I nod. "Washing of hands, hand sanitizer. Fully clean hands for anyone in your home around her, and masks if anyone shows signs of even a sniffle. Her immune system needs to recover fully, so think of keeping her in a bubble until she's grown enough to build herself back up. Now, you're free to go anytime," and she walks out. I called Cliff immediately and told him everything. I felt like he was there in record time holding a car seat at the doorway. It felt like we were escaping prison how quickly we rushed out of there and didn't look back. It wasn't until I reached the parking garage that it hit me like a tidal wave of emotions that I've held in for so long. I wept in the car silently in the back seat. Staring at my sleeping child and thanking God for saving her life as we sped home with our miracle. It feels as though it's our first time taking a baby home, even though we've done this before. This time feels more fragile, more delicate. Like she has a big Handle with Care sign waving around her. I haven't been able to bond with her like I did with all the other kids. I can't help but stare at her. I hold her little hands, which are healing from the needles they placed in her for so many weeks. I want to hold her and never put her down. I want her to lay on my chest to sleep and for me to be the first person she sees and hears when she wakes. I know this is unrealistic but in time. She is small and doesn't weigh more than seven pounds, and she was six at birth. It will be a long road of recovery. But I've been through so many battles in my life I had to fight. But the difference is this is my child. The fight is more intense and more protective. We arrive home and everyone is waiting, and when we walk in, they start cheering. Some have tears, and some can't wait to hold her and everything in between. I lay out the rules just as they were conveyed to me, and, surprisingly, everyone complies. They do so over and over. Until I don't need to remind anyone to wash their hands or sanitize before touching her. My mom is headed home, and she holds her and hugs her to her chest, and I think she too is thanking the God of the Universe for saving her. I thank her for her help and hug her tightly. A strange sense of unspoken words will always linger about my life. It will include my childhood, her leaving, and me caring for Gram. And she is leaving to go back to Texas to a man and leaving once again. But I let it go for now as if this is her way to somehow redeem herself. Or if that's what she probably tells herself. I wish her safe travels and Cliff takes her to the airport. That was October of 2019, and I've not seen my mom, Louise, ever since.

As the kids take turns with their new but old baby sister, they grew tired of her normal baby cries for food and a change of diaper. She has enough attention and love so that's not it. I tag in and they look at me in wonder at how I can take her from crying to calm and steady. They have no idea that my world was completely rocked over the past 2 months, so this is bliss for me. Waking me up every two hours, gladly.

Telling people like our church family she's home and can they visit, I say no, gladly. This time was for us. And as soon as he heard her daddy's voice, she looked around for him. He scooped her tiny body up, holding her bottom with one hand as she lay on his chest. The same nook on his chest that was designed for me, I think is designed for every baby too.

I get a call while making dinner, something I haven't been able to do but revel in right now. When I answer, it's my old boss Jay, who called when I was pregnant asking me if I was interested in a job. I thought perhaps he was checking in to see how I was, but he again said there was an opening and if I was interested. I gulped, taken out of my own bubble, and filled him in on the shortened version of what happened and is happening with Stella's care. He is empathetic as he had a preemie daughter who stayed much longer than mine, but just because she was born early. Not because she died, and God raised her from the dead. He asked what I needed to consider the job. There was no question; it needed to be remote. He compromised and said he could do four days. This is the same company and job I had before, just under new management. I consider it for a beat and say, I'll agree to interview, but I'm not giving him a yes because you need a body to fill the job. Well, I started in two weeks. At a salary he doubled from the last. I couldn't say no, not under the current circumstances. Cliff makes it work where he can stay longer hours at work and have off Mondays to care for Stella as that was the day I had to be in the office. The office was the size of a waiting room at a doctor's office; it smelled of burnt coffee and no one was ever there, including my boss. I drive home each Monday and cry because I have been through so much as of late. I'm on barely any sleep, I miss my baby, my body looks like a mac truck ran over it and I wonder what the point is of only going in one day. My baby needs me. And I went through hell and back just to leave her for 15 hours a day including commute. This goes on for months and the holidays come and go. Stella is growing and stacking weight like a sumo wrestler. But it takes a while, much longer as she's still fighting to get her immune system back in top shape. When I'm home I like to keep the Today show on in the morning after my early calls to recalibrate my mind. And I see breaking news—outbreak of a global pandemic called Covid-19.

Chapter Forty-Three

I listen intently to the developing story as they need two weeks and for everyone to remain on lockdown until they figure it out. Two weeks turned into two years. All hospitals overflowed. Makeshift tents in various cities were full, too. Death from this awful disease took over the world. The shortage of hand sanitizer and masks we had in plenty of already, but not for Covid-19, but so Stella could live. But even with that lingering thought in my mind, a new adjustment to life was again imminent. Schools shut down, jobs were now being done remotely, and all businesses closed. And each of you have your own good or bad memories that you went through individually, so I won't belabor it. But if you're reading this, know there was good in those moments of isolation. People were forced to know their family whom they may have just passed once a week on their way out or in. People learned how to cook and find what their passions were. As for us, forcing us inside couldn't have proven every death demon wrong. For us later that year, Cecelia started her first year at her dream college and was living in a real college dorm! Stella picked up her head from her belly for the first time. Then she learned how to sit up. She learned how to army crawl to an eventual full-blown crawl across the floor.

And she did this with her whole family encouraging her on at every milestone. Then she learned how to walk and, like I said before, I knew be the loudest kid in the house. This was all while learning remote school for all the kids and adjusting to this "new normal." But if life taught me anything, it's that if you have lemons, add a little sugar, and make lemonade.

Stella celebrated her first birthday that August. The same August a year ago, she was rushed and declared dead and brought back to life. As she dove into her pink cake, taking fistfuls into her mouth, clapping, and smiling. While surrounded by all the people around her who haven't left her side. I squeeze Cliff's hand and without a word he squeezes back, knowing what I'm already thinking. No matter what fire we go through, we come out not just unscathed but never smell like smoke and not even a scuff of soot on us.

Chapter Forty- Four

Restlessness can be described as the quality of being unwilling or unable to stay still. As humans, we attempt to silence this restlessness in a variety of ways. Because if we can mute our restlessness, then we don't have to deal with it. People choose to numb restlessness by drinking or substance abuse, which is a form of anesthesia to cause a numbing sensation. But food, shopping, busyness, and social media consumption can serve as socially acceptable numbing agents as well. It is only when these behaviors become compulsive that we typically flag them as problems. But many of us turn to retail therapy or binge-watching to cope with uncomfortable or unsettling feelings. But spiritual restlessness is something entirely different. This is an unsettling of your soul, like you know there is more than the life you're currently existing in. Maybe because we live between Eden and eternity. As a result, we're spiritually restless people until we get into the thing we were made for. We were put on this Earth to fix a problem only we can fix. Helping the people who need to know why you don't smell like the countless fires you've been through needs to know how to cope with theirs. C.S. Lewis so eloquently put it, "If I find in myself a desire which no experience in this world can satisfy, the most probable explanation is that I am made for another world". As the world began to reopen, a series of awful, orchestrated events struck our house. The one we called home after being home*less*… started to turn on us. Since we had stopped in the south years prior, it still hadn't left our minds, or our hearts. And it was a spiritual pull we never felt went away. But what we weren't feeling was just a pull, but an all-around uncomfortable sense of being pushed out of this home. The dryer broke numerous times, and the landlord never could spring for a new one. Then the mice arrived. Yes, mice. It's okay to wince; I did. But we figured we lived near woods, and it was cold, so they were looking for a place to stay warm. We laid traps in the basement and filled every day with stuck rodents on sticky glue coaxed by none other than peanut butter. I lived in the city my whole life and I never saw anything like this, ever. We had exterminator after exterminator put traps. They say it's supposed to eat it and take it back to the commune of its family and share it and they all die. Sounds fantastic. As I saw the little blue packets, resembling laundry pods, being taken away from their locations I thought we were in the clear. So, I worked, went about life and was just grateful for all we had endured, this included. However, I had a very high tolerance for things as life had thrown me an insane number of battles to fight, but not this time; I had zero. Now I see them under the stove when I cook, and under the fridge, **NO WAY**. This I have no tolerance for. We aren't living in some tenement, and I have kids here and my landlord does *nothing*. I feel like I must order pizza all the time just to avoid one popping up under the warm stove while I cook. It gives me the heebie-jeebies just thinking about it…. but we started noticing a trend. If we turned a space heater on, it would blow the fuse of the whole house if you ran the microwave. And the circuit breaker is in the dungeon of a basement no one dares to go. We've been here almost 5 years and suddenly I feel like I'm in Lemony Snicket's A Series of Unfortunate Events, as all the unfortunate events start playing out. But spiritual discernment requires a skill. It must distinguish between opposing forces. It's the ability to perceive and recognize the difference between truth and error. And to tell the difference between God's will and human desires. Our desire was to stay here, let our kids be okay and Cliff work for the state until retirement and we drive off into the sunset. The kicker was the new lease increasing our rent by $200 a month. Ok God, I see you. You're pushing us out. This was for a season but now the season's changing. We are now at the end our rope and I don't care who likes it or who is on board; I must start looking for somewhere else to live. I'm a pro at starting over...just not with a family of seven. I log on to every home website, looking at the town we currently live in. But we live on the other side of the tracks, blue collar, where the hardworking people are. And all that's available are houses with circular driveways that probably house CEO's and surgeons and the like. And they are way out of our price range and stature. As I'm about to give up for the day, I'm led to looking south near the church we visited. I laugh to myself. Come on, we've been there *once*; what is so great about it? I keep telling myself. But as I researched and humored myself, I saw the homes were big, affordable, and nothing I've ever dreamed I'd be able to live in. Just like the very ones I was looking at locally. This was not a me choosing to go there thing as I had nothing to go on but a one-day pass memory. And I asked all the practical questions like where the best place is to live, and what are the schools like. And that killed me because the kids loved their school, but this was like a pull-type feeling, like we needed to escape a looming fire. Cliff was so miserable at his job, and even though it had great health benefits and a pension, it had practically aged him ten years as they were working him to the core. I showed him a few houses and he really liked them but scoffed when I said I was applying for one. He didn't give me a second thought except to say, "If it's God's will then it's already ours". Since Thanksgiving was upon us, I refocused, hoping I wasn't met with any unexpected "guests". As I served the meal, I had a sudden feeling come over me, like a voice I hadn't heard before, and I stopped and hitched in a breath. I said, "This is the last time we will celebrate this time of year or any holidays in this house ever again." All eyes locked on me thinking maybe I left my brain on the stove or drank too many glasses of wine. But this was deep in my soul, and I couldn't shake it. We had to move, and we had to move quickly. No other day like the first of the new year to start making some changes. I kept up my search and I found a perfect place, 4 bedrooms, 2 bathrooms, and so on. All of which I kept to myself. I paid the fee and applied, saying I was involved in a church there (or a one-day pass memory) and I wanted a better life for my children. I think they had a pretty great life except for the constant series of unfortunate events that were too many to count. I heard nothing, crickets for a week. Thinking they had just denied us, I overthought and threw a pity party for one. And the constant loop of thought "ugh I'm stuck in this house forever" played like a broken record in my brain. It didn't stop until God had Linda, a lovely woman who called me randomly one day asking me if I had heard anything on the house I applied for. I think she could hear my apprehension on the phone, as she told me she was a realtor at the same firm of the home I inquired about. Okay, that makes sense, so I allowed the conversation to continue acting blasé about it and said no, I hadn't heard anything. She paused, then told me it was off the market but happy to help me find something and to just let her know what I wanted. I know how realtors are; heck, I worked for one who was a super manipulator to make a sale. So, I asked, "Why do you want to help me?" She responded quietly, "Honestly, I just felt really compelled to call you." I sat down on the floor stunned. Because the last time someone called me from number in the south, they too felt "compelled" to call me. And they didn't know who I was then either but wound up blessing me beyond measure. God sent Linda my way because He knows I don't do anything without a fight. Was He in charge of the series of very unfortunate events to push us to where He wanted us? My brain flooded with a fast slurry of flashbacks. Like I was at the end of a movie, and they were capturing the main character's good and bad moments and all the people along the way. Linda said my name and I was immutably jolted back to the conversation. "What are you looking for?" When I don't say anything, she says, "In a house, bathrooms & bedrooms to accommodate your family, I'm happy to see what's available and email you over some listings." I respond, "Right, of course-at least four bedrooms, two bathrooms, and a yard for my kids." I don't ask for much because I don't come from much. Having two bathrooms seems like luxury to me. The house we are in is 900 square feet not counting the attic which does span the house and one bathroom. And we've managed for several years to be a family here with no complaints until now. So,

I kept it as simple to Linda as possible and she said she'd be in touch. When I told Cliff, he said, "Nothing surprises me when God's involved. I want to be wherever He wants us to be". I love that about him; he's optimistic to a fault. But as for me, I'm as stubborn as they come.

The next morning, I bundled up and got ready for a run in the freezing cold, but I didn't care. I've been doing this so long there are certain times of the year that I love to run. In the middle of summer, where you sweat every toxin out of you. And the dead of winter, where the cold air fills your lungs, and you can see your breath as you exhale the toxins out. After several miles and playlists later, I arrived back home. Dreading walking in and pondering what unfortunate event or thing happened in the short time I was gone, I took off my gloves and headband, which covered my ears standing there just waiting. The house seemed eerily normal. Maybe it was the endorphins, not wanting to ruin my high. I got in the shower; the warm water stung my cold extremities, even my face. After a few moments, I warmed up, then I heard my phone buzzing with a flood of texts. It was still in its holder I wrapped around my arm when I ran because I threw all my stuff on my bed when I came in. I could hear it as the bathroom was right next to my bedroom, and the sound continued. I hurried the rest of my shower as the rolodex of worst-case scenarios was spinning feverishly in my head. I grabbed a towel and tore out of the bathroom as if the looming fire was getting closer. I tugged the phone out of its holder—Linda, 11 messages. I just talked to her yesterday, and she said she'd email me over listings. I really hope she's not an overbearing realtor who just wants to make a buck. I opened the messages, and there were eleven videos.

I opened the first one, then the next, until I made it to the last message: "I saw this and knew I had to view it for you. Call me and let me know what you think!" As I stood there still dripping from the shower, I knew I had just watched an entire walkthrough of the house we were going to live in. I get dressed and find Cliff and show him what she sent over. I said, "Before you ask, no, I didn't ask her to do this; I came back from my run, and she was spamming me with videos while I was in the shower." He looked at me and said, "Did you tell her our budget? That looks way over it. It's huge." He chuckled in disbelief. I said firmly, "We prayed for a big house and gave specifics, and this hits every single one and we *cannot* stay here." He responded, "Just call her back and see how much it is." I pick up my phone and called Linda back; she answered on the first ring, "Do you love it? I think it's perfect. I saw it and had to drive to do a tour for you." I said, "Hi Linda, thanks so much for doing that, it all looks amazing, the house is really beautiful." She went on about how it's in a community and has a pool, amenities, playgrounds, and is maintained well, even considering the time of year. I asked her how much it was and when she responded with it being lower than our max allotted, I nearly dropped the phone. But I came back to logic and reasoning and said, "Wow that's great, but what's the catch." She said, "I knew you'd say that. There are multiple applications already on this house, but I'll put yours in since I already have it for the other house. I'll call the person who is handling it and let them know you're being represented by me and my firm and see what happens." I let out an internal sigh. Why, if there are many people vying for a house already, did you even *show it to me?* Show me a house no one wants. Then no competition! But I graciously agreed, and she said she'd be in touch. She asked me to send her proof of income, assets, all things that would be required for an approval. She sounded way too happy, all things considered. But not too soon thereafter, I got an email. "Congratulations" and a bunch of other words. We were approved for the house. I immediately showed Cliff and we looked at each other in shock but some form of elation and disbelief all at the same time. If we agreed to this, it would mean Cliff would have to quit his job, but since mine was remote it didn't matter where I was. Linda called and congratulated us. But also said we needed to act quickly as if we didn't put the earnest money down in 24 hours, they were going to the next interested person. Cliff instructed me to do it and said if we followed what God wanted, we couldn't fail. Again, with the optimism. My whole life has been a series of unfortunate events, and I was just waiting for the other proverbial shoe to drop with this too. I was given instructions to log into a portal that would allow me to sign any paperwork electronically and make the deposit. I clicked on the link, and I sat there watching this screen for what felt like a very long time. As I waited, I recounted all the hellacious and difficult experiences. But also, the good and glorious moments that have brought me to this very moment. I've done a lot of hard things, but this is a big hard I'm asking my family to do too. If I go, it may be a chance at a new life. But if I stay here in this house, I'll metaphorically die. I ran through the scenarios in my head to make it somehow mane sense; Cecelia is in college now and Ava is graduating high school. The screen fades as if the computer is about to go into sleep mode, and I come back to the life changing moment in front of me. I've never done anything without thinking about how it would impact anyone else. I've always been the one to sacrifice, go without, and help anyone I can even with the little I may have had. I always tried to be what I didn't have to my kids, and not giving them a life that they deserve is not doing that. I make the transaction and wait for my confirmation to appear. I log out and close the laptop while the tears form in my eyes knowing everyone's life is about to change.

Communication was received from Linda that the house was now off the market. Nope, there was no turning back now or we would lose a few thousand dollars we had saved. It was all the money we had, so nothing like jumping into the deep end. We were given a sign-your-documents email following a pickup your keys end of February. Once we had confirmation, we told the kids and showed them the videos. They were elated and I said they'd all have their own room too. They were sold on that alone. Since Cecelia was in college living in the dorm in her dream school, I wasn't worried about an impact a move would have on her. She was independent and rarely came home. But Ava still had a few months to go until graduation and I was at a loss as to how to handle that. And she wasn't happy that we were moving, to say the least. She had a boyfriend, Mark, who was a great kid and parents that were hardworking, modest like us, and loved Ava like their own. His mom, Tammy reached out to me after Ava shared the news with them. She was probably in tears and who knows what other horrors she told them. But she said Ava could stay with them and she'd make sure she had her own room, and so on. I almost said no, but she said, "We love Ava, like our own. Please let us take care of her until she's done with school. Don't sacrifice giving your kids a better life, giving *you* a better life, just for a few short months of Ava being here." So, I agreed reluctantly. She was so happy and couldn't wait to "redecorate" for her arrival. Cliff gave ample notice at his job and suddenly everyone, even the difficult people who made his job harder, were sad to see him go. We started packing and just preparing so we weren't waiting till the last minute. We purged and got rid of a lot, which the dumpster divers had no problem taking when we left items on the curb. I scoured prices for moving trucks, but since Covid, so many people were leaving that the prices had skyrocketed. I found a place called Pack U. They drop off steel packing bins for three days. Then, they pick them up and deliver them to your destination, and the cost was reasonable, plus we wouldn't have to drive a giant moving van. But the only thing we had in our accounts was our paychecks. Then Cliff said since he was leaving his state job, he was going to borrow from his pension and close it out. After he submitted the application, and after taxes, it was enough to cover the Pack U and clean up the house, with some left over. We decided that when we got the keys and went to the new house, we'd stay the weekend, this way Cecelia and Ava could go too. Then we'd come back for two weeks and do the final clean up and painting. We didn't want to be dinged by this ruthless landlord. I told Linda when we'd arrive, and she would meet us at the house to do the walk through. We drove for ten hours and stayed in a hotel the night before as we had an early time to meet with the other agent. We entered the glass building and told the receptionist who we were, and she asked us to have a seat. I felt like my breakfast was about to make a reappearance when a nice older lady named Lynn greeted us. We sat at a small table signing various things, and she handed us a welcome bag and the keys to our new house. She congratulated us; we thanked her and shook her hand. Then we walked out as if we'd done this several times in our lives and this was just another transaction. What she didn't know is I could hear my pulse whoosh in my ears and my heart raced a thousand beats because I'd never done this before, ever. But Cliff grabbed my hand on the way back to the car and squeezed it. As our unspoken words again can convey volumes to each other of elation, and what the heck did we just do? We got back in the car and held up the keys and the kids cheered, well, all but Ava. We set our GPS to our new address and turned into a beautifully manicured development. We came upon the home that we agreed to live in, sight unseen, just a simple view of eleven videos. We pulled up and it was like nothing I've ever lived in or even visited before. The street is quiet, but it's chilly and understandable for this time of year as it's still winter. We're used to ambulances and sirens and cars driving by at rapid speed, so this sound of quiet was welcoming. The house is gray with black shutters and black trim, and the front door is a deep big black steel door. Not like Grams' green one, but close. Olivia stands near me as I can feel the presence of her light in the space around me as she waits eagerly for me to open the door. My hands are trembling, and she says, "Mommy is okay, open it." My hands trembling, I open both locks, turn the knob, and open the door. I am met with dark hardwood floors, high ceilings throughout the whole front space. And a multitude of big windows everywhere. They are topped with white, floor-to-ceiling curtains and heavy blinds. They let in so much light, I don't think I'll ever need a lamp. Isn't that like God to see you sitting in darkness for so long that when he gives you something there is so much light attached to it. I see the kitchen is to the right, and it is draped in white cabinetry, gray and white granite coun- tertops with a island that holds the sink and the dishwasher. I've never seen anything like this in person. This is a far way away from that rowhome in Philly and me pillaging for scraps. The kids run up the stairs that held a stained banister to claim their rooms. In the back there is another bedroom and a full bathroom as if it was made for a guest area. There is a 2-car garage and enough space just on the first floor for us to live comfortably. I head upstairs where I hear the patter of footsteps running back and forth. Olivia and Xavier have claimed their rooms, and they both have more floor space than we have at our Jersey house combined. I see a smaller room off to the side next to the full-sized laundry room. It has a small built-in bookshelf nook with a dim light overhead. Stella sat on the floor and said this was her room. I cannot argue with that as it was a perfect Goldilocks-sized room as if made just for her. Cliff and I enter the giant master bedroom, and both look at each other in awe. For some, this may seem normal or even small, and possibly wouldn't even hold all their things. But for me, this is the kind of bedroom you see on TV, not in real life. This is a far way to go from the little brown room I stayed in for so many years at Grams. There are double doors that are closed, and I think they open to a small en suite bathroom. Cliff opens them and I'm in shock. I am met with a bathroom the size of the bedroom we are leaving in Jersey! It has a separate tub, a stand-up glass shower to the right, a vanity with his and hers sinks to the left and a separate room with a toilet. Then beyond another door is a giant walk-in closet as if it was designed with two separate sides in mind, his and hers. At the Jersey house we have a small closet that Cliff kept his work clothes in. But I kept my clothes on the floor and hung up in a makeshift closet that was so cold from no insulation that many of my shoes and things would be ruined over time. But not this closet. This is again floor to ceiling built-in shelves and racks to hang clothes on both sides. I was hit with a sudden memory of asking the girls next door if they had any old clothes they were getting rid of because we had no new school clothes. And they graciously piled a trash bag full of things for me and Sam to wear. I lived out of trash bags not just that time, but too many more to count. And I was standing in a room of *shelves* for clothes, not bags, or floors. The kids came in shaking off the ghost of my past and stood there in awe just like we did. They asked, "Is this your *bathroom*?" I stand there just as in shock as they are and just nod my head. And instead of standing there in unbelief, I asked to see the rooms they chose. Olivia picked the back room with the mirrored closet doors. It also is a walk-in closet just a smaller version of ours with the built-in shelves and racks. Xavier is already planning where his things will go in the giant oversized room he chose. Cecelia and Ava did their own tour and found the fenced-in back yard with the patio we can put a table and chairs and can even string twinkling lights overhead. I hear from the front door "Hello? Anyone home?" I know that voice, Linda. I greet her with a giant hug and start to cry. I whisper, "Thank you for listening to that feeling and calling me that day". As a few tears fell; she looked at me wiping my tears while she was holding back hers. She has daughters and, in that moment, she treated me just like one of her own. We did the walk-through and she showed me some "normal" things for the southern homes. They were in fact the closets and even a tilt-out drawer in front of the sink. I thanked her for all her help, and we would be back in two weeks as we had to wrap up our other house back in Jersey. We said our goodbyes and just like so many before her, came into my life for a short season and did what God needed her to do. And then just like that, she was gone.

We slept on air mattresses for the weekend as we familiarized ourselves with the area. But we were only there for a short time as everyone had to get back to school and life. And before I knew it, we were back in Jersey packing up the last of our things in the steel bins. Painting the nicks on the walls, filling holes from photos that hung. Almost erasing the life and love held over time here. When we finished packing the Pack-U's, and the guys came to pick them up. I watched as our lives were craned into those steel bins and loaded onto flatbeds for the trip to our new home. Far, far away from the series of unfortunate events. The night before we left, I followed Ava as she drove to Mark's house with her belongings packed up in her trunk. It was frigid in Jersey this time of year, but that night felt much colder. Even if just for a few months, a part of me felt so guilty for leaving her here. Even though she's staying at the same high school, same area, and nothing changes. But so much of me feels the pain resurface from when my mom left. It's not the same, and I know it's short-lived, but I am leaving a part of me behind, and that's what hurts the most. I wonder if my mom ever felt like she left a part of her behind. Mark, Tammy, and his dad, Mack, were so happy when Ava arrived. Tammy couldn't wait to show her to her room. She had turned what was a storage room into a beautiful room made for a young woman with bedding and closet space. Even flowers and pictures on the walls. I hugged Tammy, thanking her so much. Mark stood there looking awkward; then he and his dad went and got Ava's things from the car. I knew she'd be in good hands. But I still went over the doctors' details and when to use her inhaler. She stopped me and said, "She's going to be okay. I got it. Take a breath." I know you have a lot to do, so say goodbye, and you know she's already here more than she is anywhere else. So now she just sleeps here too." Ava walked me out to the truck, and I reminded her to take care of the car and herself. I told her I'd let her know when we got there, and I just droned on in the frigid night air until tears started to fall. I hugged her tightly and breathed in the scent of her hair and vanilla sugar cookie scent so I could remember it. "I love you to the moon and back," she said. I kissed both of her cheeks like she was a small child and told her to go inside; it was too cold for her asthma. She rolled her eyes and said, "Love you," and disappeared into the house. And then I cried the whole drive home. Once I got back to the house, Cliff had set up the air mattresses, as we were leaving early. I was trying to avoid a walkthrough with the landlord, who never cared about the issues his home gave us. I barely slept. It was just, so, empty. Even though where we were going held so much promise and it was much bigger, this was the place we came out of homelessness together, the place we brought Stella home to *twice*. And the place we came together as a family when we couldn't be anywhere else. This was a place that, despite the series of unfortunate events, held just as many fortunate ones, too. We woke in the morning and packed all we could into the trunk and took one last look through the house to make sure we got everything. Including all the memories I could bank in my mind because it was time to make new ones. As we pulled away, I looked through the rear-view mirror knowing if I return to this place, I won't be the same person I was leaving. 10 hours later, we pull into the driveway of our new home and the first thing I notice is the sunshine. The brightness of the sky emanating light everywhere. The air isn't frigid and there is a sort of stillness in its place. The Pack-U truck isn't scheduled till later in the day so we get what we can inside. And the kids find their little nooks and spaces to watch videos on their tablets. I call Cecelia and Ava and let them know we've arrived, and I'll see them soon. The next time I'll see them will be for Ava's graduation which seems so far away. My heart is breaking; I miss them so much. Did we make the right decision? A sudden heaviness and a sense of doom hit me. I got a text from someone I knew at the church I had a "one day pass" to and they asked how the trip was. I told some people I was moving, and they were excited as perhaps I'd want to volunteer once I arrived. But I *just* got here. I told them I'd be in touch once we got settled. All our belongings arrived safely, and I had the WI-Fi people set us up the same day. I only had one day off and I had to get back to work even if it was remote. We unpacked the steel boxes a lot faster than we packed them. Once everything was set up it was like another Goldilocks moment; everything fit just right. Things we stored in one house fit as if they were custom made for this one. Cliff is the designer in our home so I let him do his thing and helped where I could. He's extremely creative so when he has a vision of what a room should look like, I just let him take the wheel. The kids' rooms got set up first with their beds and their belongings so they could feel a sense of something familiar. I worked at the side counter as that seemed like as good a place as any, as that's where I had been before. But I helped to unpack and organize any chance I got during my workdays. The kids started their new school about a week later and after some adjusting, they seemed to like it just fine. There were more kids than at their last school and this seemed bigger. I still had that looming thought of whether we made the right decision. They are only in school for all but two months and it's the end of the school year. They end early June here, not like Jersey where they go until practically July. Needless to say, they were happy they were out for summer. I was too, hoping it would give them time to adjust to life here, make memories, and just feel a sense of home. We were planning on taking another road trip back to Jersey at the end of the month as Ava was graduating, and with high honors to boot. Things seemed okay but I still had this unsettling feeling I could not shake, chalking it up to adjusting to a new place. Working as a project manager, you have early calls due to time zone differences with other teams. So, my work calls are as early as 7am. Eastern time every day. I conclude all the early calls and around 9am then I usually take a few to regroup, grab some coffee, and plan the day. Until I hear my laptop Teams call coming through the speakers with the awful ringtone. Thinking it's now business hours, I see it's the woman from human resources calling me. Oh no, she found out I moved, and I was supposed to fill out a form. Or maybe I can't live here and work remotely. I scanned through thoughts overwhelming me in panic, but I answered in a happy good morning tone. Then I scanned the names on the call and someone else was on, the grumpy VP named Mike whom I was now reporting to. My other boss Jay got let go during 2020 with a bunch of the team so

I was happy to have stayed on. But this new guy was not a kind human, so I tried to keep my distance. When I saw his name and hers, the rage I felt started to erupt inside of me like a volcano. Woosh, woosh, is all I hear as in my ears, as my blood pressure raised. They rattled off something about being acquired and they unfortunately were closing shop at the end of the year. And there it is…today was my last day. Same lady that came into my office all those years ago and walked me out the back like a prisoner was doing the same thing again. Only behind a screen. We just moved, Cliff hasn't found work and I start to flip through that good old book of worst-case scenarios again. I hear them say they are paying me till the end of the month and a six-week severance will be forthcoming. As much panic as I felt I responded, "Okay, thank you. I'll look for the paperwork and send it back as soon as it's received. Also please let me know where to mail the laptop." No one said anything for a beat as I think they were expecting me to freak out considering I was doing the job of three people. The HR lady said, "Thank you for your professionalism, we wish you the best." I ended the call without a response and just stood there in this beautiful kitchen feeling like the world was caving in on me; on us, again. I muster all my courage and walk into the room where Cliff is and tell him trembling, "well, I just got laid off." I told him about the severance and pay till the end of the month. He stared at me for what felt like several heartbeats and stood in front of me and said, "Babe, it's okay, that place was no good to you. God got you out and that means He has something better coming." He hugged me and told me it's going to be okay. And all I can think is I'm going to start calling him Mr. Glass Half -Full, from now on. Because he's always looking through those rose-colored glasses, I wish I could see out of too. We headed back to Jersey to see Ava graduate. Seeing her with several honor cords around her neck made all my guilt about leaving her disappear, if just for a moment. She applied to at least a dozen colleges and universities and got into most. But she settled on the one that "gave her the most money," as she calls it, and accepted the offer for a school in Florida. Tammy and Mack threw a graduation party for her and Mark. They set up several tents outside and had everything on the menu. And more cakes and desserts than one can count. I thanked them personally for all they did for Ava. From making sure she got to her senior trip on time to helping her get ready for prom. And for being there through all the milestones I missed. Great, now the guilt I feel is back tenfold. We stayed briefly and talked about when Ava would be heading home to be with us, even if briefly, before she headed to school in August. She fought me as if to say she'd leave from there and not stay with us, as technically "it's not her home." She's just as stubborn as I am, but just days ago, I was let go from my job, and I had no energy to argue. Mack said she can stay as long as she wants but would make sure Mark drove with her when she headed there. That was assurance enough for me, as my brain couldn't process how to do anything else but survive in this moment. We left and headed home the next day, and for the first time, I wasn't sad leaving as I was the last time, even if it was a few months ago. We had been attending the church we only had a one-day pass memory of, and it was nothing like the one time we were here before. I had expected to have people remember me, or even just do so much as reach out and say hello, but nothing. We even got told we couldn't sit in certain areas with our kids as it was "live" streamed. Listen super usher, how do you know this isn't the day my kids have an actual encounter with God themselves? This is not the same place I visited before and had people waiting for me upon entry. And those very people, avoided me like the plague, especially knowing I had just moved in right in their backyard. So, we paused on attending the actual campus church and stayed home; I felt so rejected. But thought maybe a few bad apples can't ruin the whole bunch. Oh, but yes, they can...I reached out to the guy whom I knew from that very church and told him I had some "free time" now so I could help only with only online serving. I didn't want to be angry with God because people in His house were as fake as three-dollar bill and all I wanted to help people. So, I chatted with him as I simultaneously applied for unemployment, again. This was a team that people went to for financial help, sort of a benevolence team. Oh, the irony. I couldn't make this up if I tried. They have teams that care for people at the actual churches that need help, but this was for those who watched from afar, like I had done. So *now* the online team has the funds to help those in need? And we're not just going to offer to put them in a shelter like they did for me many years ago? Again, oh the irony. I met the outreach lead, and he filled me in on the work they do. Then, he connected me with the team lead, who lived in Pennsylvania. I was on this team for about a month until I saw no one and I mean *no one* from this church was helping anyone with *anything*. Even a mom who lost her job with 4 boys and volunteers on 2 teams and tithes to the church, zero help was given. I felt like giving someone a spreadsheet and helping them map out a budget was not being the hands and feet of Jesus. If anything, it was portraying a very Judas spirit towards these people who looked to the place they served their God for help. Additionally, the team knew I had just moved and lost a good job and didn't offer once to even help me, one of their own. I never asked, but it was mentioned to me many times, "What are you going to do? You have *real* needs." I got my severance and was on unemployment. That would only hold us for so long. But, I replied, "Don't worry. Next time you talk to me, I'll have a job." This team was a bunch of dream crushers and death demons to people's hope and faith. This "church" was deceiving and gave such a false representation of who they were that I felt ashamed *for* them. We had a meeting with another group they wanted to join with to make one big team. But I was not sticking around to find out how that would work, I had made a huge mistake on a one-day manipulation pass. But an older gentleman was on the call, surely someone's dad and pop-pop kind of age. I guess my pensive face was palpable though the screen as he asked me what I thought this team should look like. And without thinking about it, I blurted out, "Church should be like a hospital. And we should be able to care for any illness, sickness, struggle, addiction, whatever the need, in any way possible, without any judgment. Maybe it's the ER they enter first and they get triaged and sent to the right specialist, but that is not what is being done now. We are sending them away without so much as an instruction on what to do, let alone help them through their suffering." All eyes were on me, and I could hear a pin drop. I was in no mood for these people, and I was sick of playing this game while I was having an internal and existential crisis of my own. I heard, "I completely agree," said the older man. "My name is Chaplain Garrison Evan and I have never heard anyone use the hospital model like I do in all my years of service to the Lord. And I worked as a hospice chaplain for 10 of those. Let's connect at your convenience; I'd like to hear more of your thoughts and see how we can align better." I nodded and said I was free anytime, cause, well, I was.

Ava arrived in mid-July, found a serving job, only for us to drive her to Florida a month later. I was becoming exhausted from looking for jobs and applying, only to be met with rejection. Until I had a few interviews and landed a gig with a major health insurance company starting in September. It wasn't nearly what I was making, but we'd have to make it work in the interim. We got Ava to Florida, and we got her the items she needed: bedding, food, and the like. But what she didn't know is that we only had $600 left in our bank account, and we still had to get home. We set her up in her dorm, but you could tell she wanted none of us there for too long. Florida is hot and it's uncomfortable, stifling, but this is her element. The beach, the water, the sun. Just not mine. When we arrived home, I had an email from Garrison Evan asking if we could chat this week. Oh, great, you are apart of this fraudulent church too? Could things get any worse?

Chapter Forty- Five

Garrison set up a Zoom call for the following day. The first thing he said was, "The pensiveness in your eyes is a sight I will never forget for the rest of my days." I took an audible gulp. He chuckled and said, "What I mean is you were very Christ-like in that moment. When he was flipping tables over the merchants selling in the temple. When he said it was a sacred place of prayer, he was savage. Though loving, he couldn't tolerate sacred things being twisted for gain. And you showed that just by the way you looked that day; you were disgusted for the same reason. You need to help those in real need, and I believe I have an opportunity for you to do just that. I run a mental health coaching team outside of the "church". We train individuals just like yourself to work with people in need for five to six months. And we help them through whatever they may be struggling with." I responded, "Wait, you want *me* to be someone's coach to help them with *their* mental health?" totally caught off guard. I asked myself, does this guy doesn't know anything *about* me? My own mental health is so jacked up how on earth can I help someone else through their mess? He said before I could think about it any further, "you have story and a tough one at a that, one that was hard and not easy; that I can easily tell. And there is no more perfect person to go through what you've gone through and be a light for someone else. Letting them know they are seen and heard and can get through whatever it is they are facing. And you are a living epistle of that." My eyes welled up in that moment. I felt a tug at my heart saying you always wanted to help those who didn't have a voice like you didn't, now's your chance. He said, "The course is about four months, and it's quite pricy but I will get you a scholarship if you agree to do it. If I can guarantee your placement, will you do this?" I felt like Tom Cruise in Mission Impossible with the looming question "should you choose to accept your mission." But he always did because there was always someone or something important at stake. "Ok, I'll do it." I said without thinking about it. Garrison smiled and left me with words that still stay with me to this day. "The courses are tough, and they cover some tough topics so if you need to pause, debrief, I'm here." I got access to the courses and finished in 10 days. TEN days. Not four months as originally told. It covers everything from showing how to deal with suicide to psychotic breakdowns. Well, if I haven't experienced all fourteen lessons personally, I don't know who is more prepared than me. Garrison met me again on Zoom once I had completed the courses to debrief. "Young lady, you don't cease to amaze me. I knew you'd get through that, and I knew giving to you was the right thing to do because you lived each one, haven't you?" I responded with just a nod. "Great. I teach a course on Critical Incident Stress Management. It's a fancy way of saying Immediate Crisis Intervention and I'm willing to teach it to you to combine with your coursework. No charge, just about 40 hours of your time and my investment in someone the Lord showed me is worth it." I took him up on the offer and I learned so much. I must take breaks because it hit so close to home. If someone did for me what I could now do for someone in a time of crisis, I'd have avoided so much hurt. All my teaching concludes, and I have my first client, then my second, and my third. All while helping them on the sidelines gain their lives back is what I know I was made to do. I am now a Board-Certified Mental Health Coach and in Crisis Intervention. I can be called on by any hospital, accident, or police issue at any time to de-escalate a person or situation. I've committed to this and there is no going back. I have my fourth client, then my fifth, then sixth, and all in different situations, but seeing in real time their lives change. I'm helping people who are suicidal be talked to about how they matter and to not give up is such a place I never thought I'd be. I called Garrison and thanked him. He only said, "Glad I listened when I did. You have a gift, young lady; you are God's hand on earth that these people need." I started working my regular job while still managing to help these amazing broken people. But watching them come back to life after just a few months of listening, guidance, and faith in them ignited mine. I didn't do the work for them. I just made sure they followed through, and I was committed to each one because no matter what they were dealing with, I knew what to do. People were in crisis from abuse, domestic violence, suicidal thoughts and ideations, death, grief, and complete mental breakdowns. Also, those with anxiety and panic disorder, depression, divorce, or facing homelessness. I knew what to do because I had survived it all myself and living *with* it. So, I gave them what I would have needed done for me in those situations. And the countless women and men I've helped are etched in my heart and my soul as a testament to whatever you go through, your story is not just someone else's survival kit, but, in fact, the big light they need to see through their own darkness.

So…

Fight, no matter how much you want to give up.

Stay, no matter how much you want to leave.

Because you matter to me, and you matter to God.

Conclusion

My life has been anything but picture-perfect, and my story is still being told. Much more has happened that are not yet in the pages of a book. But I can say I never stepped foot in or affiliated with that church again. I was so impatient with God that I went on a one-day fast pass thinking anything was better than where I was. No matter how big your bathroom is, or how many rooms your have, all that happened was it brought distance to our family. But I did birth this book out of that place, so yes, no matter how difficult it seems, God works all things for our good. We've since moved back to Jersey as the grass is certainly not greener on the other side, in fact it's a quiet liar in your ear thinking there is something better. So many thing have changed, and many other things have happened that I can't wait to fill up more pages for you and tell you all about in time to come. But no matter how many pages I write, what I learned is that even though I didn't have a blueprint of what to do or how to do it, I had God with me every step of the way, and so do you. The dream version of my life consisted of going to Juilliard and learning from the best so I could be a smashing success on Broadway. I dreamed of a life on stages, and captivating audiences portraying stories and characters that weren't my own. But none of those dreams had come true for me. Would I change it? Never. Because when God imparts His dreams to you…we then understand why we were made. Maybe some of those things you dream for yourself will be peppered in there somewhere, just not in a way you expected. My life now is not a version I expected for myself, but I wouldn't trade it as it's made me who I am today. But I do still want to be on stage, just not my version. My dream now is to be on stage speaking to thousands of people on the idea of not giving up. And sharing my story of not just survival, but the reason to stay and why you matter. I want to give a keynote speech at Juilliard speaking to all the young hopefuls about to step into the world and that rejection is nothing more than redirection. I want to open multiple safe houses around the globe to help people find the immediate help they need. Like a compass from anywhere, you can find us. I also want to be a published author, so if you're reading this, at least one of those God dreams has come true. As my new story unfolds, I promise to keep talking to you all about it, as perhaps it will be a piece you can add to your very own survival kits for times to come.

And I promise the big light will always be left on, for you.

About the Author

Nicole is Board Certified as a Mental Health Coach and in Crisis Intervention. She is dedicated to helping others find hope and healing through life's most challenging moments. In her debut novel, *The Big Light*, Nicole shares her personal journey of trauma, and a vulnerability into her own mental health struggles. Through her story, she offers a beacon of hope to those struggling in the dark, showing that no matter how difficult the path, there is always a light to guide the way. Nicole Legerra is a writer who believes in the power of true stories; the kind that hit somewhere deep and stay with you. She's a mom to five amazing humans and married to her best friend. When she's not writing, you'll find her hitting the pavement running with an audiobooks or playlists in her ears while escaping into the world of words and sound. She owns more vintage rock band T-shirts than she'll ever admit and still holds out hope for that one unforgettable Broadway stage door to be opened...just once.

You can connect with me on:

🌐 https://authornicolelegerra.com

🖊 https://www.instagram.com/authornicolelegerra

Subscribe to my newsletter:

✉ https://authornicolelegerra.com/mailing-list